Boundaries of Identity

Boundaries of Identity

A Quebec Reader

Edited by William Dodge

Lester Publishing Limited

Lester Publishing Limited acknowledges the financial assistance of the Canada Council and the Ontario Arts Council.

Canadian Cataloguing in Publication Data
Main entry under title:

Boundaries of identity : a Quebec reader

ISBN 1-895555-11-6

1. Quebec (Province) – History – 1976- *
I. Dodge, William, 1956-

FC2925.B68 1992 971.4'04 C92-094235-0
F1053.2.B68 1992

Lester Publishing Limited
56 The Esplanade
Toronto, Ontario
M5E 1A7

Printed and bound in Canada.

92 93 94 95 5 4 3 2 1

CONTENTS

The Gender of Sovereignty

Marks of Identity: Immigrants and 'Other' Citizens

"Maudits Anglais?"

Writing the Future

Between Ourselves: An Inconclusion

Objets tangibles, ils requiérent une relation constamment renouvelée, confrontée, remise en question. Relation impalpable, exigeante qui demande les forces vives de l'action.

Ce trésor est la réserve poétique, le renouvellement émotif où puiseront les siècles à venir. Il ne peut être transmis que transformé, sans quoi c'est le gauchissement.

Que ceux tentés par l'aventure se joignent à nous.

Au terme imaginable, nous entrevoyons l'homme, libéré de ses chaines inutiles, réaliser dans l'ordre imprévu, nécessaire de la spontanéité, dans l'anarchie resplendissante, la plénitude de ses dons individuels.

D'ici là, sans repos ni halte, en communauté de sentiment avec les assoiffés d'un mieux-être, sans crainte des longues échéances, dans l'encouragement ou la persécution, nous poursuivrons dans la joie notre sauvage besoin de libération.

— — — — — — — — — — — —

Real things require relationships repeatedly renewed, or challenged, or put to question: relationships impalpable, exacting and dependent on the vivifying force of action.

Our treasure is poetic resource: the emotional wealth on which the centuries to come will draw. It cannot be passed on unless it is transformed, and lacking this it is deformed.

Let those who are inspired by this endeavour join us.

We foresee a future in which man is freed from useless chains, to realize a plenitude of individual gifts, in necessary unpredictability, spontaneity and resplendent anarchy.

Until then, without surrender or rest, in community of feeling with those who thirst for better life, without fear of set-backs, in encouragement or persecution, we shall pursue with joy our overwhelming need for liberation.

Paul-Émile Borduas
From *Refus Global*, 1948
Translated by François-Marc Gagnon
and Dennis Young

Preface

No matter what Quebecers may decide about the future, one thing is certain: Quebec is not a monolithic society that speaks with one voice. But how well known are the views of native leaders, authors, political thinkers, artists, journalists, and scholars in Quebec whose conflicting ideas and allegiances are at the core of Canada's constitutional crisis?

The dream of sovereignty continues to both inspire and divide French Quebecers. But the desire for recognition and power in Quebec today goes beyond the historic divisions between French and English. This reader brings together many of the different views of sovereignty that exist within Quebec – differences noticeably absent from the polarized debates that have preoccupied Quebec and the rest of Canada since the demise of the Meech Lake Accord in June 1990.

While one of the aims of this reader is to explore the increasingly pluralistic and hybrid nature of Quebec's identity, it is clear that every society has to operate on some common ground or with some shared sense of citizenship. Whether this common citizenship is affirmed through collective rights, individual rights, or a combination of both, it draws its strength from the recognition that human identities are not formed in isolation. Our differences, and the meanings attached to these differences, are dependent on our contact with and knowledge of each other.

The views presented in this reader are explored through a variety of sources including essays, briefs, quotations, literary excerpts, manifestos, film scripts, and newspaper articles. Each section of the reader has a central theme. Rather than divide the book into chapters, I have adopted a more lateral approach which gives emphasis to shifting points of view and unusual juxtapositions. I wanted, as much as possible, to reveal some of the conflicts and contradictions in Quebec society, thereby enlarging the space in which different or competing views coexist.

In Cree, there are no words for sovereignty, self-determination, or self-government. The Cree language does not even have a word for lawyers – the professionals who perhaps have done the most to entangle the search for a new constitution in debates over legal abstractions and amending formulas. By situating the native perspective at the beginning of this book, I wanted to remind readers of the diverse aboriginal cultures that existed in Quebec before the arrival of European settlers. Ironically, many politicians and historians continue to neglect the contribution of native peoples to the development of "Quebec" and "Canada" although they use these native words daily to distinguish their own nationhood.

For the many people both in and outside Quebec who are concerned about Quebec's survival as a French-speaking community, there have been some significant advances. The proportion of Quebecers who speak French reached 93.5 per cent in 1986. In Montreal, where the language conflicts have been most pronounced, the circulation of the three French-language daily newspapers increased from 387,200 in 1960 to 555,100 in 1990. In contrast, there were two English-language dailies in 1960 with a circulation of 304,600. By 1990, the one remaining English daily newspaper had a circulation of 178,400. As this evidence suggests, the enhancement of French – one of the primary concerns of most Quebec nationalists – has been achieved without political separation. This fact points to some of the important differences that continue to exist between Quebec nationalists and "souverainistes," differences which are not always understood or appreciated outside Quebec.

Although many Quebec "Anglos" remain wary of the exclusive interests of Quebec nationalism and an "official" culture which seems preoccupied with erasing signs of "the other," there are also many Anglophones who support the cultural aspirations of French Quebecers. The 1986 federal census reported that 57.8 per cent of young Anglophones in Quebec (25 years old or younger) are bilingual, compared to 19.2 per cent of Francophones in the same age group. But Anglophones are also leaving Quebec in alarming numbers. Between 1966 and 1986, demographers estimate that 20,000 Anglophones left Quebec each year. Over the past 20 years, enrolment in Quebec's English school system has dropped from 250,000 to just over 100,000. As the section "Maudit Anglais?" reveals, Quebec Anglos have strong but often contradictory responses to their community's diminished influence and political isolation.

For immigrants who want to feel at home in Quebec, the historic tensions between Canada's two official languages can create special hardships – hardships that are often compounded by the cultural insecurities which a French-speaking community experiences living on a continent dominated by English. Nearly two out of every three immigrants decide not to stay, according to demographer Jacques Henripin. But most newcomers are aware that cultural tensions are not exclusive to Quebec. The section entitled "Marks of Identity" explores some of the tensions experienced by different ethnic communities in Montreal – home to the majority of Quebec's immigrants.

In many ways this book represents a meeting place. Quebec – in all its complexity and indeterminacy – can only be understood through the efforts and perspectives of many people, and this book is a direct beneficiary of the many unexpected and fascinating exchanges that have taken place at Ficciones, a small literary bookstore in Montreal. Situated in a labyrinth of one-way streets close to Mont-Royal, Ficciones is devoted to international writing and reflects the linguistic and cultural awareness of Montreal readers, many of whom are bilingual or trilingual. There is a simple conviction that I have brought to this book: when it comes to understanding the past, there simply are no "facts" independent of interpretation.

I would like to thank the project's associate editors, Ruth Abbey and Craig Ryan, for their important work, as well as Jennifer Allen for her assistance in proofreading the manuscript. I would also like to thank Sheila Fischman, Richard Fidler, Linda Gaboriau, Chris Korchin, Susanne de Lotbinière-Harwood, Craig Ryan, Ruth Abbey, and Caspar Sinnige for their fine translations for this book.

A special thanks also goes to Carole Baldwin, Ron Burnett, Lee Davis Creal, Harold Crooks, Louise Dessertine, J.D. Dodge, Peter Dodge, Michael Dorland, Hazel Field, Gary Geddes, John Goddard, Bruce Heggen, Ellen Jacobs, Benedicte Kruse, David Oancia, Shelley Pomerance, Berel Rodal, Gail Scott, George Stedman, Fred Ward, Janice Weaver, Merrily Weisbord, and Mary Williams for their helpful suggestions while the work was in progress. I am also indebted to Pierre Menard for his insight into the fiction of *the past* and his insistence, at every turn of the page, that reading is always more decisive than writing because it continually interprets the text anew.

William Dodge

Berel Rodal

Berel Rodal was born in Montreal in 1943 and was educated at McGill University, Montreal, and Balliol College, Oxford. His professional experience as a senior official in the Government of Canada includes policy and executive responsibilities in a variety of fields in the defence, foreign affairs, international trade, economic, and social domains, and in federal-provincial relations. This essay is abridged and adapted from a paper prepared by the author for the joint Boston University / Renner Institute consultation on State and Nation in Multi–Ethnic Societies, held in Vienna, January 11-12, 1991, and published in State and Nation in Multi-Ethnic Societies: The Breakup of Multinational States, *edited by Uri Ra'anan, Maria Mesner, Keith Armes, and Kate Martin (Manchester University Press, 1991).*

State and Nation in Conflict

The debate in Canada, historically and in its particularly sharpened form since 1960, has been fundamentally about ways of thinking about "state and nation." The present crisis came upon the country almost unexpectedly. Separatism was written off only a few years ago: yet today, as a result of the failed attempt by the government of Canada to gain Quebec's full and formal assent to the 1982 Constitution Act, Quebec nationalism and the demands for forms of self-rule on the part of aboriginal peoples dominate the Canadian national agenda. The puzzling thing for many is why there should be talk of the country's being at breaking point, when so little appears to be at issue.

English-speaking Canada has come to see the nation and the state in highly pluralistic terms – in terms of ten provinces of disparate size, population and wealth, each marked by a distinct resource endowment and economic base and ethnic and linguistic composition. Canada outside of Quebec is an immigrant society. The proportion of Canadians born outside of the country is considerably higher than in the United States. The "British," those tracing their ancestry to the British Isles, were less than 40% of the Canadian population in the 1981 census, and this proportion would be lower today. In the four Western provinces (Manitoba, Saskatchewan, Alberta, and British Columbia), those of other than British or French descent outnumber those of British and French combined. The principal source of stress has been seen as economic regionalism, amplified by the imbalance between centre and periphery.

The Québécois, however, did not and do not now see themselves as part of the voluntary confluence of separate ethnic and cultural mainstreams making up Canada. They long saw themselves as the only real Canadians, denied both partnership in the colonization and westward expansion of the country and their communal/cultural rights outside their heartland in Quebec. Quebec's evolution since 1960, the year of the "Quiet Revolution," has been truly radical. It is a remarkable story of a society's transformation from a defensive minority sheltered in a linguistic and cultural enclave, to a self-confident majority and, in its own terms, a distinctive "nation" ready if it wishes to assume control of its own national state.

The 1960 election brought to power a Quebec government which saw itself as having to build in a short time and in a coordinated way much that had been built up gradually and incrementally over many years in other provinces and societies. It saw its role not as that of local administration, but the transformation of Québécois society. The Quebec state recruited the best and brightest to politics in order to build the new Quebec. The view was that economic circumstances and imperatives powerfully shaped one's way of living and thinking; that French-Canadians had little control of their economic destiny; and that remaining in an economically inert cultural enclave out of phase with conditions outside the community's boundaries would accelerate rather than protect French-Canadians from assimilation.

This "Quiet Revolution" led to the creation of the Royal Commission on Bilingualism and Biculturalism (the B&B Commission) in 1963 which warned that Canada, unconscious of the fact, was in crisis, and proposed that if Quebec was to be challenged, Canada needed to become a more credible "national center" for French-Canadians. The Commissioners advocated wider recognition of "cultural dualism" and a vastly expanded acceptance of and space for French-Canadians in Canada at large – in concrete terms, the acceptance and institutionalization of equal partnership and full participation of French-Canadians in political and economic decision-making in Canada; policies for the protection of the French language and culture; and bilingualism.

Indeed, federal policies to bring French-speaking Canadians into the upper reaches of Canadian government and enterprise, policies introduced by Prime Minister Lester Pearson and further developed by Pierre Trudeau, and continued by every succeeding Prime Minister, have become a major element of Canadian governance. French-speaking Canadians have held every critical portfolio in Cabinet in recent years, occupy almost a third of all Cabinet posts, and head important Crown Corporations, state enterprises, and national cultural institutions. It is virtually unthinkable today that a Canadian Prime Minister would not be bilingual; indeed, the Prime Minister of Canada has come from Quebec in thirty-one of the past forty-two years, and twenty-three of the past twenty-four years.

One of the prime ministers to come out of Quebec, Pierre Trudeau strongly opposed the focus on the Quebec state while a law professor and intellectual activist in Montreal. He rejected the link between ethnicity and territoriality, a link which he saw as leading to illiberalism. The ideal was the multinational, pluralist state. In his essay, "La nouvelle trahison des clercs" [originally published in *Cité libre,* 1962], Trudeau quotes Lord Acton:

> A great democracy must either sacrifice self-government to unity or preserve it by federalism . . . the coexistence of several nations under the same State is a test, as well as the best security of its freedom. It is also one of the chief instruments of civilization . . . the combination of different nations in one State is as necessary a condition of civilized life as the combination of men in society . . . where political and national boundaries coincide, society ceases to advance, and nations relapse into a condition corresponding to that of men who renounce intercourse with their fellow men . . . a State which is incompetent to satisfy different races condemns itself; a State which labours to neutralize, to absorb, or to expel them, destroys its own vitality; a State which does not include them is destitute of the chief basis of self-government. The theory of nationality, therefore, is a retrograde step in history.

As Prime Minister of Canada after 1968, Trudeau forcefully articulated a stance and policy which went beyond the removal of discrimination and irritants and the containment and accommodation of Quebec's demands for increased autonomy. Trudeau's policy was specifically to depoliticize ethnicity, to separate the concepts of the ethnically-determined "nation" from the "state" and to strengthen the Canadian "state" as a liberal, secular, pluralistic polity better able to serve the interests of justice for all citizens, ensure equitable prosperity, and provide the space and scope needed to preserve French-speaking Canadians' language and culture.

Trudeau's dominance on the federal scene, in large measure due to the forcefulness, clarity, and consistency of his vision and approach, made the debate in Canada a dramatically clear conflict of alternative visions of the state and ethnicity, though the terms may have been obscured by the stresses, over the same period, of Canadian regionalism, and the waxing and waning of the intensity of nationalism within the Québécois population. Trudeau amplified and sharpened the focal points of conflict with Québécois nationalism.

In Trudeau's "territorial" approach to the issues of "state and nation," it is the state which is at the base of the nation, and nationality is a matter of citizenship and residence. For the Québécois, it is the nation that is at the base of the state – citizenship is a matter of territoriality and residence in the Quebec state in which the Québécois are the ethnic group that defines the state, constitutes its core, and provides its elite and culture. The centrepiece of Trudeau's vision and political arrangement was citizenship, individual rights, and uniform entitlements across Canada, a regime in which no one should be subjected to territorial majority rule and relegated to dependent minority status with respect to basic political and cultural rights.

Quebec for its part meanwhile proceeded with the transformation and "francisation" of Quebec society. Bill 101 made French the language of work in Quebec, and opened enterprise, its upper reaches in particular, to francophones and the products of Quebec's new educational and managerial system. The rise of a successful middle class under the auspices of the state has been a development of central importance. The paradox, again, is that Quebec has managed to achieve all that it has under the existing constitution, and under the aegis of a supple, accommodating federalism. Why the thrust to sovereignty, whether defined as "renewed federalism" or full independence?

The key element is Quebec's sense of distinctiveness, buttressed by the creation of a successful and autonomous society, and allied to a sense of historical grievance; the memory of subordinate status and insults; demographic strength and vulnerability; the sense that on the larger issues, Quebec thinks and feels differently from English Canada; and the attrition of over 25 years of discussion of constitutional change.

Quebec distinctiveness seems all too obvious to Québécois, whether comparing the legal systems in English Canada and Quebec, municipal and provincial institutions, corps intermédiaires, arts, literature, educational systems, social and health care networks, religious institutions, financial institutions, language, or political culture. To the Québécois, Canadian provinces resemble in all or most of their essential aspects, US states – except for Quebec. There is little knowledge or cognisance of an "English-Canada," seen as at once amorphous, yet rejecting and culturally and demographically threatening. In the new circumstances, there is renewed, perhaps deepened opposition to the 1982 Constitution Act and the values it enshrines – to strengthen an encompassing pan-Canadian citizenship and political identity, embodied in the reform and the provisions of the Charter of Rights and Freedoms.

The concerns are both material and symbolic. Québécois are concerned about the declining weight and therefore weakening influence of both Quebec and French-Canadians in Canada. French-Canadians now represent about 25% of Canada's population, concentrated nearly 90% in

Quebec, where they constitute 83% of the population. The highest French-Canadian share in another province is some 30% in New Brunswick (numbering some 217,000), the highest number being 330,000 in Ontario (under 4% of Ontario's population). There are fewer French-speaking Canadians than "allophones" (persons of a mother-tongue other than English or French) in every province but Nova Scotia and tiny Prince Edward Island. There is an acute sense of this precarious status as a French-speaking island and culture in an English-speaking sea. There is deep concern about demographic trends within Quebec, and the preference of immigrants for the English-speaking continental mainstream. The Québécois view has been that without the application of state power, special protection and unilingualism, the reality would be domination by those speaking English. Québécois appear unwilling "to tolerate a conception of Canada where they become 'citizens' by virtue of a set of rights adjudicated by a national Supreme Court where any 'collective rights' legislation must rely on the notwithstanding clause which is then open to criticism from the Rest of Canada." [Thomas Courchene, submission to *La Commission sur l'avenir politique et constitutionnel du Québec*]

Indeed, as Courchene observed, bilingualism and *le rayonnement du français*, may well have changed English-Canada more than French-Canada. While it created acceptance for the "French fact" across Canada, and to a certain degree has become part of English Canada's sense of national identity, it has been minimised in Quebec to the extent that it was seen as an aspect of a policy which involves denial of special status for Quebec and the legitimacy of the Québécois approach to "state" and "nation."

Canada, then, is at a defining moment in its history, one turning on the potency of symbols and interests, but also on the meanings that attach to terms, and the consequences which attach to such meanings. With the evolution of opinion following the collapse of the Meech Lake Accord, both Quebec parties are territorial and "sovereignist." The Parti Québécois is for classical independence. The governing Liberal Party, traditionally though conditionally federalist, is presently committed to the achievement of political autonomy, involving "exclusive, discretionary, and total control" of significant areas of governmental activity. Canada represents a partnership to be reformed "on the basis of the free and voluntary association of the participating states," in the language of the Report of the Liberal Party's Committee on the Constitution (Allaire Report). Quebec would assume exclusive jurisdictional authority in a very wide range of areas of activity, including powers germane to its "national economic development," including investment, industrial policy, research and development, and corporations. Responsibility for foreign relations would be allocated on the basis of which government held jurisdictional authority for the field in question domestically. Quebec would obtain jurisdiction in any field not specifically allocated, as it would in the great majority of fields allocated. The federal government, at least as regards Quebec, would have exclusive powers in only four areas – currency, customs, defence, and financial equalization – with new rules to determine how Quebec participates in formulating policy and arriving at decisions federally in these areas. The Charter of Rights would be limited in its application to Quebec, and decisions of Quebec Courts could not be appealed in the Canadian Supreme Court.

Even when characterizing the positions taken by the Allaire Report as negotiable, Premier Bourassa's core conception remains, in his own words, that of a federalism in which "Quebec aims to obtain all the powers for managing its social, cultural, and economic development," noting, en passant, that "in the international arena, Canada and Quebec are very respected states." English-speaking Canada is unlikely to recognize federalism or indeed a country in any of this.

Canada, then, is something of a battlefield on which fundamentally different concepts of state and nation continue to be tested. The Québécois preference has been to achieve, retain, and expand control of their own territorial state, and not to be satisfied with equality, language and cultural rights in an overarching multiethnic state. The grounding and legitimation of the Québécois position essentially (though not exclusively) in a conception of nationality that is based on cultural and historic identity has also brought about dramatic change in the scope of political claims made by aboriginal people in Canada. These claims are now embodied in the assertion of an inherent right to "self-government." Many federalists hope that the consequence of the developments of the last few years, of the last thirty years particularly, will not be the fragmentation of Canada into two or more independent states, but new arrangements which will accommodate the needs of the "distinct societies" coexisting in the Canadian community, without enfeebling pluralism and the Canadian state itself. While there is a preparedness in English-speaking Canada to contemplate and undertake significant reform, including forms of decentralization that would accommodate regional diversity, there is also a growing realization that accommodating two majorities and several minorities is one thing, but different concepts of nationality and statehood quite another.

Boundaries of Identity

Our Home and Native Land

The first enduring European settlement within the present borders of Canada was not established until 1608, and in 1663 there were still only 3,000 Europeans living in New France, no more people than constituted a small Iroquoian tribe. Moreover, these Europeans remained dependent on goods imported from France, many did not intend to remain in the colony, and those who did were only slowly learning to adapt to life in the New World. Yet, at that time, every part of Canada was settled by native peoples who possessed cultures that had evolved over thousands of years and that were adapted to a diversity of environments. In the first half of the seventeenth century, the French were in contact with native groups totalling more than 125,000 people. Not only their numerical superiority but also their knowledge and skills allowed native Canadians to play a far different role during the Heroic Period than history books have ascribed to them.

Bruce Trigger, ethnohistorian
From *Natives and Newcomers*, 1985

Matthew Coon-Come

Matthew Coon-Come is the Grand Chief of the Grand Council of the Crees of Quebec. The following speech was part of a conference, "Lessons from Oka: Forging a Better Relationship," organized by the Aboriginal Law Association of McGill University on February 13, 1991.

Different Laws for Different People

Quebec has invented the concept of English Canada, and English Canada has accepted the myth of an English and French Canada. Meech Lake described a Canada based on a falsehood, the racist notion of two founding peoples. The debate once again attempts to push the real founding people, the first peoples entirely aside. I understand the reason for this. Canada has an unsavoury history in its relations with my people. While the French and English are arguing about which of them came first, they both know that their arguments fail when they are forced to confront the truth. May I ask a question? Have I become your enemy because I tell you the truth? Indigenous people lived in Canada and governed themselves for thousands of years before the spoilers of this land came here and began squabbling among themselves. It is ironic that these people do not want to recognize our existence and rights now. It is because our presence spoils their arguments. That is why Canada prefers to make this a debate between the French and the English.

Prime Minister Mulroney could never bring himself to acknowledge the role that Elijah Harper had in stopping Meech Lake. There is a reluctance to concede that the first peoples, the original people of this land should have an interest in shaping its future. Elijah Harper made it clear we are interested. We do not want to be pushed aside or shut out. The Mohawks showed Canada in the summer of 1990 that they will not be left out. We are looking for solutions and the question is always asked: What about the treaties, what about the James Bay Northern Quebec Agreement? Is that a solution? Is that a model that can be followed? The answer is no.

Neither Canada nor Quebec really wishes to acknowledge the right of the indigenous people to participate in decision making. We, as indigenous people, are excluded from the process of government. Nothing makes this more obvious than James Bay I and the history of the James Bay and Northern Quebec Agreement. The decision to build the complex around 1975 was made in Premier Bourassa's office. Little acknowledgement or consideration was ever given to the presence or the rights of the Cree that live in James Bay.

Archaeologists have shown that we existed and lived there for 5,000 years. No one from the Government of Canada even thought it necessary to come to the Cree committee to discuss the proposal to build what was then the largest hydro-electric project in the world in the middle of our communities, in our own backyard and on top of our graves and hunting grounds. As far as Quebec was concerned, we did not exist.

But let's look at the position that the government of Canada took. I don't need to remind you that the federal government has the constitutional responsibility for Indians. It is required to protect our interests. Well, when the James Bay project was announced Canada did nothing. Canada, as I think you know, has the well earned reputation for doing nothing when Indian rights are threatened. James Bay was the biggest grab of Indian land in Canadian history and the government of Canada was entirely silent. Canada did later lend the Grand Council of the Crees of Quebec money to cover some of the costs of the court cases. But the fact is that Canada took no initiative on its own. Quebec ran over our lands and our rights. They did as they damn well pleased with no consideration for the people that lived there. In every way the construction of the James Bay project reflected the unilateral behaviour of the governments toward indigenous peoples. And when we did object, when we did raise our voices in protest, Quebec said our actions were against the law. We were told that in the eyes of the law we had no title to the land. According to their law, we were squatters. I ask: what kind of law is it that makes squatters out of people who have been living in a territory for thousands of years?

Certain laws can be unfair. Look at the laws that Hitler's regime developed against the Jews. In Africa, they developed laws against the black people. Just because something is law, doesn't mean that it is just or fair. You may be surprised to learn the James Bay project, James Bay I, was never subject to environmental impact assessment. It was just built, in spite of our objections and in spite of the objections of environmentalists and human rights activists. Why is it that everytime you build projects, whether they are mega-projects, whether they are forestry, mining, or tourism projects, they are built on indigenous lands? James Bay is not a good model. It has not set a precedent. It simply follows the old tradition of the government when it comes to indigenous rights, do exactly what you want to do. That's the reality. Different laws for different people.

I think we all know what has happened to the James Bay Northern Quebec Agreement. The governments of Canada and Quebec have used the implementation process to minimize government obligations to the Crees. They pick and choose which provisions they are going to interpret and what is going to be in their interest to build. They even attempted to force the Crees to make one final settlement for all the agreement benefits by holding up their explicit obligations and instituting an elaborate communications policy to create a false public perception that the Crees received more than their due.

As for the agreement itself, the Crees negotiated for rights to which we should have been entitled whether the James Bay project was built or not. Why should Indian people have to sign a land claims agreement to gain control over the education of our children? These are the things we negotiated for. And for most other indigenous people in Canada, the level of control we achieved in the agreement has still not been reached. The agreement contained the basis for Cree self-government. The first, and still the only constitutionally-based Indian self-government in Canada. Cree self-government was affirmed as a constitutional right. This has not yet been achieved by any other indigenous people in Canada.

These rights have never made much of a difference to Canada. Even though the Cree are no longer under the Indian Act, the government still insists that we come under the control of the Department of Indian and Northern Affairs.

Is there really a solution? In British Columbia, the Gitskans, like all the other indigenous people in Canada, want the basic democratic right to govern their own people. There appears to be some fear in the non-native community that the Indians might win their case. It has led to speculation on the dire consequences that could follow. Some have complained that the Indians would impose their own rules on non-natives. What is wrong with that? Some people in British Columbia went crazy when a lawyer for the Gitskans suggested that the Indians would constitute a third order of government. I think we have to recognize that the Indians already are a third order of government, but that the government under which the Indians live is a dictatorship.

The federal minister of Indian Affairs exercises arbitrary power over the lives of Indian people. He determines who is an Indian. He controls the right to education, Indian land, Indian resources, health services. He even has the power to invalidate the last will and testament of any Indian. He does not provide any rationale. Maybe we should have special legislation for Greeks, Italians, Jews. Why Indians? I think Canadians need to realize that Indian people live in a dictatorship. We are beneficiaries under a trusteeship which has been terribly abused. And under the law we have little power to refute our trustee. Look at Oka, look at James Bay. What good are treaties that are broken over and over and over again. No I do not see any good models that we can follow.

If we are to succeed, we need to do something entirely new, not confine ourselves to Quebec. We have to go farther than that. We need to stop lying about the history of Canada. We need to end the racism and deceit that denies us our basic rights. Canada claims us as subjects. Quebec claims that it also will treat us as subjects if it separates from Canada. We were nations long before Canada or Quebec came into being and we will not agree to subjugation no matter how it is legally construed. There comes a time when people cannot take any more abuse. The time has come. Enough is enough.

Billy Diamond

Billy Diamond is the chief of the Waskaganish Band of James Bay Cree and the President of Air Creebec. As the grand chief of the Cree in 1975, he was the main Cree signatory of the James Bay and Northern Quebec Agreement. The following article is abridged from Arctic Circle, *November/December 1990.*

Villages of the Dammed

Hydro-electricity is very important to Quebec, and the Cree homeland provides approximately 40 percent of Quebec's capacity of 25,000 megawatts. However, unlike some Scandinavian countries, where hydro-electric flooding is confined by mountain walls, in the Cree territory hydro-electric projects flood vast areas and devastate the land.

The La Grande Project has a total reservoir area of about 14,000 square kilometres, of which about 10,500 square kilometres is flooded land. If James Bay Phase II, the massive expansion of the Northern Quebec hydro-electric system currently being planned by Hydro-Quebec, is completed, this total will rise to 25,835 square kilometres of reservoir, of which 15,519 square kilometres will be flooded land. This is comparable to submerging the whole of Northern Ireland.

At this moment, we have no idea how far the consequences of James Bay I have gone. We know that our people cannot eat certain species of fish because they are contaminated with mercury. We know there are fewer and fewer geese each year. We know that whole fisheries have been wiped out, and that hunting, fishing and trapping areas have been severely reduced. We know that 40,000 non-native people each year use the hydro-electric infrastructure to hunt and fish in the region, without controls. We know there have been impacts on the wildlife of the region, and on James Bay and Hudson Bay.

Hydro-Quebec has carefully prevented public environmentalists and other scientists from learning the full impact of the La Grande Project. How can they build another project, cut more trees and flood more land without knowing this? We know about the destruction of the Amazon forests, but what about the destruction of the northern Quebec forests? Premier Bourassa says he is going ahead with James Bay II. He says he does not need Cree consent to destroy our rivers and flood our land. But he is wrong. Cree consent is required, and we want these projects stopped.

In the Great Whale River Project, Bourassa intends to flood the lands of the Great Whale River Basin, the Nastapoca Basin, the Coates

River Basin, the Boutin River Basin and the Little Whale River Basin in order to produce some 3,000 megawatts of electricity. Each of these rivers has important fish populations, and each contributes to the ecology of Hudson Bay, which supports populations of beluga whales, seals, polar bears and arctic char. As well, rare inland freshwater seals depend upon this water. The flooding of Lake Bienville to turn it into the major reservoir for this project will destroy important wetlands and ruin caribou calving grounds. And it will release mercury into the environment which, for many years to come, will contaminate remaining fish, mammal and bird populations of the reservoir area.

The Nottaway-Broadback-Rupert Project, the next major complex after Great Whale River, will produce 9,000 megawatts of power when the ten proposed power plants are completed.

As with the Great Whale River Project, these power plants will operate to supply the demand for electricity in the South. It will replace the natural cycle by draining the reservoirs in winter and refilling them during the summer. The Nottaway and Rupert Rivers will be diverted toward the Broadback River system where, on the present channel of the Lower Broadback, the power plants will be mainly located. Water flow in the Lower Broadback River will, in winter, be ten to twenty times the present natural flow. The plan is to build the upstream power plants first, and build others downriver as required.

Over a period of years, this increased flow will scour out the Lower Broadback River channel. Reservoir depth will fluctuate annually between six and more than eighteen metres, and, as the reservoirs are shallow, this will leave vast bands of mud around each reservoir. The impact of this project will be devastating. Many Cree families will lose the most productive parts of their hunting, fishing and trapping areas. Because the Nottaway-Broadback-Rupert Project is to be built in low-relief forested areas and in sensitive wetland environments, the project will cause mercury contamination of the fish in those reservoirs at levels as yet unseen in Northern Quebec.

These river basins form an intricate and complex pattern of wetland environments and small lakes. They are major nesting grounds for ducks, herons, and all of the other migratory waterfowl which come to our northern region every spring. The spilling of forty cubic kilometres of fresh water into James Bay and Rupert Bay every winter will have a negative impact on the trout, cisco and whitefish populations as well as the snow geese that use Rupert Bay for a staging area during their migration.

For the Cree communities, local effects, in addition to social problems and damages to the hunting and trapping way of life, will include loss of community water supplies, contamination of local bodies of water, erosion and silting problems, and problems in transportation. My community, Waskaganish, will be greatly affected by this project. Our very existence is at stake.

Besides all that, these projects do not produce clean energy from an atmospheric standpoint. The projects will allow Quebec and northeastern United States to avoid implementing energy conservation as recommended by the international Brundtland Commission. In addition, the rotting vegetation from these projects will dump 100 million tonnes of carbon dioxide and methane into the atmosphere, contributing greatly to the greenhouse effect. Major power transmission lines will have to be built and will cut through our region as well as populated areas in southern Quebec and the United States.

The real crime about these proposed hydro-electric projects is that they are not needed, and there are much better investments available for the people of Quebec. It is only because of a few interested parties, including Premier Bourassa, that the projects are proposed at all. Hydro-Quebec is not a publicly regulated company, although it is a public company and has all of its debts underwritten by Quebec taxpayers. Hydro-Quebec proposes to spend $62 billion on mega-projects and related works over the next ten years. This is approximately twice the level of spending proposed by Ontario Hydro.

In Brazil, developers argue, the enormous population increase in the next century will require the power that they hope to get by flooding parts of the Amazon Basin. In Quebec, the population is expected to start declining by the year 2006. Quebec presently uses the same amount of electricity as New York State, even though it has about one third of the population of that state.

To increase the demand so its projects can be rationalized to the public, Hydro-Quebec has aggressively marketed electricity in the United States. Moreover, Hydro-Quebec sells electricity at well below cost to aluminum smelters which, incidentally, have been exempted by Quebec and Canada from environmental review. In 1984 when Premier Bourassa was re-elected, Hydro-Quebec sold what it called "surplus electricity" to the United States at bargain basement prices. This was not surplus electricity; it was the margin of energy security, as stored water in the reservoirs.

The alternatives for Quebec will cost less than these mega-projects. Eight thousand megawatts of power can be accessed through conservation. As new technologies are developed using sun, wind and perhaps fusion, it is likely that the cement and gravel pyramids in Northern Quebec will be monuments to the abuse that 20th-century man has heaped on the environment.

Yves Beauchemin

Born in Noranda, Quebec, Yves Beauchemin spent much of his early childhood in the small village of Clova, Abitibi. He is the author of the phenomenally successful novel, Le Matou *[translated as* The Alley Cat*], which sold over half a million copies in Quebec and France and was turned into an award-winning movie by Jean Beaudin. The appearance of his most recent novel,* Juliette Pomerleau *(1989), was a major publishing event in Quebec. The following is excerpted from a letter written by the author to Greenpeace. This excerpt appeared in* Le Devoir *(November 5, 1991).*

Greenpeace's Dubious Ties

For a long time I have admired the courage and ingeniousness Greenpeace has brought to the defense of a cause I hold dear to my heart: the environment. Greenpeace has done more for my own future and the future of my two sons than all of our smooth-talking, weak-kneed politicians. Politicians who, alas, often serve as little more than smokescreens for certain interests with their blind, "fast-buck" obsessions – and to hell with future generations.

So it is with great sadness that I read in the October 22 edition of *Le Devoir* that your organization had participated in the publication in the *New York Times* of an advertisement that savagely attacked Quebec on the issue of the Grande-Baleine. I was flabbergasted by what I read. Many of its claims are a flagrant contradiction of the truth.

While reading it we feel breathing down our necks the Grand Inquisitor himself, so obsessed by the desire to further his cause that he will resort to any means. Is this advertisement part of the smear campaign that has been unleashed on us over the past year, and which gathers momentum as the national liberation movement deepens here at home?

Has Greenpeace signed on with the Trudeaus, the Richlers, and other Warriors whose goal seems to be to relegate Quebec culture to the history books? In joining this great symphony of slander, have you taken the trouble to inform yourselves about the conductor of that symphony? Some curious forces converge in these fanatical and widespread attacks, forces that seem to serve the interests of English Canada.

You know as well as I do that certain parties in English Canada are working ferociously hard to ensure that Quebec independence dies in the delivery room so that the unity of this artificial and heterogenous Canada, which for Quebecers has always proved to be more of an iron collar than a cradle, might be preserved. In this affair, the environment and the constitution make a suspicious blend. Are you serving as an instrument in a battle you do not want to lead, but which is being led because of you?

Grande-Baleine is a complex subject; and I don't want to suggest that in this affair goodness and truth are lined up on the same side. Which is one more good reason not to spread confusion and engage in extreme oversimplifications. Why are you doing just that?

A single instance: The *New York Times* text affirms that the Grande-Baleine project will trigger a catastrophe "comparable to that of the devastation of the Amazon." The Amazon basin, according to the "Robert" [dictionary], covers 6 million square kilometres. But I suppose we shouldn't worry about minor differences . . .

The defense and protection of this planet's ecosystem is a sacred cause, for in its success hangs, as everybody knows, humanity's survival. Nonetheless it does not justify the use of half-truths, gross oversimplifications, and lies. So you will appreciate that, under the circumstances, I feel obliged to withdraw my name from the ranks of Greenpeace and suspend my aid to your organization.

Translated by Chris Korchin

KAHN-TINETA HORN

Kahn-Tineta Horn is a Mohawk National of Kahnawake Territory in Quebec. She was one of the people charged with the Mohawk Warriors and their allies at Kanesatake during the Oka Crisis in the summer of 1990. She conducts seminars in North American Indian History and Contemporary Issues. The following is abridged from Harbour *(vol.1, no. 3, 1991), an interdisciplinary magazine about art and everyday life published in Montreal .*

AFTER OKA: A MOHAWK'S PERSPECTIVE

Language rights are basic human rights, and I commend the French-speaking Canadian people for the efforts they have taken to hold onto their mother language. The Mohawk Nation now wants to do the same to save our language, our land and our race.

ON JULY 11, 1990, THE MOHAWK TERRITORY OF KANESATAKE, QUEBEC, WAS attacked by the para-military forces of the Sûreté du Québec (S.Q.). To support and save the lives of our Mohawk brothers and sisters in Kanesatake, the Kahnawake Mohawk blocked off the Mercier Bridge and the entire territory.

Emotions from July 11 until the end of August proved to be volatile. Sometimes the Mohawk Territories would be calm for lengthy periods and other times the hostilities and resentments shifted locales. During the middle of August things had become so calm that I, like the majority of Canadians, had figured the crisis had come to a halt.

I took my two daughters with me.

Shortly after I arrived at Kanesatake, the Territory was surrounded by the military. The military were then surrounded by blockades of the Sûreté du Québec. Outside them were the racist mobs, and our supporters. Tensions became extremely high. It wasn't long before I found myself with about sixty other people holed-up in a building known as the Treatment Centre.

Things inside the encampment were calm. The only dangers lay on the other side of the razor wire fencing the army had put around us. Daily there were reports of Mohawk people who had left the Treatment Centre only to be beaten and arrested by the S.Q. (police). Many of these reports were gruesome and they made us fearful of the authorities that were said to be in place to protect us.

Also, Indian people were beaten by members of non-Indian radical groups, while members of the S.Q. stood by and watched.

The scary conditions outside and inside the army's barricades would not lift for almost another month. On September 26, 1990, all Mohawk people trapped inside the Treatment Centre felt the only way we could leave safely would be to leave together and suddenly. During this peaceful evacuation, many women, children, and men were injured by the army, including my sister, Waneek, then fourteen years old, who was stabbed in the chest by a soldier.

We were arrested by the army, interrogated by the S.Q. and taken to court. I was charged with three different criminal counts. As well, I was fired from my job at the Department of Indian Affairs in Ottawa because I am a Mohawk Indian. I will prove racism and discrimination by the Department when my appeal is heard. I was also served with papers which claimed possession of my youngest daughter, Ganyetahawi.

Today, I doubt Mohawk people facing criminal charges will receive fair hearings. Every possible jury in Canada has been prejudiced. The Minister of Justice herself, Kim Campbell, called all Mohawk Warriors "criminals." In other court cases there would be special provisions made for juries they feel have been prejudiced.

My great grandfather, Ranakarakete, meaning "carrying the horns of Chieftainship," helped re-establish the traditional spiritual beliefs of the Iroquois and helped bring back the political system of the Hodinosanunee, meaning the people of the Longhouse, to the Mohawks on Kahnawake Territory. This was after a long reign of English domination which controlled both our politics and our religion.

My grandfather, Karonhiankeniate, a Longhouse Chief, felt that Indians would find their way if they traced their spiritual roots. My grandfather was the youngest condoled Chief of the Iroquois Confederacy, condoled through the traditional ceremony of installing Iroquois Chiefs.

My father taught me to accept discrimination on a physical level and to strengthen my cultural beliefs internally, so that one day Indian people would be left alone to believe what they wanted, even if it meant fighting for this right.

I was born a Mohawk of the Six Nations Confederacy. As Mohawk Nation citizens, we do not consider ourselves to be Canadian, as per the original agreement between the Mohawk and the non-Indian people which stated that "We would retain our separate nationhood and live side by side, neither side absorbing the other."

Our "Warriors" have been given a bad rap from the press and from the politicians. The Warriors are "Ratiskenhaketeh," the "carriers of the burden of peace." "Skenha" is a state of complete peace, tranquility and enlightenment.

The clans elect the "Sachem" or head of the clan in time of peace and the war chief or leader for war. The clans could depose the war chief when deemed necessary and could even call a war party back from the field. It is said that in time of war, the warriors must have their moccasins made by the women. This symbolism implies that it is the women who make the decision as to whether the men will go to war or not.

All Iroquois people are born warriors and it is the duty of every male to become protector of the boundaries and the people. The "Gai'Wiio" instructs us to try everything within our power to resolve issues peacefully. If peaceful resolutions are impossible, the issue is brought before the people "who have no positions," the Warrior Society.

In the past, if the opposition did not pick up arms, there was no reason to settle problems with aggression. But the newcomers who came to our land had a different conception of life. In Kanesatake the politicians and the bureaucrats pushed the Mohawk people so far because they wanted the last of our land, a ceremonial and a burial site, to build a golf course. They pushed the people to the point of having to defend themselves against a para-military force. The Mohawk had no choice but to defend themselves. Our Warriors had to rise up and say, "No more! You can't take that land" to the authorities who felt it was their god-given right to take whatever they wanted from the Indian people.

Oka is first a land issue. Because of our stand to defend ourselves and our land, we were threatened, intimidated, abused, labelled and treated like criminals and terrorists. Before we walked out of the Treatment Centre, we went through a purification ceremony so we would not be touched by the violations of others. It was a spiritual suit of armour to protect us against the violence of the unknown, to help us go from one reality to another. It was not a surrender, but a freedom march home. We did not run. We went headlong into the armed soldiers who awaited us, who pushed us with their guns and bayonets into the razor wire and into the ground. We screamed to protect ourselves against the grotesque reactions of the young men who were attacking us.

Oka had to happen. Everything needed to be brought out in the open for the Canadian public. The Mohawk needed to find out who our enemies were. Now we know. Oka was a resistance movement of the aboriginal people, and the Québécois will be free when the aboriginal people of Canada are free. The politicians and bureaucrats in Canada and Quebec have not only threatened the Indians who live inside the Quebec borders, they have threatened everyone.

What were the effects of Oka? The Indian people have told the rest of Canada that we want a new relationship with government. We want control of our land, our resources, and to speak our mother tongue, and most of all, to be free. These are basic human rights. These were guaranteed through treaties and agreements made between the Indians and the newcomers to our land. These will have to be honoured. Indians recognize this, and now, so do most Canadians.

The summer of 1990 will be remembered as the summer Canada grew up. The summer that Canada lost its innocence. No longer can Canadian people assume that everything is rosy and that the big people will take care of everything. The big people have abused this power to serve their own ends.

Let the politicians and bureaucrats do whatever it is that they can do. But let us continue to keep up the fight for democracy and justice. The minorities of Canada must now unite to save our cultures, our races, and our mother, the earth.

Note: In the summer of 1992, most of the natives who faced charges stemming from the Oka Crisis were acquitted.

Dan Gaspé

Dan Gaspé is a Mohawk from Kanesatake. He was special administrator to the Kanesatake Mohawk Council from January to March 1990. He now does public relations work for the Akwesasne Mohawk Council and is a partner in Gaspé, Tarbell and Associates, aboriginal affairs consultants. This article first appeared in Rencontre *(January 1991), a magazine on aboriginal issues published in Quebec City.*

The Mohawk Struggle

Many grievous errors in the spring and summer of 1990 have led to the most distressful event in the history of Mohawk-Quebec relations. It is difficult for me to write about these events because it pains me to express the reality that some of my own people participated in the series of errors and crimes that led to the conflict. The actions of Canada and Quebec prior to and during the confrontation are equally hurtful.

The media made much ado about the Warriors holding their own people hostage. But the press did not focus on the innocent Mohawks who were simultaneously hostages of the Warriors and under siege by the Sûreté du Québec and later, the Canadian Armed Forces. Mohawks had to endure harassment and racist slurs at army and police checkpoints followed by insults and petty power trips at Warrior checkpoints.

The ordinary people – the majority – in Kanesatake and Kahnawake went through hell. On one hand, the Warriors, supported by a minority faction (or is it the other way around?) set up the barricades in Kahnawake and Kanesatake, while on the other hand, the police and army surrounded our communities. Despite a mandate given by the Mohawk community to the Chief at Kahnawake on July 12 to take the barricades down, they stayed up. In fact, the silent majority was being punished by the police and the army for the wrongs of a small group.

Meanwhile, on the inside, the Warriors and their supporters took over effective control of the community. Democracy and accountability to the people were noble concepts which were suspended during the summer, leaving tyranny and might to rule over our communities.

Historically, the Mohawks were never conquered by any military force. In that sense, conquest cannot be used to justify the small land base left to us on our "reserves." What is the justification for Quebec and Canada to have sufficient land and political power while the Mohawks do not have the same? It cannot be superiority of numbers or majority rule, since there is still plenty enough land and resources to go around for everybody including the aboriginal nations. It is a sense of justice and fairness that is in short supply.

Could it be that the Mohawks once had sovereignty or signed treaties but that they no longer apply today? You would have to search long for a Mohawk who has not been brought up with the teaching of the elders that we never relinquished our sovereignty or lands and that every successive generation must continue the struggle until we once again occupy our rightful place amongst the nations of the world.

Our rights have been consistently repressed and denied and an entire legal and political system was developed by Canadians to deprive us of our traditional lands, not to mention similar actions in the United States. We have an internationally recognized right to self-determination as a people.

Mohawks, like other First Nations, accept people of European descent in North America; we simply want a fair share of our original territories, and adequate powers over our own affairs. We also want to negotiate compensation for past wrongs which have left us in a disadvantaged position in relation to the dominant society. The forced taking of our lands and disempowerment of our governments are an historical wrong that must now be made right for the sake of both First Nations and Canadian society.

As a first feeble attempt to correct past wrongs, Canada and Quebec agreed to negotiate with us the unification of the checker-board lands in Kanesatake in 1989. It was our first direct participation in Mohawk land matters since the early 1700s. There were limitations imposed which were unacceptable to the people of Kanesatake but those could have been worked out in negotiations. However, discussions were broken off at a time of internal political difficulties in Kanesatake.

One serious flaw in the process is that federal and provincial policies demand that municipalities get involved as much as possible in reassigning land and jurisdiction to Natives. Individual members of municipal councils and the people they represent are often the local land owners, who are naturally reluctant to let go of lands they view as theirs. It gives the innocent third party, an individual land owner, the right to prevent justice to a whole nation or one of its communities. Federal and provincial laws also give municipalities the right to order the police to enforce their will. That is what happened at Oka on July 11, 1990. Giving municipalities a veto on land claims is no way to ensure fair negotiations with First Nations.

Sadly, a small group of Mohawks invited help from the Warriors to prevent the municipality of Oka from cutting trees and making a golf course on land that we claim as Mohawk land. The defence of land is commendable but the use of guns for defence goes against Canadian, Quebec and

Mohawk laws. The majority of Mohawks are assertive but peaceful in the pursuit of legitimate claims. The movement to organize resistance to the mayor of Oka and the town's plan to build a golf course began on April 1, 1989, with a peaceful march of 300 Mohawks through the streets of Oka. The community was organizing the 1990 protest in an equally peaceful manner when the faction that supported the use of guns took over. Most Mohawks watched the barricades from a distance because it was no longer a community-run movement after the first week of March, 1990. The array of peaceful tactics available to us was pushed aside in favour of armed resistance by a minority.

The police raid on July 11 and the Warrior response left one policeman dead, with many frightened women and children placing themselves as a shield between the two "rambo" forces. I don't know who to believe as to what exactly happened that day but I cannot condone police attacks in these types of situations any more than I can accept that unaccountable Mohawks carry assault weapons in my community. They were both wrong, and as in most wars, the real victims are the innocent civilians.

I worked in Akwesasne during April and May, 1990, when Warriors and pro-gamblers stepped up their campaign of violence and shooting against peaceful Mohawks who were protesting against the gambling on their territory. I was there when the news of the death of Matthew Pyke, a young Mohawk anti-gambler, pierced the hearts of a hundred or more people who had gathered for a community meeting. The Warriors were involved in incidents where three sacred lives were extinguished in less than three months.

It was reported in *The Gazette* [Montreal] on May 9, 1990, that Warrior spokesmen at a press conference in Kahnawake had boasted the Warriors were implementing a plan to take over control of all Indian communities in northeastern North America through the election of their own supporters or through other undisclosed means. The "other means" I have witnessed include fear, intimidation, coercion, deceit, cult techniques, beatings, arson and death. They have forsaken our traditional ways for resolving disputes and for ensuring harmony and strength of the community and the nation.

The recent history of the Warrior Society is one of greed and lust for power. Since the early to mid-1970s, traditional Longhouse people began asserting themselves in Kahnawake and Akwesasne. In the early 1980s, divisions surfaced when some traditionalists defied their Chiefs' councils and the clans who had refused their request to set up bingo and were trying to stop them from smuggling. Cigarette smuggling and gambling casinos became lucrative operations bringing in hundreds of millions of dollars per year to be distributed to a small élite.

The actions of the Warriors today exist primarily to preserve those illegal business operations. The Warriors' public image had suffered greatly at Akwesasne in the spring of 1990 when they were shown on national TV firing automatic weapons on their own people. Their involvement at Kanesatake was later proven to be motivated largely by their business operations so they tried to improve their public image by attaching themselves to broadly supported land claims issues.

There were two types of Warriors at Kanesatake: those ordinary, patriotic people who picked up guns to protect the land in an honest belief that their lives were in danger after the initial police raid, and those full-time, military-trained, salaried Warriors who had economic interests to defend. The latter's greed and their wish to take over control of the communities to maintain the necessary conditions for the continued operation of their illegal businesses are the simple reasons why they will not let human lives stand in their way.

Generations of Mohawks and other Indians have been cheated and lied to. The early seventies saw a new land claims process adopted by the federal government. Despite almost 20 years of Mohawk research and petitions to the federal government, the land claims were rejected. In 1989, our community had had enough of land theft and with our new found skills in mounting political pressure, our community began a campaign of organized, peaceful protest.

As good, law-abiding Mohawk people struggle to maintain control of our communities, we will need the support of Quebec and Canada. The federal and provincial governments must understand that it is in their interest to help us maintain orderly communities controlled by reasonable people. Otherwise, they and all the population of Canada will have to face some Mohawks who favour, as we have seen, armed resistance.

Québécois and Canadians must not allow our young people to feel that they have exhausted all peaceful and legitimate means to have our land claims and our rights to self-determination respected. Otherwise, the call to arms by a misguided minority of Mohawks may be heeded in the future. The events at Oka show us that, as neighbours, Mohawks and Québécois must learn more about each other and learn to respect each other more.

Good people in Kanesatake, Kahnawake and Akwesasne are trying hard to heal the wounds in the communities. The truth, no matter how harsh, must be told.

I pray to the Creator that the power of the good mind and the ways of our great Peacemaker will prevail.

Sean McCutcheon

Sean McCutcheon has worked as an exploration geophysicist in the north and was a contributing editor to The Junior Encyclopedia of Canada. *He lives with his family in Montreal. The following is abridged from* Electric Rivers: The Story of the James Bay Project, *published by Black Rose Books (Montreal, 1991).*

Changing Native Society

THE KEY TO ADVANCEMENT IN NATIVE COMMUNITIES NOW IS POLITICS. THE BRIGHTEST and the best-educated of the Natives of northern Quebec – those who bridge the gaps not only between elders and youth within their communities, but also between the culture of the Crees and that of the non-Native world; those who are at ease arguing with ministers and deputy-ministers; hiring money managers, tax lawyers, consultant energy analysts, and Madison Avenue public relations firms; flying from meeting to exhausting meeting, articulating their peoples' discontents to the world – hold the few prestigious, well-paying jobs that exist in the James Bay region. Wits have wondered whether there are enough Natives in the James Bay region to attend all the meetings the complex new political order requires. There are; they constitute one of the most remarkable impacts of the agreements, and thus, indirectly of the hydroelectric project: the creation of a politically-sophisticated Native elite.

Once, on the desk of Walter Hughboy, chief of Wemindji, I saw an enormous stack of documents held down by a rifle – apt symbols, I thought of the two cultural modes, hunter and bureaucrat, in which Native leaders function. There is continuity between these modes; getting power and money in a hostile environment calls for shrewdness and self-reliance just as does harvesting furs and meat. But there is a rupture too; in order to preserve their traditional hunting culture, Native leaders have had to abandon it, to become what they call "briefcase Indians."

Despite the fact that the contractual provisions of the James Bay and Northern Quebec Agreement and its related agreements have been incorporated into both federal and provincial laws, and embedded in the Canadian constitution, some of the promises made in these agreements have not been honoured. Both Crees and Inuit have been dragging the government before the courts, trying to force them to provide promised money for, among other things, education, health, infrastructure, and for houses – of which the Natives, with their expanding population, are chronically short. At the beginning of the 1980s, for instance, an epidemic of gastroenteritis, a disease associated with poor sanitation and the lack of running water, killed eight children and hospitalized 80. The Crees mainly blamed Quebec, which had not yet funded promised sanitation facilities. A federal review of the problems in implementing the Agreement, organized in response to the Natives' bitter complaints, accused government bureaucrats of honouring the Agreement only in the narrowest sense, and of taking no pains to make it work. In 1983, the federal government decided to give $60 million more to the Crees.

The main problem with implementing the Agreement, from the government's point of view, is that in signing it they promised to deliver services the costs of which were not made explicit and which have turned out to be higher than predicted. (Between 1975 and the year 2000 the number of beneficiaries of the Agreement will have trebled, and the costs, per person, of providing services such as health care to distant and widely scattered communities are huge.)

The native leaders complain that they have not been able to exercise any significant control over decisions affecting their region. The mechanisms, such as joint committees, which were to give them power to participate actively in economic development in their land – not just as beneficiaries, but as controllers – do not work. For instance, the Crees have not been able to stop the loggers who, with Quebec's permission, are now clear-cutting most of the harvestable timber in the southern portion of the Cree homeland (including lands which Hydro-Quebec hopes to flood in the Nottaway-Broadback-Rupert complex).

The developers claim that the Crees exaggerate the social as well as the ecological impacts of the hydroelectric project. The developers acknowledge that they might have made some better choices of technical fixes; rather than building access ramps to the La Grande complex reservoirs, for instance, they should have built snowmobile trails so Crees could set up fishing camps on distant lakes. But the developers insist that though the Natives had to adjust, moving to fresh lakes and to fresh hunting grounds, even with the La Grande complex built they can continue to live off the land, and some do. The developers agree that Native lives have been changed, but claim that this was bound to happen, and that the Natives have been generously compensated for their inconvenience. "Why do Natives never say anything positive," Jacques Guevremont has asked. "Why do they never talk about the benefits they have received?"

They do not do so because they feel so much resentment. They resent the pressure on them to sign the Agreements from which these benefits flow, pressure exerted by the massive scale and momentum of the James Bay project. They resent the physical changes to their land and lives caused by its intrusion. They resent their growing dependence on the State. They resent all the changes that have swept through their communities in the past two decades, and they blame these changes on the developers. But the Cree leaders have more to do than resent the past; they have new problems.

A few years ago, hunters from the community of Great Whale River, who hardly ever encountered strangers, Native or non-Native, began seeing helicopters zooming overhead, landing pads hacked out of the scrawny forest, surveyors' ribbons and stakes. Surveyors, hydrologists, and geologists were exploring and mapping the routes for more roads and power lines, the sites for more construction camps, the pits from which more rock will be excavated and dumped into more rapids, the ground on which more dams will stand, and the land which more reservoirs will inundate. They were starting work on the Great Whale hydroelectric project, the first of the James Bay II megaprojects. The Cree leaders are focusing their formidable political skills on stopping it.

In Quebec, where the fate of the Great Whale River will be decided, the struggle for power between the bulldozer coalition and the Crees grows more polarized and the arguments more strident. The grassroots coalition of opposition groups in Quebec has been attempting to mobilize public opinion in ways similar to those used south of the border. In the summer of 1991, for instance, a group including Natives, environmentalists and trade unionists toured the province to drum up support. Quebecers remain ambivalent and confused. A poll conducted by Hydro-Québec during the summer of 1991 found that 56 percent of Quebecers are in favour of the Great Whale project; at best a slim majority, if this poll reflects reality, and a declining one, since public support for Hydro-Québec was much higher a few years ago.

Hydro-Québec has mounted an expensive public relations effort aimed particularly at the United States and at Europe. This attempt to restore its image as an environmentally-sensitive corporate citizen is of some importance because, as its image deteriorates, it loses the confidence of the investors from whom it borrows. In media such as its annual reports, beautifully illustrated with photos of unspoiled nature, or of romantic old poles carrying power to snowbound villages, the utility praises itself for its fastidious care of wild nature, and for its concern for human needs. It arrogates the rhetoric of its opponents; its chairman and chief executive officer, Richard Drouin, speaks of sustainable development now, and of "negawatts." In advertisements aimed at Quebecers it plays on fears about the steady supply of electricity.

The proponents are frustrated by what they see as the unrepresentative but hyperactive opposition in the United States, and by the intransigence of the Crees. Both Bourassa and the chief of the Parti Québécois fulminate about tiny minorities getting in the way of the majority of Québécois.

The magnitude of what is at stake has grown with the recent growth of nationalism in Quebec, and with the resurgence of the possibility that Quebec could separate from Canada.

Behind the few thousand intransigent Crees, some Quebecers see the manipulative hand of the federal government. If Quebec were to separate, some say, the federal government would support the Cree and Inuit claims to their homelands, and would take back Nouveau-Québec, the northern half of the province, from Quebec, and give it to the Natives. The new nation-state of Quebec would occupy only the old territory of Nouvelle-France, the land France colonized along the Saint Lawrence River.

And what would happen to the James Bay project? Would the federal government take it over? Would the Crees form Hydro-Creebec, and run it themselves? Would it become the economic base of the sovereign nation which the Crees say they will form if Quebec separates, a nation which has no other visible means of support? Or will the threat of losing the James Bay hydroelectric project, which *indépendantistes* see as Quebec's entry card to the planetary club of nation states, be what keeps Quebec in Canada?

Boundaries of Identity

Québec Libre

At the end of this film [Arcand's Comfort*], I was so disgusted by the whole referendum issue – not by the actions of one side but by the actions of both sides. They were both appealing to the same lower instincts. I guess they couldn't do anything else, because otherwise people wouldn't vote for them. Once I understood this completely, I stopped being interested at all in Canadian politics. I could never really read a newspaper after that.*

Denys Arcand, filmmaker
Interview in the *Globe and Mail*, November 4, 1991

Christian Dufour

Born in Chicoutimi, Quebec, Christian Dufour was admitted to the Quebec Bar in 1972. He worked for ten years in the Quebec civil service in the area of federal-provincial relations and recently served on the staff of the Bélanger-Campeau Commission on Quebec's constitutional future. He now teaches a course on Canadian federalism at Laval University and coordinates the study of Quebec's "distinct society" for the Institute of Research on Public Policy. The following is excerpted from his best-selling book on Canadian and Québécois nationalism, A Canadian Challenge / Le défi québécois, *co-published by Oolichan Books & The Institute for Research on Public Policy, 1990.*

A Little History

Under the French regime, New France was already known as Canada, the inhabitants as Canadians. That was the only name for Quebecers' ancestors until the Union of 1840. The others called themselves "the British." The term "Canadiens" is used in this sense in the following . . .

Today, the only event that most Quebecers still remember about the English Conquest of New France is the battle of the Plains of Abraham. There has been a recent tendency to consider it a mere skirmish, rather than something of real importance, probably because of the small number of soldiers involved and the fact that the matter was settled in less than half an hour.

And yet, Wolfe's victory over Montcalm on September 13, 1759, on a plateau overlooking the Saint Lawrence where Quebec stands, is mentioned in every respectable book of world history. To the shrewd observer, that battle was the first clear signal that world hegemony was passing from France to England and that America would be Anglo-Saxon. In this sense, the battle of the Plains of Abraham is more important than the formidable defeat – in all its noise, fury, and glory – of Napoleon at Waterloo, fifty-six years later.

We usually remember the Plains of Abraham, but almost everyone has forgotten that this battle, and the Conquest of New France in general, came after a long and terrible war, by far the most trying that has ever taken place on Quebec or Canadian soil. In September 1760, the winners were faced with a prostrate people. The losers were really a pitiful sight. This fact is not irrelevant to what follows.

New France, during the war, had lost one-seventh of its estimated 1765 population of sixty-five thousand, according to Lionel Groulx. The countryside had been devastated. The British army had torched, systematically, every village from Quebec down both sides of the St. Lawrence, to Baie Saint-Paul on the North Bank and the River Ouelle on the South. After two months of siege and bombardment, only one house remained standing in Lower Quebec City. The majority of the "Habitants" had been under arms for several years. Those who were not had sought refuge in the surrounding woods during the last days of the invasion. The war brought misery and, at its close, famine.

And there was fear, nourished by French and English propaganda. Wolfe's famous proclamation of June 27, 1759, gave enough food for the imagination: "If, to the contrary, misplaced stubbornness and careless valour cause them to take up arms, they (the Canadiens) can expect to suffer the most cruel effects that war has to offer . . . if they are comfortable in imagining the excesses of fury of which an unleashed soldiery is capable."

French propaganda had had no difficulty convincing the Canadiens of what they risked if the English won: at best, they would be deported, at worst, summarily executed. The Deportation of the Acadians, one of the dishonourable chapters in English colonial history, had just taken place, at the beginning of this war, and was still fresh in their minds. Some of the unfortunate deportees had fled to Quebec, which could not help but spread doubt about the magnanimity of eventual English conquerors. We must keep in mind that we look at the England of 1760 in the light of the evolution of that country, and the West in general, to a higher level of tolerance. For the Canadiens, the British were the hereditary enemy (with all that implies of hatred and fear).

Between the surrender of Quebec City and Montreal, France sent notice that it would suspend redemption of the paper money which the Canadiens had been forced to accept for many years. This was practical confirmation that the motherland had truly abandoned the Canadiens. (She had not sent any ships since 1758.) It was an end of the regime worthy of the colony's scandalous wartime administration under the infamous Intendant Bigot. As a final stroke of bad luck, between the two capitulations the abandoned Canadiens lost their last natural leader. The last Bishop of New France, Mgr. de Pontbriand, died May 8, 1760.

The people really touched bottom during the surrender of Quebec City in September 1759, and of Montreal a year later. In a country where each colonist still had his own gun, the disarmament of the Habitants, during ceremonies which brought together many parishes, was an emotion-filled event. Everyone was involved: highly symbolic, the act was lived as a disgrace. The people were "disarmed" in every sense of the word. Defenseless. Vulnerable.

The worst – military occupation – was yet to come.

But while Montreal was still French, Quebec was already under English rule. And the people began to breathe more easily – there had been, at least thus far, no summary executions.

From the surrender of Montreal in September 1760 to the entering into office of the first English civil governor, James Murray, in August 1764, the colony was occupied by the British Army: the country was under martial law. The Conquest was not yet a *fait accompli* and the war between England and France continued elsewhere. Quebec was no longer under the French regime, but not yet under the English.

These four years would be crucial. They would permanently mark the young, developing Canadien identity. It is difficult to understand the problems faced by the Quebec and Canada of today if we do not take into account what happened during that period. While the Canadiens were in a state of shock and entering a phase that should normally have been the most devastating, the behaviour of the British military proved to be correct. Even exemplary.

Michel Brunet, a Quebec historian unlikely to be accused of compliancy on this topic, writes that "the generosity of the Conqueror, his kindness, care for the general interest and his spirit of justice won the hearts of the vanquished." Not only were the Canadiens free from any kind of physical threat, it quickly became clear that there would be no question of deportation. To the contrary: there was some fear that the Canadiens would emigrate, as the Treaty of Paris would give them the right to do in 1763.

The occupiers vied for superiority in intelligence and kindness during this period when it was not yet known whether England would keep Canada. The basic characteristics of the French Regime were preserved. The judicial system was still divided into three administrative regions: Quebec City, Trois-Rivières, and Montreal. When the English made changes, it was generally for the better, like paying cash for army purchases. During this time of shortages, and to avoid speculation, the military governors wisely fixed the price of staples such as meat and bread.

At times, the occupiers even proved gentle and considerate. Approximately £8000 were gathered from the English officers to help the most needy of the Canadiens, and soldiers were ordered to salute religious processions in the streets. The Canadiens expected Attila: they got Caesar Augustus. Twenty years after the "Please fire first, Gentlemen of England!" of the Battle of Fontenoy, the spirit was that of a petticoat war.

The Canadiens were deeply touched. This is a delicate subject that embarrasses some historians, but the facts are incontestable. During that period, the Canadiens were more or less seduced by their conquerors. The historian Burt's expression for this period implies something terrible: "the moral conquest."

Numerous examples, not always from the occupiers themselves, are proof of a feeling of content among Quebecers' ancestors. In 1763, the captains of the militia, or what remained of the military elite of New France, sent the governor nothing less than an "affectionate address." The next year, another address was ended with this seemingly unbelievable closing: "Duty is enjoyable when accompanied by affection." Finally, and as incontestable proof, were the forthcoming marriages of Canadien women to British soldiers.

Seduction would be reciprocal, to a certain degree. The military governor of the Quebec region, James Murray, pitied the vanquished. Four months after the fall of Montreal he wrote to Amherst, his Commander-in-Chief, concerning the miserable situation of the Canadiens: "to describe it is really beyond my powers and to think of it is shocking to humanity." He preferred these Canadiens to the few dozen English adventurers who followed the British armies and settled almost immediately in Quebec and Montreal.

Murray was to have an important influence on the Canadian identity. It is important, therefore, to take a look at his personality. Brigadier James Murray, the son of Lord Elibank, came from a good Scottish family. Some have said that he was a little like Wolfe, the victor of the Plains of Abraham. Authoritarian but fair, intelligent, muddle-headed, and impetuous, Murray was the product of the old England, aristocratic and rural. As a soldier, he fought fiercely against the Canadiens during the war. (His army ravaged the islands of Sorel and their surrounding region during the summer of 1759.) As a victor he was moved by the distress of those he had conquered.

At first, Murray found the Canadiens ignorant, dominated by their seigneurs and priests. But a military governor about to manage an occupied country appreciated their docility. With time, the gentleman would be seduced by their good manners, reminder still of Old France. In a petition to the English Minister of the Colonies, he described them as "perhaps the best and the bravest race on this globe"; later, he "would speak of them as a people he loved and admired."

Such turgid descriptions would not prevent Murray from thinking that the assimilation of the Canadiens would not only be unavoidable, but desirable, and for their own good. But the military governor of Quebec was somewhat disgusted with the evolution of the English society of his time. This society was losing respect for the aristocratic and military values he so cherished. In England, the pragmatic, mercantile spirit which prevailed was on its way to making the small island off Europe mistress of the world.

The governor found he had affinities and community of interest with a society that had always been militarized and that kept its feudal ways. In 1762 he gave the name Beauport to the property he purchased in England, with the intention of retiring there after his service. He later decided to spend his last days as a seigneur in Canada. He would devote a great deal of money and energy to his seigneury of Lauzon, near Quebec City, when the colony's English merchants succeeded in having him recalled to England.

In retrospect, this uncommon "love story" between the defeated and the occupiers is not that surprising on the Canadien side. After fearing for one's life in a terrible war, and while still in a state of shock after the defeat by the hereditary enemy, and with the increasing signs of France's disregard, surrendering to such kind English people was not merely the only possible objective outcome but it must have been experienced with relief. Almost like a liberation. The Church, the only Canadien elite still politically functional, in spite of the death of the Bishop, had sent its flock an unmistakable message. Even before peace had been officially declared between France and England, a solemn *Te Deum* was sung in the churches in honour of the English victory.

This is analogous to hostages who fall in love with their abductors, when these reveal themselves as captivating individuals. But no comparison is perfect, for the English were far more imposing than vulgar kidnappers. They were the Conquerors.

During the latter days of military occupation, London and Paris had already agreed on the colony's destiny. This was sealed in February 1763 by the Treaty of Paris, which put an end to the Seven Years War. Canada's abandonment by France was confirmed. In the months that followed, the Board of Trade, the English department responsible for administration of the colonies, drafted in London the Royal Proclamation. This would give what used to be New France its first civil government under the English regime.

The Canadiens did not yet know it, but they were about to be officially abandoned by France and conquered by England. They and their descendants would take some time to grasp fully what had happened.

It is clear that what did happen during this period was as much France's abandonment of its colony as it was England's conquest. If France had wanted Canada, it would have been able to keep the country during the signing of the Treaty of Paris, in the context of negotiations concerning not only Europe, but India and the West Indies as well. But France, obviously, didn't want Canada. First and foremost a European power, it had invested a great deal less in New France than had England in its American colonies.

While one Englishman in six lived in the New World in 1760, the ratio for the French was only one in three hundred.

The historian Mason Wade noted that French Canadians used to call the Conquest the Cession. This was probably to take into account the aspect of the event that had particularly hurt them and that reflected on France's honour: its only inhabited colony, the only part of itself that had started to take root elsewhere, was yielded freely and without regret to the hereditary enemy.

The young Canadien identity had as yet no existence independent of France. Understandably so, that identity would be deeply marked or bruised by this desertion, which would be emotionally perceived as rejection. That experience would certainly tarnish the image Canadiens would develop of themselves. It probably explains the traditional francophobia of Quebec's "little" people, which has always contrasted with the love of France of some of the elite.

There was never a serious plan for reconquest. In France, Canada was quickly forgotten. During the American War of Independence, the chivalrous Marquis de Lafayette dreamed of a Franco-American expedition to free Quebec, but the affair was never seriously considered in Versailles. When Alexis de Tocqueville visited Canada in 1831, he expressed his astonishment at finding a French nation completely unknown to Paris. There, those who knew their history thought that the Canadiens had been assimilated.

It was not until De Gaulle's "Vive le Québec libre" in 1967 that an emotional link between the motherland and its old colony was really re-established politically. With his extensive knowledge of French history, the great man felt that he was settling part of "Louis XV's debt," according to his biographer Jean Lacouture. Because of the unique way in which he represented his country, and because of the era, which was still open to this kind of effusion, De Gaulle was the last Frenchman in a position of authority to be able to say to the Canadiens' descendants: France is sorry, France recognizes you as French, France loves you . . . Most of the message was heard, to the great displeasure of the English Canadians, who reacted bitterly to the outburst. The Québécois identity emerged stronger than before.

But the reality of 1763 was abandonment, rejection. This transforms a defeat, which you can always hope to reverse, into something permanent: a "conquest." Without France's support, it was totally unrealistic for the sixty-five thousand Canadiens to hope to liberate themselves from England, the greatest world power. But being abandoned made the Conquest easier to accept at the time.

There was no choice; even France was in favour of it. Later, when the motherland was swept by atheist revolution, the Canadiens even managed to convince themselves that, all things considered, this was a blessing from heaven.

People are often very surprised that Quebecers say they are still affected by an event that took place over two hundred years ago, while other peoples have already overcome more recent, more devastating defeats. They forget the fundamental difference between defeat and conquest. A conquest is a permanent defeat, an institutionalized defeat.

In 1760, France suffered a major, humiliating defeat by England. She had her revenge fifteen years later, giving the Americans, in their War of Independence against the English, the support that proved the deciding factor. The Canadiens were not really defeated during the Seven Years War: in general, they had won the battles for which they were responsible. The Canadiens were conquered in 1760.

In accordance with international law of the times, England acquired, in principle, limitless power over them. That is the ultimate catastrophe for a people: being taken over, totally and permanently, by the hereditary enemy. Contrary to the vanquished, the conquered is affected at the heart of his collective identity. He becomes the conqueror's creature, to do with what he may. That the conqueror is magnanimous changes nothing in this reality. On the contrary, it makes the conquest more humiliating because the conquered also has to be grateful.

But these are only concepts – juridical terms. Merely words. A conquest is lived. As Kenneth McRae, a critical observer of Quebec nationalism, wrote in 1964, "To the Canadiens, it was a cataclysm beyond the power of the mind to grasp." Literally, the unthinkable.

Lionel Groulx

A renowned philosopher, priest, and professor of History at the Université de Montréal, Lionel Groulx is regarded today as the father of Quebec nationalism. He was one of the first historians to portray the French-Canadians as a potent national entity, and since his death in 1967, many public monuments have been named after him. A product of the right-wing thinking of the Catholic Church which reached its zenith in the 1950s and the Duplessis era, Groulx admired the Italian dictator Benito Mussolini and believed the interests of the nation or collective should come before the rights of the individual. He has been recently criticized in Quebec for his anti-Semitic views. The following excerpt is from "The First Obligation," an essay from Pourquoi nous sommes divisés *(Éditions de l'Action Nationale, 1943).*

The First Obligation

In Quebec let us be strong with all our strength. Let us take heed of the incomparable value of our geographic position. In 1867 Confederation could not have been made without us; we have remained indispensable to Confederation. We are the arch that links the east and the west. By the river we guard the great door to the sea; through our territory we give passage to the transcontinental railways on their way to the ports of the Atlantic and the Pacific.

Quebec, the nearest Canadian territory to Europe, furnishes aerial transport with its most convenient bases and landing fields. There may be richer lands than ours; nevertheless, we possess some of the most opulent riches of Canada and of America. We possess them in sufficient variety to build one of the best-balanced economies of the world. These riches should no longer be offered to the stranger for some handfuls of cents and dollars.

Let us regain those we have lost by every means that we can learn from our economists, particularly by the co-operative system. We have considerable purchasing power. Following the example of the whole world, let us use it for our own benefit first. Would certain mercantile races insult or frown upon us if we ceased to make their fortune for them? We have labour; let us not lower the market for it. Let us exact a just return from those who live and grow rich at our expense. Let us not abandon our workers to leaders from beyond our borders or elsewhere who ask nothing better than to sell us a Trojan horse.

Translated by G.O. Rothney

Jean-François Lisée

Jean-Francois Lisée is one of Quebec's most respected journalists and the author of In the Eye of the Eagle. *The following is abridged from an interview published in* L'actualité *(November 1991).*

The New Look of Independence

Jacques Parizeau is a man in a hurry. He's anxious to do battle with the Liberals in the next election. But the leader of the Parti Québécois must put up with a certain delay: his dream of holding a referendum in 1991 went up in the smoke of the Bélanger-Campeau report, and he's not even sure he can count on the one promised for October 1992. He doesn't think Quebec premier Robert Bourassa will keep his word. That's bad timing because Parizeau has worked out a recipe for the sovereign Quebec he'd like to create: lots of sovereignty, not much association. He explained that he wouldn't want to commit himself to major negotiations with the federal government before sovereignty is achieved, and studiously avoids any talk about creating a Canada-Québécois Brussels. Mention the shared institutions of the association discussed in René Lévesque's 1979 white paper on sovereignty and he quips: "That's archaeology!"

Lisée: Was there a time – I'm thinking of your own "outstretched hand" speech on the night of the death of Meech – when you thought that Mr. Bourassa could bring about sovereignty?

Parizeau: One thing is still clear today, conversely, which is that should Mr. Bourassa decide in favour of sovereignty, my first reaction would be to say: "Bravo, let's do it together."

Lisée: Do you still think that he will perhaps do it?

Parizeau: The likelihood of that has been over since the end of the Bélanger-Campeau Commission [on Quebec's political and constitutional future], when it became very clear that the Liberal orientation was going to be very, very federalist. And it explains why, since then, the outstretched hand has been withdrawn.

Lisée: Despite the rise of sovereignist feelings last year, as soon as you talk to Quebecers about new federal offers, the polls have always shown that the majority would buy it. In the end, your biggest ally is Clyde Wells. You need Canada to say no to Quebec.

Parizeau: For twenty-five years my best ally has been the majority of English-Canadians. They don't want us to break up their country. I have a lot of sympathy for them. For example, they want a national education policy. That's obvious. Is there such a thing as a country without an educational policy? But it's impossible because Quebec doesn't want one. They're fed up, and quite rightly. Clyde Wells is simply the one who gives a voice to that kind of sentiment. And look at some of the things that have been written in English Canada recently, saying good riddance to Quebec. In a sense it's one of the underlying ideas of the Reform Party. That's how far we've come.

Lisée: Let's look at your scenario. No referendum but an election in late 1993, early 94. You say that if you're elected, you'll begin the sovereignty process immediately and not hold a referendum until later. But are you going to start that process even if you're only elected by a minority of Québécois?

Parizeau: In 1867, when Quebec joined the federation, there were a great many requests and petitions in Quebec for a referendum on the matter. They were all turned down. So this time we're being very nice, very democratic. We say, you don't pull out of the federation simply through a parliamentary vote, you'll need a referendum. Now just between us, we would be granting something that was never granted to us in 1867.

Lisée: So it's possible that 45 percent of the people could elect you, you'd start the process, hold a referendum, and 55 percent of the people would vote no to sovereignty?

Parizeau: There are people who would like us to have 65 percent of the vote in a referendum. If we put more obstacles before the horse, even if he's frisky it would be most unusual if we couldn't stop him from jumping. [laughter]

Lisée: But wouldn't you be up against a brick wall? No federal government will want to negotiate. Ottawa will wait for the referendum results before they return your call.

Parizeau: My only questions to the federal government will have to do with "maintaining" certain things. We're already making progress in that debate. Most of the analysts who have been consulted recognized that if Quebec wants to keep the Canadian dollar, it will do so. What might come out of those discussions as far as a monetary policy is concerned? We'll see. What's important initially is that everyone be quite certain the decision is Quebec's to make.

Lisée: Would those decisions be made during the transition period, before the referendum?

Parizeau: We must acknowledge a certain number of points. Take maintaining the free flow of capital. It's possible that Toronto would decide to set up exchange controls aimed solely at a sovereign Quebec. That would be unheard-of, but we must examine all the assumptions. It means that our money would be obliged to make a detour via New York. . . . It would also mean that the commissions on these operations would all be taken in New York. So I ask English Canada, Do you agree with that? They, obviously, say no. And so I tell them, Then we agree on the free flow of capital. That's what I mean about "maintenance." When things are presented from that point of view, plenty of emotions fall away. The last thing I want are "wide-ranging negotiations with Ottawa" that would change matters profoundly. In the atmosphere that will prevail at the time? Unthinkable! It's obvious that the federal government will refuse to negotiate and I won't ask them to. I simply ask them to tell us if they agree to maintain certain things to which I know very well it's impossible for them to say no.

Lisée: But that's not true for all the components of the Canadian economic space.

Parizeau: Customs union presents problems, that is to say tariffs for products from third countries. Should we decide unilaterally to follow Canada's policy, we would have to modify our tariffs at the same time and in the same direction, for example towards Asian textiles. We'll have to ask ourselves if it's worth having our own policy, which would imply setting up customs at the Ontario border, but only for transporting goods. I'm not dogmatic on that point. Circumstances will determine our decision. As for the free flow of services – our banks and their banks having the same rights in the two countries, for example – that will require either harmonizing legislation or signing an agreement. The big challenge will be to find a formula for settling disagreements, and for that we could use the mechanisms from the free trade accord with the U.S.

Lisée: Are you sure you'll be able to remain part of the free trade accord?

Parizeau: There are hundreds of agreements of all sorts between Canada and the United States, and we have two choices. We could look at them one by one – free trade, the Seaway, and so forth. Do you realize what a shambles that would lead to? It would take forever. Or, we accept them all. As is. With a simple adjustment in the case of agreements that require a bipartite presence. In those cases, we'll have to find a supporting role for Quebec somewhere. Then, on the normal dates for renewing those agreements, we will re-negotiate them as required. I've often tested that approach with the Americans. Some tell me, we'll have to re-examine this or that. And then I bring up NORAD, and they say: "Oh no, not NORAD!" So then I say, "Look here, it's not selective. Either we take everything, or we negotiate everything." They admit that it's more convenient to take everything. With English Canada, it's a little more complicated, because for a while their reaction will be emotional. That's why we must talk about it often, which I do, deliberately. We have to wave the red flag at the bull every week, provoke vindictive editorials in the English-Canadian press. Once the emotion has passed, the calm discussions can begin.

Lisée: But negotiating the debt and credits, that can't wait!

Parizeau: What pleases me enormously – and in that respect, Bélanger-Campeau was a marvellous operation – is that the debate has got underway very properly. This summer there were astonishing articles in some newspapers, English-Canadian mainly. It's marvellous that subtle distinctions between the kinds of federal debts should be established so far in advance of a Quebec election. I'm convinced that when negotiations really get underway, much of the groundwork will already have been done.

Lisée: You talk about maintenance, about the debt and credits, but you haven't mentioned economic association. It will require "wide-ranging negotiations" to arrive at an association.

Parizeau: I don't think that would be useful. I never bring it up. What's important is that we have just what we need at the outset to ensure free circulation and the same currency. Once that has been established, we'll see as far as the rest is concerned if we want more formal mechanisms. Time will tell.

Lisée: The constraints of the free trade accord spare the provinces. But if Quebec becomes a country, its financial institutions, for example, could be bought by American companies.

Parizeau: Do you think no one has seen that one coming? And why do you think all the mainsprings of Quebec's financial structure have been set up [he finishes the sentence in a whisper] so that they can't be bought by American companies! If you want to talk about collusion between successive Quebec governments over the past fifteen years, here's a good example. La Laurentienne is a mutual, Les Coopérants, the Industrielle-Alliance, which also controls Trust Général – they're all mutuals. The Caisse de dépôt [which manages Quebec's pension fund]? Can't be touched! The Caisses populaires? Can't be bought! The Fonds de solidarité?

Lisée: You say that Quebec products such as milk will have protected access to Canada because of the GATT, which Quebec would like to be part of. But if Canada is opposed, Quebec can't automatically join the GATT.

Parizeau: In practice, it doesn't happen that a country, new or old, is refused admission to the GATT. There's no precedent for it. Once a country has been recognized, it's accepted.

Lisée: Yes, but what if Canada didn't recognize Quebec? Ottawa would declare a trade war. At that crucial point there would be a legal void and it is false to say that Quebec is protected by the GATT.

Parizeau: And if you're telling me that international recognition has a certain importance, I would tend to say yes. This is why we have our own contacts in the United States, France, all over.

Lisée: Give me a sense of the possible cost of sovereignty, in terms of the GNP or unemployment or the cost of living during the first five years of a sovereign Quebec. What could that represent?

Parizeau: I'd be crazy to name a figure! What we'll have with sovereignty is the chance to do things that we can't do now. The question is, will we be amazingly intelligent about it, rather stupid, or somewhere in between? The figures depend on that. Certain things strike me as obvious. We can't set up effective manpower training programs in the present framework. That's in large measure the explanation for the fact that after seven years of unbroken prosperity, until 1990, we're still stuck with ten per cent unemployment.

Lisée: For a certain number of years there would be a significant process of political transition. There will be uncertainty, even in the best of scenarios, and a price to pay.

Parizeau: Why don't those who think there'll be a price to pay come out with numbers? Let's talk about uncertainty. We had two strikes against us when we [the Parti Québécois] came to power in 1976: we were socialists and we were sovereignists. Uncertainty should have dealt us a serious blow. Aren't you struck by the fact that from 1977 to 1980, investments in the industrial and manufacturing sectors increased more rapidly in Quebec than in Ontario? I ask lovers of uncertainty to explain that to me. No one can. On the other hand, at the time, Quebec was starved for capital. Were the money markets in Toronto, New York, Montreal shut down? Yes, they were. Did that stop us from organizing ourselves? No. I've borrowed in Japan and Europe, at almost the same rate as Sweden. Then the American market opened up again, naturally. So I think that if we conduct our business more or less correctly – and I can see what we'll be able to do – there are only gains to be made.

Lisée: Don't you risk ending up, after sovereignty is achieved, perhaps for reasons unrelated to your policies, surrounded by economic problems for which you won't have prepared Quebecers, making them wonder if sovereignty was such a good idea?

Parizeau: In 1980 we went into the referendum campaign with enthusiasm and it ended in numbers. This time, we want to start with the numbers and finish with enthusiasm. We'll also have to convince Quebecers that once they've become responsible for themselves, the results will depend largely on their work and their efforts. I've always been struck by the degree to which Quebecers tend to hand over responsibility to others. Psychologically, that has done us considerable harm.

Lisée: Your conversion to Canadian currency has caused some skepticism. With your criticisms of Canadian monetary policy and what you claim to be its harmful effects on Quebec, logically you should be hoping to control that lever by creating your own currency.

Parizeau: I sang the praises of a fluctuating Quebec currency throughout the 1973 election campaign. Everybody got nervous! Technically, creating a Quebec currency isn't really complicated. But to do so in such a way that the people have confidence in it is another kettle of fish. What's the best way for them to have confidence? Tell them we'll keep the Canadian dollar, even if the Canadians don't agree. I know very well that we'd be giving up an important economic instrument. But it completely changes the monetary argument. You don't hear any more talk about a Quebec dollar worth 65 cents.

Then we move onto the next stage: a lot of business-people, who were the first to spread fear a few years ago, come to see me and say: If we keep the Canadian dollar, we'll have no influence over monetary policy. I tell them: "If enough of you ask, I'll see what I can do!" [laughter] After all, I've learned some political lessons in the past twenty years. This time, the demand for a Quebec currency will come from the public and the business community. But it won't happen overnight. Ireland took twenty-five years to create its own currency, which was very wise.

Translated by Sheila Fischman

Pierre Vallières

Pierre Vallières was one of the main theorists of the separatist and terrorist Front de Libération du Québec (FLQ). Born in 1938 to a working-class family in Montreal's East End, he wrote most of his seminal book on Quebec independence, Nègres blancs d'Amérique/ White Niggers of America *(1968), in the Manhattan House of Detention while awaiting deportation with Charles Gagnon for demonstrating in front of the United Nations on behalf of the FLQ. Jailed numerous times in connection with his FLQ activity, Vallières threw his support behind the Parti Québécois in 1971 with the publication of* L'Urgence de choisir. *He is now the chief editor of* Vie ouvrière *in Montreal. The following article appeared in* Le Devoir *(August 18, 1990).*

The Demagoguery of Consensus

From now on in Quebec, working towards independence no longer means building a free society, but simply doing business, very big business.

When it's heating up as it is now, the national question automatically brings happiness to sovereignists of all persuasions, whether on the left or the right. It spurs on the politicians who make a living off of it and who hope that the popular fever, reignited once again, will swiftly lead them to the head of the affairs of state.

Unfortunately, the political haste of these public debates called for by the party leaders too often has the effect of excluding the majority of the population that is being invited to speak broadly, and of course democratically, about their collective future.

Since the failure of the final (and less than open) discussions surrounding the Meech Lake Accord, there has been no shortage of superficial praise for democracy and the "sovereign people." The shortsightedness of holding constitutional talks behind closed doors has been energetically, and rightly, condemned. It has now been proposed that the future status of Quebec (independence, sovereignty-association, neo-federalism . . .) be discussed at the public level by all groups and individuals who wish to do so.

In short, an attempt to move from the backroom into the town square. But this fine plan is nothing but a base lie, a demagogic deception.

In effect, the political leaders, especially the most nationalistic among them, define at the outset this democratic practice of the people, referred to as "sovereign," as the necessary pursuit of social unanimity, which is to say a form of consensus that excludes straightaway the right to dissent, to healthy criticism, indeed to any kind of genuine opposition.

So, even before giving the green light to the forthcoming public discussions, people in high places have hastily decreed that any political plan for a departure from capitalism cannot and must not be put on the table. In sum, Quebec, whether sovereign or not, is sentenced by its leaders to the economic and social status quo. Research on the specificity of Quebec in North America precludes any kind of alternative to primitive capitalism.

In consequence, groups and persons who have been wronged by the dominant system are resigning themselves to it. Natives, the jobless, poor people, "hewers of wood and drawers of water" of all types, your opinion is not required. What's more, your calls for justice are ill-timed. For heaven's sake, leave your protest signs at home! Don't soil the halls of the new aristocrats with your tantrums!

In this way, social peace, absence of protest, and submission to the elected – no matter how politically bankrupt the latter might be – are being presented as prerequisites to debates which are at the same time supposed to be broad-based and democratic. It has been argued that the urgency of defining a new constitutional arrangement for Quebec is such that we must unanimously, and without discussion, stifle all divergences, stuff our differences into the closet, and, in effect, "erase" our historical consciences. In short, we are to be less a people, than a flock.

The shepherds, Parizeau, Bouchard and company, repeat it over and over: the discussion must be limited to staking out the legal-constitutional ground for an eventual Quebec-Canada-U.S. free trade triangle. In agreement with Bourassa, they demand that these talks be presided over, directed, and concluded, by bankers. Money is the final boundary of our "liberation." Alas, when you are poor, marginalized, scorned by bankers, politicians and lawyers, liberation might just bring you hard times. It has been seen elsewhere before.

Who cares if Quebec is, in the words of Lise Bissonnette, a "profoundly non-egalitarian and dangerously negligent" society, the financial spokesmen of the 1990 version of "Québec libre" intend to use all means, including censorship, to keep the debate on the national question from becoming an occasion for collective and pluralistic thinking about an alternative social plan. There is no question of activists taking on the battle against poverty, among other things, by pointing a finger at the system that is the cause of it. No.

Better to give the business people and their publicists the time to manipulate at their leisure the symbol and slogans of political sovereignty. From now on in Quebec, working for independence no longer means building a free society, but simply doing business, very big business. It's a money matter, which, because it's costing a lot and should pay off handsomely, must be dealt with by professionals, by experts, by political economists, and not by "hewers of wood," let alone by socialists, greens, women, or natives.

It hardly matters that in everyone's eyes, the business milieu is far behind the times in dealing with the problems and expectations of the majority. What's good for the Banque Nationale is, on the face of it, good for the entire nation.

WE will work for independence just as WE voted in favour of free trade: captives, all, of a system which confounds democratic practice with the jungle-law of the market. Our politicians, driven by the urgency of gaining the maximum advantage from the nationalist momentum, have forgotten that pluralistic debate is the necessary condition for all democratic practice.

Without pluralism, the consensus obtained can be nothing but the product of the most vulgar political obscurantism. Social unanimity, knocked together out of dictates and hollow slogans, is the opposite of liberty. And where have we seen a democracy without liberty?

The impatient nationalism of Parizeau's and Bouchard's business troops does not serve democracy. To build a society, a truly free country, we must move away from a performance democracy, a show-biz democracy, towards a democracy of participation that is pluralistic and creative, where no one will be left out in the cold.

Translated by Christopher Korchin

Donald Brittain

One of Canada's foremost filmmakers, the late Donald Brittain (1928-1989) worked briefly as a police reporter and foreign correspondent before embarking on his film career with the National Film Board in Montreal in 1955. His prodigious output included more than one hundred films, many of which brought him international recognition. Among his best-known works are Bethune (1964); Ladies and Gentlemen . . . Mr. Leonard Cohen (1965); Volcano: An Inquiry into the Life and Death of Malcolm Lowry (1976); Canada's Sweetheart: The Saga of Hal C. Banks (1985); *and* The King Chronicle (1988). *The following script is abridged from the* The Champions (1978, Part 1&2; 1986, Part 3) *and is presented with the kind permission of Brigitta Brittain and the National Film Board. The films are available on video cassette from the NFB.*

The Champions

[. . .] symbol indicates where the original script has been abridged

Narrator (*Donald Brittain*): In the fall of 1967 René Lévesque was 45 years of age. He had spent seven years as a television personality. He had spent seven years on the front benches of the Liberal Party. In both careers he had been a huge success. Now he had a new career – he had become a Separatist.

Voice (TV): Well, let's put it this way. Let's get right down to the real cases – there's a novel out on this very subject – would you fight if you had to?
Lévesque: Would you what?
Voice (TV): Fight.
Lévesque: You mean fight with arms?
Voice (TV): Yes.
Lévesque: Would the rest of Canada fight to keep Quebec in against its own will?
Voice (TV): I don't know.
Lévesque: I know. It won't. Because I think the rest of Canada first of all has no illusions on that score and second is civilized. Next question.

Narrator: On the eve of the Liberal Convention Trudeau arrived in Ottawa. On the opening night they said goodbye to beloved Mike Pearson. Paul Hellyer was desperately trying to convince everybody that he was two years younger than Trudeau. He was actually four years younger than Trudeau but nobody believed him. [. . .]

Going into the fourth ballot, Trudeau's margin was shrinking, but by the time Hellyer and Winters finally got their act together it was too late. Trudeau needed 1200 votes.

Voice: Pierre E. Trudeau, 1203 . . .

Narrator: Almost immediately Pierre Trudeau went to the nation at large. Three days before the general election he was in Montreal. "Be master in your own house," he told the Québécois, "but let that house be all of Canada." He planned to end his campaign at the parade honouring Jean Baptiste, patron saint of Quebec, but he had recently compared the FLQ terrorists to the assassins of Robert Kennedy and this had enraged all Separatists. Pierre Bourgault and the Rassemblement pour l'indépendence nationale (RIN) had promised a surprise for Trudeau if he showed up at the parade.

Voice (*Brittain*): The Jean Baptiste affair, which was talked about a great deal, what was your role in that?
Bourgault: I led it.
Voice (*Brittain*): And it was a deliberate situation which was well-planned?
Bourgault: Of course. We had decided that since we were not very numerous, we could gather about 2000 people in the streets at the most, so we decided to hold it right down here so that we could use the 100,000 people who were there. The police will come on us, we'll go on them and after a while they'll have to go through the crowd, the crowds will turn against the police and that's what happened. [. . .]

I was supposed to be there for ten minutes and then go home and then they would have started the rumour Bourgault has been arrested so that the militants would be mad. But it happens that I was arrested, so I didn't have to go home. I was thrown in jail right from the start . . .

Narrator: On schedule the RIN let loose a barrage of bottles and rocks. The police charged. A lot of innocent on-lookers were hurt. But the nation watched Trudeau stand his ground and swept him back into office. He was given the first majority government in ten years. He brought new faces to Ottawa. Eric Kierans believed that Trudeau would create a true federalism. "Now," thought Kierans, "the entrenched bureaucrats will be cleared out and the provinces treated with respect." Bourgault and his rioters had only ensured Trudeau's victory. They had committed political suicide. Lévesque severed all connections. [. . .]

Bourgault announced to his followers that he was disbanding the organization. The only hope was Lévesque's new party. Lévesque would not take them in en masse – they would have to join one by one. In October, the other major separatist party, the

Ralliement Nationale, joined Lévesque's movement, and together they founded the Parti Québécois. There was never any doubt as to who would lead it.

Lévesque: I'd like to say we've got no lesson on that score to take from the McConnells – from anyone that has been dominating Quebec like a bunch of Rhodesians – the white group! If we had colours here you'd feel it, and that is something we will not stand for any more, this paternalistic wasp – and it is that typically – the wasp arrogance of the ones that have been leading our government and through the slush funds they contribute to, leading both of our hack parties by the nose for too long.

Pauline Julien: I don't want to lose you either, but we have to change, to really be free both you and me, and every people in the world just want that.

Narrator: Pauline Julien, Quebec singer and separatist, being interviewed by Patrick Watson.

Voice TV (*Watson*): I'm just asking you now . . .
Julien: We have just a few years to save ourself.
Voice TV (*Watson*): Is there an answer from where you sit to all the people like Pauline Julien who talked to us earlier today and who is an extremely eloquent propounder of this statement of personal need to exist as a cultural entity?
Trudeau: Well, it's like someone who would say, you know psychologically I have to stay within the British Empire, this is a psychological need, so I make sure the sun rises and sets on parts of me – how do you argue with a person like that?
Voice TV (*Watson*): No, but that's an enormously contemptuous thing to say about people who feel profoundly that they have been pulling themselves up from – you know all about that . . .
Trudeau: Well some Colonel Blimps felt very profoundly about the British Empire. All that I can say is that we're living in a different world now, whereas Miss Julien or Colonel Blimp are living in the 19th century.
Voice (TV): But are you equating the passion of a person like Miss Julien or the ambitions of a man like Lévesque with the instinct to hold on to a fading power that Colonel Blimp stands for?
Trudeau: People – many persons of this type – say, you know I can't argue with you, you talk economics, you talk sociology, you talk politics, you talk history – this may sound good but it's a question of dignity, it's a question of feeling. What do you say? Go and feel your own way, you know – I'll feel mine.

Narrator: This was all very well for Pierre Elliott Trudeau, but the English-speaking residents in his home riding of the Town of Mount Royal had a lot of houses for sale. Many of them weren't waiting for the spring election. For the first time in Quebec there was a viable separatist party, with a leader who was once a Minister of the Crown.

Voice (TV): What chance do you have of becoming premier of Quebec in the next election?
Lévesque: If we get less than ten or twelve ridings it's rather catastrophic.

Narrator: He got only seven seats – he lost his own – but the Parti Québécois got 23 per cent of the vote and Lévesque was a hero.

October 5, 1970 – James Cross is kidnapped. October 10, 1970 – Pierre Laporte was kidnapped. The Prime Minister calls out the troops to guard potential victims.

Voice (*Protester*): Sir, what is it with all these men with guns around here?
Trudeau: Haven't you noticed?
Voice: Yeah, I've noticed them, you people decided to have them.
Trudeau: What's your worry?
Voice: I'm not worried but you seem . . . I'm worried about living in a town that's full of people with guns, running around.
Trudeau: Have they done anything to you? Have they pushed you around or anything?
Voice: They've pushed around friends of mine.
Trudeau: They have? What were your friends doing?
Voice: Trying to take pictures of them.
Trudeau: Aha.
Voice: Is that against the law?
Trudeau: No, not at all.
Voice: Doesn't it worry you having to resort to this kind of thing?
Trudeau: It doesn't worry me; I think it's natural that if people are being abducted that they be protected against such abductions. No, I still go back to the choice that you have to make in the kind of society that you live in – well, there's a lot of bleeding hearts around that just don't like to see people with helmets and guns. All I can say is, go on and bleed, but it's more important to keep law and order in a society than to be worried about weak-kneed people who don't like the looks of . . .
Voice: At any cost? At any cost? How far would you go with that – how far would you extend that?

Trudeau: Just watch me!
Trudeau (*TV Speech*): It's a democratic society – to continue to exist it must be able to root out the cancer of an armed revolutionary movement that is bent on destroying the very basis of our freedom. For that reason the government, following an analysis of the facts, including the requests of the governments of Quebec and of the City of Montreal, for urgent action, decided to proclaim the War Measures Act. It did so at 4:00 A.M. this morning in order to permit the full weight of the government to be brought quickly to bear on all those persons advocating or practising violence as a means of achieving political ends. At the moment, we have been forced to include the right to search and arrest without warrant, to detain suspected persons without the necessity of laying specific charges immediately, and to detain persons without bail. . . . These are strong powers, and I find them as distasteful as I'm sure you do.
Voice: You will find the body in the trunk of a green Chevrolet bearing license number 9J2420.
Trudeau: I want to express to Mrs. Laporte and Mr. Laporte's family the very deep regrets of the Canadian people, of the Canadian government, and our desire as Canadians to stick together in this very sorry moment of our history.
Voice: Could you tell us about the kind of people you're dealing with?
Trudeau: I can't tell you anything more. [. . .]

Narrator: Lévesque who had fought to keep his movement free of violence condemned what he called "an act of barbarism" – a stain on Quebec. Pierre Laporte, who had been Lévesque's Cabinet colleague and Trudeau's schoolmate, was buried. James Cross was saved. The kidnappers were apprehended. Trudeau had arrested 419 people – 281 were never charged but as his supporters pointed out, there were no more kidnappings. The Parti Québécois was on the edge of ruin. Lévesque readily admitted that because of his open policy some violent men may have found their way into his party and that they would have to be removed. But he was not alone in condemning Pierre Trudeau for overkill. Trudeau had spoken of a great dark insurrection, but he never produced any evidence that there was anything more than a handful of mad dogs. Eighty per cent of the country was on his side. The others, who thought Trudeau had debased individual liberties, were an embattled minority.

In 1972 he called an election, announced that the land was strong and declined to campaign. His Cartesian logic and Socratic dialogues did not go down well in a Drummondville cafeteria. He offered Quebec little but half of them voted for him to save him from political oblivion. He was more in his element with the great men and issues of the time. Here he could realize his dream of Canada moving with stature through the international community. Lévesque had called him a citizen, not of Quebec, or of Canada, but of the world.

Trudeau himself had said, however, that if he were not a French Canadian by birth, he would be one by adoption. Among Lévesque's followers were those who talked about ethnic purity and the dangers of cultural contamination. To Trudeau this was cultural suffocation, a crime against humanity.

Lévesque believed that Canada did not exist, except as some artificial concoction and that the sooner this was recognized, the better for all concerned. In the 1973 election he told the Québécois that a vote for him was a vote for separation. Bourassa's Liberals demolished him. He considered quitting but he'd got 30 per cent of the popular vote and decided to stay on and give it one more try. Even Lévesque's arch enemy, Marc Lalonde, admitted the PQ was the best organized party in Canada. The RCMP was spying on it until Trudeau told them to stop. Lévesque claimed to have 75,000 card-carrying members but he had decided to change his tune – he would fight the next election on good government. [. . .]

Bourassa: I'm very used to relatively strong attacks – the union leaders are attacking me very strongly. As you know, the separatist leaders are attacking me in a vociferous way, so I'm used to that. You know, it's not an easy job to govern Quebec. [. . .]

Narrator: Bourassa could sense a decline in popularity. He conceded that his majority might be somewhat reduced. It is November 15th, 1976.

McNeil (TV): The polls in Quebec have been closed for more than an hour and the returns that are coming in now show that this could be one of the most important provincial elections in Canadian history. The reason we say that is because the public opinion polls that came out five days before the election showed that the separatist Parti Québécois headed by René Lévesque could cut heavily into the Liberal majority of Robert Bourassa's Liberal Party and after one hour we are seeing that that's exactly what's happening.

Narrator: Lévesque's astounding victory must have been the dark moment in Pierre Trudeau's political life. By achieving power, the cause of separation had taken a quantum leap. The movement was now credible. It had a momentum and Lévesque had in his possession the awesome weapons of office. Trudeau could no longer stay removed from the battle for Quebec. [. . .]

In the aftermath of the election the Royal 22nd Regiment stood firm at the Citadel, but a lot of other people didn't know if they were coming or going. They set tables in New York to listen to Lévesque, who claimed he was George Washington. Then Trudeau went to the States and claimed he was Abraham Lincoln. The Americans were confused. The only people who weren't confused were the French. A guard of honour was drilled incessantly in preparation to receive a new officer of the Legion of Honour, René Lévesque. [. . .]

In the tunnels under Bourassa's bunker, Prime Minister Lévesque swiftly rams Bill 101 through the legislature. It is a repressive bill, imposing language requirements on business and limiting English education to certified descendants of Quebec educated anglophones. A nation, he once said, is judged by how it treats its minorities, but this must now be forgotten. [. . .]

Trudeau: My attitude has always been, and I've taken this in the worst years of the Duplessis era and of other governments, my attitude has always been, if you don't like the laws, if you think they're that bad, don't go running after your mother's apron strings. Take your responsibilities and defeat that law in the courts – if it's bad – and if you can't do it in the courts defeat it at the polls.

Narrator: Lévesque probably knew that Trudeau would not intervene. It would not be logical or politically smart. Lévesque himself is embarrassed. The Bill is more reactionary than the one he rejected nine years earlier, but many of his followers have an obsession with language. [. . .]

Trudeau had once quoted Plato – "the heaviest penalty for declining to engage in politics is to be ruled by someone inferior to yourself."

As Lévesque is briefed for his question period in the legislature, he knows that he too may be charged with suppressing individual freedoms for the greater good of the state. One Quebec writer calls it majority rule with a vengeance. But in Lévesque's case, as in Trudeau's, there seems to be no great resentment on the part of the people. The times had changed, the old street fighter, Pierre Bourgault, had been appointed to the Board of the Montreal Museum of Fine Arts. The final battleground would not be in the streets. [. . .]

Jim Coots (*adviser to Trudeau*): There were a lot of us who thought, you know, maybe the thing was going to come unstuck. Maybe there wasn't going to be a country. What we found in the Quebec surveys – the disturbing thing which I think has been known to everybody – is how many Quebecers toyed with the idea of separation at that time. It looked like a generational thing at the beginning and one had to say, if another generation in another five years, or whatever, coming as voters, as youths, as people in the work force, have the same ideas, the balance of this thing is going to tip. [. . .]

Narrator: Unlike Trudeau, who was losing good cabinet ministers out of sheer neglect, Lévesque knew how to find good men and keep them. His cabinet was the best educated in Canadian history. It was also dynamic. A mass of legislation had been passed. The party itself was fiercely democratic and remarkably honest, but everyone was waiting for the other shoe to drop.

The referendum question hung heavy in the air, but Lévesque's master weaver would not be rushed. Claude Morin would spend years carefully constructing the question itself. Less than 40% of voters were ready to launch a new ship of state. Morin's polls had told him that if he were too blunt or too quick, that ship would sink without a trace.

There was one good omen. Trudeau's popularity in English Canada had plummeted. In four months he had to call an election. Trudeau had one burning dream, and he threw his final energies into making it come true. For a half century Ottawa and the provinces had wrangled over the definition of their nation. As a result, Canada was the only country in the world without its own constitution. Trudeau called the provinces together in a last desperate effort to end this national embarrassment. For Lévesque and Morin, the conference served another purpose. They had promised that an independent Quebec would be associated with the rest of Canada. They needed the friendship of the other provincial leaders. To get a constitutional agreement, Trudeau was prepared to offer huge concessions but he had made too many enemies. [. . .]

Trudeau (*meeting of premiers*): You know, if we're bargaining what more did you want from us? We haven't agreed on everything, but at some point you should say O.K. they've showed at least . . . And I'm prepared to stand by what I said now. I don't know how long I'll be in this chair. Hey, you haven't delivered anything to me. You haven't delivered anything. I haven't asked for anything yet. I've got a second list like René Lévesque has one.

Narrator: Lévesque would save his second list for the next Canadian Prime Minister. The conference had failed. Pierre Elliott Trudeau had come up empty, and so there was little to show for eleven years in power. The great promise of a just society had not materialized, the Constitution was still a boring joke, and he would probably have to face Lévesque's referendum as a political cripple.

Trudeau: Half an hour ago I asked the Governor General to dissolve parliament for a federal general election on Tuesday, May 22nd. I look forward immensely to the campaign that begins tomorrow. It will be decisive for our country.

Narrator: René Lévesque had his work cut out for him. His time was starting to run out. He had strengthened his team. Claude Charron now sat at his right hand, as a prime strategist in the great referendum struggle.

Claude Charron: Having only 41% of the vote, knowing that in the polls sovereignty association was not even doing 41% of that vote . . . we had to convince even some of the people that had voted for us. We were writing orange books, green books, white books, so that people would know what we were doing at the time, and just to get sympathy and with that sympathy, try the impossible mission.

Narrator: But there was a ray of hope. French power in Ottawa was a spent force. As long as Trudeau ran Canada, he was a living example to Quebecers that they had a major place in the country. Now he was a living example of rejection by "les anglais."

Trudeau: I'm announcing today that after spending nearly twelve years as leader of the Liberal Party, I'm stepping down from the leadership and asking the National Executive of the party to call a convention for next March to choose a new leader. I've thought a good deal . . .

Narrator: He would return to Quebec and fight on as a foot soldier in Claude Ryan's army.

Trudeau: I want to assure all Canadians, as they have stood by me in every battle since 1965, so to the best of my ability I shall stand with them to fight for Canada during the referendum.
Lévesque: O.K. Well, I hope you're not asking us to assess Mr. Trudeau's career. We got the news while we were in a cabinet meeting and we didn't have much time to think about it. Very simply, after three years, one thing I can say is that Mr.Trudeau, despite all of our differences and that has to be emphasized – just the durability is something close to record – has stamina. He was a man . . . is a man of great stamina and certainly one of the most brilliant men to work on the political scene at the federal level, also a very dedicated man to his ideas. That I think we all know, and I think also his departure is well timed because from reactions in the West, in Toronto, over the last few weeks, it was obvious that, as proud as he is, he wouldn't wait until he was asked to go. He took the initiative.

Narrator: Joe Clark's arrival at the seat of federal power must have been a pretty sight for René Lévesque. The federal government was no longer a powerful francophone fighting force. It was a sitting duck. [. . .]

Joe Clark wisely decided to play no role in the referendum campaign. Christmas of 1979 came early to the watering holes of the Parti Québécois. Ryan was looking a little shaky, Clark had withdrawn, and Trudeau was a lame duck. Good things were falling into place, and Lévesque had finally announced that his referendum would be held in the spring. Joe Clark looked like he might be around for awhile. He had only a minority government, but the Liberals were looking for a new leader. [. . .]

Clark had decided to bring in a hard budget. Although a defeat in the House would bring down his government, the Liberals were in no position to force an election. They would talk tough, but when it came to a vote a lot of their members would come down with diplomatic flu. Perhaps he'd forgotten little Jim Coots. He and the other old Liberals moved through the Liberal Christmas party. Coots played for keeps, and Coots was ready to pounce. Two members were summoned from their hospital beds, they would go for Joe Clark's unprotected throat. [. . .]

There was a gentleman's agreement between opposing parliamentary parties. It's called pairing. If a member is sick or away on business, his opposite number will refrain from voting. Now the Conservative Whip was told that all deals were off. [. . .]

Now everything depended on the five Creditiste members led by Fabien Roy. They owed the Parti Québécois some favours and they knew that the Péquistes wanted Clark to stay in place. In Quebec City the National Assembly was sitting late. Claude Morin, who normally handled these matters was in Africa. Negotiations were left in the hands of Daniel Latouche, a college professor with no practical experience. Latouche wasn't too worried about the Creditistes.

Daniel Latouche: . . . Fabien Roy was phoning desperately almost, asking for instruction on how he should vote for the budget. I didn't know what to tell him. Nobody knew in the office really what to tell him.

Narrator: It is entirely possible that one word from Latouche might have saved Joe Clark and finished Pierre Trudeau. But without that word, Fabien Roy and his confused Creditistes decided to abstain. Clark's only hope now was that some of the reluctant Liberals might defy their leaders and go home to bed.

Joe Clark (*Prime Minister*): Mr. Speaker, I rise on a point of order. The government has lost a vote on a matter which we have no alternative but to regard as a question of confidence and I simply want to advise the House that I will be seeing His Excellency the Governor General tomorrow morning. [. . .]

Voice TV (*Mike Duffy*): Pierre Trudeau, the man who wanted to retire from politics to spend more time with his family, was back at the center of the political stage again today as the Liberal Party debated whether or not it wanted Trudeau to lead it in the election campaign. Mobbed by reporters and cameramen, Trudeau met with members of the national Liberal caucus this morning. The cheers Trudeau received seemed to be spelling the end to the dreams of the other potential Liberal leadership candidates. [. . .]

Narrator: The Parti Québécois was in trouble. A federal election campaign was underway and Trudeau was drawing big crowds in Quebec. Lévesque had said he would never call his referendum when a federal campaign was on and loyalties were divided. A postponement seemed obvious. That afternoon in the National Assembly, Claude Ryan asked if the referendum was still scheduled for the spring. Lévesque rose to the bait. Election or no election, he said, the referendum was on. Perhaps he was momentarily confused; his supporters were stunned. [. . .]

Daniel Latouche: Claude Morin was furious. Everybody was furious as a matter of fact. Claude Charron was not very happy either. There were no words that were not said against the stupidity of what Lévesque had just done. He should have consulted them. Nothing, nothing was not said in a way. Then Lévesque walks in the room, fixes himself a drink, it's very quiet and then he looks around with his smile and says, "I guess I made an error there," and it all evaporates.

Narrator: Lévesque had just handed Trudeau a gold-plated issue. The spectre of the referendum would bring English Canada back into the fort. [. . .]

Trudeau: Now I hear that the Tories are complaining . . . that they're losing this election because of the image of their leader. Canadians couldn't care less whether Mr. Clark looks like Mr. Redford or whether I am just the shadow of a former gunslinger. [. . .]

Narrator: It was no time for bold moves. Two months earlier, as the referendum question had finally been handed to the Quebec cabinet, it did not have the ring of the Declaration of Independence. [. . .]

Claude Morin: We tried lots of questions when we had private polls made by the Parti Québécois and by other organizations, so that we knew for instance that if we asked the people of Quebec, do you want to separate, yes or no? we would have gotten no more than 22 or 23% saying yes. So this was the best question. [. . .]

Narrator: There would be no sovereignty without association, and a second referendum would be held before anything was finalized. The day before it was to be announced, Lévesque was still doodling with the wording.

Latouche: Of course we had a round table on this and we said this is a lousy question. So Lévesque took the question, threw it out and came out with a second version . . . and then everybody started to work . . . all 26 members of the cabinet started to work collectively on the question. It was eerie in the sense that everyone was trying to suggest one sentence here and one . . . Around 12:30, or 1:00 in the morning, one minister who had not said a word, you know, sort of stands up and says: "Is this a question? What is a question? Do we need a quotation mark? Interrogation mark? Or can we have a question with two sentences in it? Can that be a question if you have two sentences?" Lévesque turned to his Minister of Justice, who obviously had not thought about that, and I thought Lévesque was going to fire him right there on the spot at one o'clock in the morning . . .

Of course everybody went to sleep and it's the staff who got caught with that problem. So we assembled the best legal minds the government could get at two o'clock in the morning in police cars, and these lawyers had in my office a three-hour discussion . . . as to what is a question. It was fascinating, I mean people quoting an episode in 1946, I mean lawyers talking about this, and finally they didn't arrive at a conclusion, so they all went to bed again and I sat there and talked to the chief of staff, and finally I put semi-colons in the middle of it and gave it to Lévesque and that was the way it was done.

Narrator: The question: a mandate to negotiate sovereignty and economic association with Canada, semi-colon; a second referendum to approve any change, semi-colon; do you agree?

Bourgault: And I said, my God what a stupid question. It leads nowhere. What is a mandate to negotiate? Every government has that.

Narrator: Pierre Bourgault, the rebel-rousing separatist street-fighter, was a bad memory as far as Réne Lévesque was concerned, but Bourgault wasn't going to sit on the sidelines. He would call a spade a spade. The English were the villains and separation was the goal. . . . It was a battle for survival, he said. The English were bent on cultural genocide.

Bourgault: . . . tout se passe en anglais, la loi est anglaise, les ordres sont anglais, les affaires sont anglaises, la vie est anglaise, et nous devons prendre notre courage à deux mains, simplement pour survivre. On peut imaginer ce que c'est en dehors du Québec où les minorités françaises se font littéralement massacrées.

Narrator: But Bourgault was now just the loose cannon. Lévesque was on another course.

Lévesque: In this search for solidarity, which is quite clearly growing all over Quebec, I believe it is also beginning to be felt to a lesser degree, admittedly, among our non-francophone fellow citizens of all extraction. [. . .]

Narrator: The tide had indeed been turned. For the first time ever the forces of separation were leading at the polls. The date was set, the campaign was under way. [mixed voices]

Claude Ryan looked and spoke like a parish priest, and campaigned in the manner of an old style politician. He kissed babies, pressed flesh, and worried Pierre Trudeau. [. . .]

One of Lévesque's most persuasive friends was Lise Payette. She had been a popular T.V. host before becoming a cabinet minister, but one night Lise Payette made a terrible mistake. A little girl called Yvette was suddenly famous.

Lise Payette: Yvette, sa petite soeur, est joyeuse et gentille. J'vous prierais d'écouter, ça va vous faire du bien. Elle trouve toujours . . .

Narrator: She had called the women in Ryan's camp a bunch of Yvettes. Furthermore she said, he was married to one. Yvette appeared in a lot of school books. She was a good little girl, who looked forward to a life of cooking and sewing. Payette had triggered a storm of protest and the more she talked, the worse it got. Outside the Assembly, an army of wraths was gathering. Fifteen thousand women poured into the Montreal Forum. Those who admired old-fashioned virtues were proud to be Yvettes. Those of the liberated generation resented being Yvettes. Lise Payette had galvanized them into a single cohesive fighting force. [. . .]

The campaigners for the yes vote manfully tried to laugh it all away, but underneath the laughter they knew great damage had been done.

Latouche: You're not supposed to say it was an important turn of events during the referendum. You're not supposed to say it was a tactical error of gigantic proportions by Madame Payette, but I'm convinced that . . . I mean the figures are there. [. . .]

Narrator: The yes forces had decided on a low-key campaign and they were sticking to it. Madame Lévesque and her husband moved from schoolroom to meeting hall to church basement, handing out certificates to those who pledged support. It was a campaign without rhetoric, aimed at reassuring the voter that they were not wild-eyed revolutionaries. [. . .]

Some people accused the federalist forces of running a campaign of fear. Would all the corporations flee they asked, would all the banks close, would Quebec starve in the day of separation? [. . .]

On the economics of separation, everybody had their own set of numbers. [. . .]

Morin: The other factor was the Trudeau intervention. You see, Trudeau is a great figure of Canadian politics. He's a . . . I don't think there will be many people like him. . . . It's like Mr. Lévesque, they are monuments of Canadian politics . . . of Quebec political history.

Charron: Trudeau is, you know, one pole of our soul, Lévesque is the other pole. Lévesque is what we are, Trudeau is what we would like to be, and we are torn between these two attractions. [. . .]

Trudeau: Monsieur Lévesque continue de répéter, pis la démocracie qu'est-ce que vous en faites? Si le peuple québécois votait majoritairement oui, est-ce que vous seriez pas obligés par les lois de la démocracie de négocier? Mais non. A tous les canadiens des autres provinces, nous mettons notre tête en jeu nous, députés québécois, parce que nous disons aux québécois comme une indication que tout va bien pis que tout va rester comme c'était auparavant. Nous voulons du changement, nous mettons nos sièges en jeu pour avoir du changement.

Narrator: A no vote, he said, was not a vote for the status quo. If Quebec remained in the Confederation, he gave a commitment to build a new Canada.

Narrator: May 20th, 1980. Eighty-seven per cent of Quebecers came to vote. It was the biggest turn-out in Canadian political history. [. . .]

Less than an hour after the polls had closed, the result was obvious. Only 40% had voted with René Lévesque. [. . .]

Lévesque: S'il vous plaît. S'il vous plaît. Mes chers amis . . . S'il vous plaît. Si je vous ai bien compris, vous êtes en train de dire à la prochaine fois.[. . .]

Narrator: Canada was still in one piece, but on paper it was nothing but a British colony. Trudeau had been given a precious last chance to relieve the British of the Canadian Constitution. The British were as anxious as he was to get rid of it. Three weeks later, Trudeau invited the provincial premiers to tea. René Lévesque was not the life of the party. Trudeau on the other hand was under a full head of steam. Surely now he could convince the provinces to bring home a Canadian Constitution. He had, after all, just saved Canada. Lévesque still had a veto, but his strength was sapped. . . .

Trudeau was ready. His strategy was precise; his staff had analyzed the particular positions of each and every province. If necessary, he would use this information to divide and conquer. It was laid out by Michael Kirby in a top secret memorandum. The secret document, however, had fallen into the hands of René Lévesque. [. . .]

Lévesque passed it on to his fellow premiers. If he had to be a Canadian, he was certainly going to be a champion of provincial rights.

Brian Peckford (*meeting of premiers*): We've all talked here today about the concept of Canada, the vision of Canada, and that's what it really comes down to because everything flows from that. Both, yourself Mr. Prime Minister and Mr. Lévesque, articulated two different visions of Canada, and I would have to side with the theory advocated by Mr. Lévesque. There's no question about that.
Trudeau: Certainly all I can say is that the people of Quebec have shown last May that they didn't agree with the view of Canada held by Mr. Lévesque. And yet we hear from premier after premier that they agree with the concept of Canada put forward by Mr. Lévesque.
Lévesque: The climate of understanding in the many areas of consensus that we found this week, has been for me an extraordinary and unprecedented experience. But we hit against a wall. The wall of a rigid, even in some ways authoritarian, conception of federalism.

Narrator: Pierre Elliott Trudeau had reached the limits of his patience. He would declare war on the provinces. Trudeau rammed a proposal through an angry House of Commons announcing that the Canadian government, with or without the consent of the provinces, would ask the British government to deliver up the Canadian Constitution to Ottawa. [. . .]

René Lévesque had called an election and buried Claude Ryan. Quebecers might not be ready to separate, but they wouldn't be pushed around by Ottawa. Lévesque was still their champion. He would fight Trudeau's constitutional scheme. He would need help; he would join the Gang of Eight. Three days later, Lévesque made the gamble of a lifetime. He surrendered Quebec's historic right of veto in return for an alliance with seven other provincial premiers. For Lévesque it was written in blood. It was an agonizing compromise and his bottom line. For the gamble to pay off, the Gang of Eight had to stay rock-solid. They had agreed on a constitutional formula which protected the provinces. The object was to stop Trudeau.

Not only the Gang of Eight, but the entire nation, waited for a Supreme Court ruling. When it came, it was not clear cut. Trudeau's unilateral patriation was legal they said, but without some agreement with the provinces, it was unconstitutional in the conventional sense.

Roy Romanow: Clearly it was a victory for nobody. Clearly the impact and the importance of the Supreme Court decision was that it was a message to us: you get around that negotiating table one more time. I don't think the Canadian public would have tolerated any one of the two competing camps taking the position that they were not going to attend another conference.
Morin: They said, and the other provinces agreed more or less with them, they said the people in Canada are fed up with those discussions and we have to come to a solution. It must be the last meeting of the kind and so forth. Again what was at stake for them was much less important than what was at stake for Quebec.

Narrator: If Quebec lost control of its schools and its language, it would lose everything. Morin had no room to negotiate, and they'd given up their veto. He had begun to sense that the unthinkable might happen. The Gang of Eight might come unstuck. Romanow of Saskatchewan was talking to Chrétien of Ottawa, but Romanow had a different view of the alliance.

Romanow: . . . We told Quebec, we told all of the members of the Gang of Eight, I remember saying so myself, that this was a position from which we would bargain. [. . .]
Latouche: I think where Trudeau outmanoeuvered Lévesque is that Trudeau knew his team, literally knew that the premiers of the other provinces of Canada were a bunch of Kiwanis presidents, with no vision of history, that could be turned with two cocktails, a bit of pressure, more money on a factory . . . [. . .]

Narrator: On the third morning, Trudeau came with a firm offer. It was bound to appeal to Lévesque. Let us agree, he said, to bring back the Constitution and put a moratorium on the contentious issues, the amending formula, the Charter of Rights. If we can't agree within two years, we will go directly to the people of each province and decide it by referendum.

Eddy Goldenberg (lawyer): He threw it out at a private meeting to Lévesque and he said, hey Lévesque you can't be opposed to a referendum. You guys,

you just had one, and Lévesque said, no I'm not opposed to a referendum. I'd like to fight the Charter of Rights, in Quebec.
Romanow: I remember sitting right beside Newfoundland. We were stunned and shocked at this, and the last thing that they wanted of course was another referendum. They disliked Mr. Trudeau's idea of a referendum. Can you imagine a debate in Canada on some very divisive and emotional issue, say like language. So nobody liked the idea of a referendum, and all of a sudden it was being advocated by a leading member of the Gang of Eight, and of course joined immediately in the debate by Mr. Trudeau.

Narrator: Whether this was a serious offer, or a Machiavellian manoeuver may never be known. If Lévesque was the open book, Trudeau was the enigma. [. . .]

Trudeau: We would put the whole question of a charter to the people of Canada. Do you want it? Do you want this charter modified or otherwise? Or do you not want a charter? And the people of Canada would decide if they want a charter, and Mr. Lévesque agreed with that, so we have a new alliance between the Quebec government and the Canadian government . . . [Pause] And the cat is among the pigeons.

Narrator: By nightfall Trudeau's team had concocted a Byzantine referendum formula. Lévesque said it now seemed to be written in Chinese. He would have no part of it. But that wouldn't matter any more. The spectre of a referendum had stampeded the other provinces. Trudeau went home to play with the kids. Romanow and Chrétien were already cutting a deal in the kitchen. They would be joined by McMurtry of Ontario. By four o'clock in the morning, every province but one had been consulted. [. . .]

Voice (*Brittain*): Claude Morin was deeply hurt that he was not called that night or consulted. What was the reason for not calling him?
Romanow: The reason was very simple. There was nothing that could have been advanced to Mr. Morin, to Claude Morin and to Mr. Lévesque that they would have accepted. What the province of Quebec would have done is requested additional amendments or changes, in my judgement, which would have either obfuscated or delayed, and thereby killed, the process.

Narrator: Lévesque had just had breakfast with the Gang of Eight. He has been handed a "fait accompli." He will be able to opt out of any constitutional amendments, but there will be no financial compensation, and he will have no veto.

Charron: If Trudeau had not been there, nobody knows how the history of this country would have been written in the last five years. Trudeau is the only man who defeated René Lévesque, but he defeated him. [. . .]
Lévesque: Maybe second thoughts and further events will make them understand that this could have incalculable consequences. . . . What they did this morning is beyond description.
Voice (*Brittain*): What about Mr. Lévesque himself? Do you feel that he ever recovered from the shock of the constitutional . . .
Charron: No, he did not. He did not, and that was the beginning of the end for him also at that time, but he was so much stronger than me that he could last for awhile, much longer than the three months I could manage to survive. But anyway, he lost control of himself, he lost control of the party. [. . .]

Narrator: Pierre Trudeau's government had also gone into terminal decline, but he himself was walking tall. The world at large was in disarray, and he set out to save it. He wanted to rid the Third World of poverty, and the superpowers of their nuclear weapons. When American officials scoffed at his peace plan, he called them "pip-squeaks." [. . .]

Many Canadians liked the way he stood up to the USA, but the gun swinging style did not work on the world. His peace mission was largely resented or ignored. Now the dark side of Pierre Trudeau began to show. The world statesman was periodically transformed into a pork-barrel politician. In the end there would be an orgy of patronage appointments . . .

Trudeau: What the reaction of the public is . . . I really don't know. I would guess out of 24 million Canadians there's perhaps, what . . . I'd say all the members of the Opposition and their spouses and probably all the hacks in the Tory Party and a certain number of the hacks maybe in the media, would be indignant at this appointment, but I don't think the rest of the Canadian public cares very much whether Mr. Pitfield or Mr. Smith goes to the Senate.

René-Daniel Dubois

The author of more than a dozen plays, René-Daniel Dubois is one of the most colourful figures on the Montreal theatre scene. An actor, playwright, and director, he has worked for diverse theatre and opera companies as well as numerous film and television productions. Among his plays translated into English, Never Blame the Bedouins *won the Governor General's Award in 1984 and* Being at Home with Claude *was produced in the United States, London, and across Canada and was recently turned into a film by Jean Beaudin.*

October 1990

In the fall of 1988, Michelle Rossignol, the newly-appointed artistic director of Montreal's Théâtre d'Aujourd'hui (Quebec's only professional theatre company devoted exclusively to the production of work by Quebec playwrights) initiated a workshop focusing on the status of political theatre in Quebec. Several playwrights were invited to explore in an open-ended fashion the directions and forms political theatre might take in Quebec in the upcoming decade. Early in the process, the participating playwrights, all under 40, felt the need to reexamine political preoccupations in Quebec over the past twenty years, before tackling the issues of the years to come. They decided to immerse themselves in a recent chapter of Quebec's history – the October Crisis.

Over a period of twenty months, they met with many of the key figures in the events that marked Quebec politics in the late sixties and early seventies – Pierre Vallières, activist and author of *White Niggers of America*; union leader Michel Chartrand; poet, publisher and now a Member of the National Assembly, Gérald Godin; Paul Rose and Francis Simard, members of the FLQ cell who kidnapped and assassinated Pierre Laporte; Jacques Lanctôt, member of the cell who kidnapped British Trade Commissioner James Cross; and FLQ defense lawyer, Robert Lemieux, to name only a few.

These meetings made a lasting impression on all the participants in the workshop. As October 1990 approached, the playwrights, several of whom had begun writing new "political" plays, decided to organize a one-time event so they could share some of the thoughts, images and feelings provoked by the workshop experience. The event, entitled "Règlements de comptes avec la mémoire" (literally "A Settling of Accounts with Memory" or "Paying Our Debts to Memory"), was held at the Maison de la Culture Frontenac on October 8, 1990. The following piece is a translation of the text René-Daniel Dubois read that evening.

October 8, 1990. I didn't write a play on the October Crisis. Because the October Crisis never ended. So I can't seize on it, appropriate it and deliver my private version, nor can I ever hope to do so. It can't belong to anyone, it remains forever pending. The October Crisis – what we call the October Crisis or "les Événements" – constituted the acute, the visible, identifiable part, the so-called tip of an iceberg. In fact, it was the peak of the mountain formed by the tips of two icebergs colliding. On the surface: two kidnappings and the army in the streets, these are the tips. Below the surface: the revolt of many expressed by a few, on the one hand; and the contempt of a few, expressed by many, on the other.

The workshop on political theatre in Quebec launched by Michelle Rossignol and directed with determination, beautiful, dogged determination, by Linda Gaboriau took place over a period of twenty months. During that time I was able to measure to what an amazing extent the October Crisis remains a taboo: a corpse in our closet, if you'll excuse the image, but an extremely significant corpse, if only because of the energy we've devoted to ignoring it over the past twenty years, in spite of the smell. Twenty years! I've lost track of my many attempts to write about the October Crisis over the last two years. Plays, poems, essays, reflections, cries of rage. I could often feel an idea, an emotion, a wave surging, but never managed to grasp it. No matter what form my attempts took.

I believe the artist is the person in his or her society whose task is to let himself travel with the currents which run through his life, in order to synthesize, albeit in spite of himself, the currents which also run through the lives of his contemporaries, those close to him. His task is also to dive into the waves and search instinctively for the shards, the debris, the bits and pieces which decorate the ocean floor, and bring them to the surface. The artist's first responsibility is to what drives him, intimately, but in this respect, his responsibility must be total, without faults or fears, whatever the price to be paid. It is the artist's task to be the madman who provides the synthesis, the dervish who puts himself in a state beyond his control in order to spin and spin until he becomes dizzy with repeating his pain and joy, until, forgetting everything, he is filled with an immense cry that possesses him, yet is not only his, for it is also the cry of his contemporaries. At least, one of the cries, for we all carry within us, individually and collectively, more than one cry.

But being aware of this, being aware of the dervish's responsibility, and having chosen to entrust my life to this dance of the depths, how can I dance, with the voice of one of the men we met during the workshop going round in my head, repeating:

In jail, the guys I saw there . . . they never learned how to live.

And another voice:

So far, the people who have talked about the Events, have mostly talked about the day-to-day details. But it seems to me there's a myth in what happened in October 1970.

True, the image of Premier Bourassa hiding out in the Queen Elizabeth Hotel, white as a sheet, cowering at the end of a corridor lined with policemen carrying machine guns – there's something mythical about this bunker-like image. And the image of young people jumping into the void, fed up with the silence and lies masking all the suffering and determined to do something, if only to make themselves heard, yes, that's serious business, really serious . . .

And another one of the people we met in the workshop, telling us about Trudeau, well before 1970, sitting in his Jaguar, saying:

Christ, we're going to stir things up. We'll bring in socialism.

Then, the same man Trudeau had said that to, went on:

The real problem is, we come from the backwoods, and we're not out of the woods yet.

And:

Oh sure, save our language but let the people who speak it croak.

And:

It's the women who built this country.

And:

French Canadians are afraid of poverty. But not a single sociologist has ever dared study poverty and our fear of it.

And:

When you sell your soul, you don't complain about the rest.

And then:

Humanity is a man and a woman.

Another said:

It took me eight years after I got out of jail to enter the outside world.

And:

Freedom? It's a question of details.

And:

Death is another thing, we've got no right.

And another one said:

You better believe I'd do it all over again. That's what's missing in Quebec: non-resignation, hope. Our submission to the law in Quebec is phenomenal. Anger is what's missing.

I could go on quoting sentences like that, real gems, for hours. But. But I can't claim them for myself. I can repeat them for you, but I can't claim they belong to me.

I searched. In the collision of the two icebergs, in that collision between contempt and revolt, I searched for what belongs to me in the memory of October. I tried, in thirty or forty different ways, to start dancing, diving, but with no success. I couldn't submerge myself in what has remained suspended for the past twenty years, and feel what that important arrested gesture means today. I couldn't manage . . . to look the corpse in the eye. Because the eyes I saw were those of some of the men we met over a period of almost two years, and everything going on in their eyes . . . but I can't tell their story, I'm not about to ransack their lives. What really counts is what their eyes awaken, the echo, the unspoken. I can't claim to immortalize in words their lives, which they go on living. And I don't believe they ever intended to see themselves cast in the bronze of words. So why, after almost two years, am I so afraid of betraying them, of distorting, of lying?

And yet I cannot remain silent. That would be an insult to their revolt. Let me try one last time. Heaven help us. I'll try a prayer. But a prayer to no particular god, because I'm not sure I'm a believer. A prayer to courage, perhaps, the courage certain people have, and the courage which is sometimes missing. And a prayer to the belief in the necessity of helping, at least a bit.

A Secular Prayer

I am made of slums and ruins. And for a long time, I believed I was made of only that. And, for a long time, I believed I could only give birth to more slums and more ruins. And, for a long time, I believed that slums and ruins summed up life.

Seven years old, home from school, standing in the snow, in the falling dusk, shivering, silent, staring, unable to let out the slightest sound at my mother lying dead drunk, immobile, a few feet away from me, on the other side of the locked patio door. And my mother screaming one night, I must have been around nine that time, my mother screaming, then footsteps running through the house, beyond the closed door of my room, and the explanation of the screaming the next morning: drunk, but still thirsty, she had downed a bottle of alcohol, too drunk to remember she had neglected to remove the label on the bottle when it was empty and refilled with varsol; that wait in the snow, and that screaming, those hurried footsteps and the explanation at breakfast, that was life.

My mother, drunk again, having absorbed barbiturates and alcohol, carrying on a long telephone conversation into an ashtray, and my sisters and I, petrified, desperately concentrating on the television set, pretending everything was normal, that too was life.

And hours spent, morning, noon and night, sitting alone in the car, waiting for my father who was meeting friends and who smelled of beer when he finally came back, that interminable waiting, with one objective in mind: to be somewhere where you never have to wait, where you don't wait for anything and where you'll never have to wait again, that, too, was life.

The bailiffs handing me warrants I was to deliver to my parents, and their contemptuous looks, oozing contempt, as they looked over my shoulder toward our slum living room, that was life.

At eight, nine, ten years old, I didn't throw snowballs, I threw ice balls, with gravel inside. At windows, windshields. I can remember a construction site on fire. And shoplifting. And, on my way back from the swimming pool with my friend and his sister, I can remember some kids bigger than us in the woods where the Olympic Stadium now stands. I can remember being tied to a tree. I don't know whether the rape took place, or just the threats. That's life.

My mother found dead in the office of one of the directors of an important state agency, where her lover, the director, had abandoned her when she fell and hit her head, fleeing like a coward and leaving her to bleed to death, that was life. The newspaper article announcing her death . . . of a heart attack, lies to save face; deception no matter how great the horror, that was life.

Then, being torn away from my only friend and from my sisters, sent to live with my grandparents, in their dark flat where I had to kneel by their bed every night at seven o'clock to say the rosary, while outside the spring sun . . . oh, no, life wasn't about the sun, it was about the rosary, and obligation, for obligation's sake, just because.

And then, I can remember realizing at that early age, age ten I think, that if I went on like that, I can remember the image perfectly – maybe the image came from a movie or a TV police series – I remember knowing that I would die with my throat slit in some basement. And, in spite of the horror, at least death would mean peace. I can't remember having chased away the image, or having consciously decided to change my life, but my life changed.

I spent the following ten years of my life becoming, first of all, the class brain, because math is great, it's a game you can play without feeling a thing; and then, acting, because when you act out someone's life, someone else's words and feelings, at least you know that sooner or later the play will end. In both cases, it was so I could stop feeling.

And then, wait, suddenly I know why I didn't write a play on the October Crisis. And I know why I almost screamed when Francis Simard said:

The guys in jail, they never learned how to live.

And I know why I can't forgive the men and women who made October: because once the revolt had been declared, shouted out loud, by them, and then stifled, I couldn't find any way to proclaim it myself. Revolt had been muffled, gagged. I could never forgive them, without even daring to say so, because life was unbearable, with its lies, with death and suffering everywhere, suffering, nothing but suffering, years of suffering for a moment of happiness. I couldn't forgive them because life is nothing but slums and ruins, for me, and they stopped midway. I couldn't forgive them because the night the news bulletin interrupted the Radio Canada show I was watching to announce that Pierre Laporte had been kidnapped, for the fifteen-year-old character I was, the class brain who shot up math, a little echo made itself heard, deep, very deep inside me, a little echo that said something like this:

Hey. Someone's decided to rattle the cage, someone's decided to say it's not true, life can be more than that.

And then, one Sunday when, from my grandparents' balcony, I saw the Army, the unending military convoy, arrive in the city, I said to myself:

Somebody's scared shitless. The bailiffs, and the priests, and "l'Étoile du Matin" [theme song of a nightly religious program on Montreal radio] *are going to get their asses whipped.*

But then, when I heard, a few weeks later in the schoolyard at recess, that helicopters and soldiers had surrounded a house in Montreal North, and people were talking about a car on its way to Dorval Airport, or rather, to Expo, then Cuba, the little voice fell silent. It said:

That's life.

And it fell silent.

The voice came back, later. It made itself heard. But only now can I recognize it, it took so many detours and used so many disguises in order to return. I don't think that voice fell silent because it had reached the end of the line, run out of breath, it was because, on the subject of what life was all about, as far as I was concerned, there was nothing more to be said: I was nothing but . . . that's right, nothing but slums and ruins.

And today what does it say? That in full awareness of the slums and ruins, there is hope for something else. And that maybe I'll never achieve this something else. But achievement isn't the only thing that matters. If only victory mattered, we wouldn't be here this evening.

My prayer is a question. Not a question about the results of the events yet to come, but rather a question about our memories of those which have already taken place, and the memories we will some day have, perhaps, of the events that will take place tomorrow.

This question is made up of fragments. And those fragments are more difficult to bear than the memory of a dead-drunk mother, an absent father, or a rape. Because they speak of the memory reserved, the memory made available for dead-drunk mothers, rapes, absent fathers, and boys of fifteen who want to stop feeling, for fear their feelings will kill them.

There's a New York translator who, speaking of Quebec theatre shortly after reading several Québécois plays, said:

> *It's strange, but you can tell your playwrights write for small theatres.*

And something in that sentence, in the tone of voice, evokes a fractured culture, a culture that emerges in little bursts, a culture in which those to whom it belongs barely recognize themselves.

There's an Argentine director, living in exile in Caracas, who waited a full hour while we were sitting there talking before killing the horsefly buzzing around his head, because, he explained afterwards:

> *I thought that, for a Canadian, killing an animal must be a crime.*

His sentence says a lot about the out-of-this-world, from-another-planet, beyond-reality quality of what it means to be a Canadian.

There's a Nicaraguan artist I met in New York. Toward the end of a reception, on the last day of a week-long event – we finally had a chance to talk. He said to me:

> *I went to Montreal once for a few days. I've been to your country. One evening, talking with someone, I put my hand on his arm. He pushed it aside, brusquely. That struck me, because I noticed lots of things like that, during my short stay in your country. Why are you all so afraid all the time? Why do you believe the minute anyone approaches you, it's just to screw you?*

There's that yelling on the radio last summer, in a taxi, for at least twenty minutes, a call-in show (on the Oka Crisis):

> *Send in the tanks, then they'll negotiate, you just wait and see!*

And the driver refused to turn down the volume, he wanted to be informed.

There's my first lover in 1976. We met shortly before the Parti Québécois was elected. For him, the class struggle came first. Language was a *detail*. At night, he put me through my self-criticism. Because my pain was incomprehensible in his terms, he said I was a *cultural frill*. Strange. In the FLQ Manifesto, where the subject is the class struggle, there's a single word to describe how horrible Trudeau is: *faggot*.

Then there's a diplomat in Morocco, originally from Quebec City, who introduced me to one of his friends, an angry young Moroccan poet. The diplomat insisted that we had to meet, but I could sense immediately that the poet had come only out of friendship for the diplomat. Something in his way of looking at me made me lose control, and I spoke too loud in that polite party. I said to the Moroccan poet what I had said to the Nicaraguan dancer, but this time it was a cry:

Listen to me: I can't accept the contempt I see in your eyes. You're fighting for your people, for their struggle. And you consider me a poet of a people who have no struggle. But what do you know about it? Eh? What do you know about the pain of the people who live in Quebec? Just because you can't imagine their pain, you despise it? You have no right to feel contempt like that without knowing the pain of a nation that is dying in silence.

And there's the fact that I haven't written a play on the October Crisis. And I don't think I ever will. First of all, because what makes me dance is not the tips of icebergs, it's their depths. And also because I don't have any enemies. What I mean by that is there's no one in this world I am willing to reduce to that term: enemy. That doesn't mean I agree with everything everyone does, nor does it mean that others wouldn't like to get rid of me, but that's their problem. I believe that if we oppose irremediably anything that stands in our way or attempts to stand in our way, if we allow ourselves to reduce the other person, whoever that might be, to the status of enemy, nothing is possible, except slums and ruins. And I believe that as soon as we have a declared enemy, it automatically becomes a question of victory, and that is not the question. What we hate in other people is what we hate in ourselves. It's better to remember. And accept that we must take self-knowledge into account, self-knowledge in its entirety.

I'm here tonight because one Sunday evening I was asked to join a workshop on the theme: "Why isn't there any political theatre in Quebec now?" And I think I just found the answer to that question.

Because a people in the process of becoming an endangered species don't get involved in politics. Getting involved in politics means feeling that you have a legitimate right to live. It means listening to your feelings, your own feelings first, your pain and your joy. Not just your hate. To feel resentment is to admit that the meaning of your life is beyond your control.

It's because of . . .

It's not my fault . . .

If he or she or they hadn't done this or that to me . . .

Or on the contrary:

If only he or she or they had . . .

No little voice can make itself heard through resentment, because one's self is excluded, one's self is a victim – passive or, at best, acting only out of reproach.

A people in the process of becoming an endangered species, suffering from loss of memory, speaks to ashtrays and lies face down on the ground, immobile, in the middle of winter, behind patio doors. And they're afraid of getting screwed. And they find poets boring, compared to tanks.

A dying people is not made up of people who have ceased to live, but people who have ceased to remember. They have forgotten what it is that killed those who suffered before them.

There's a journalist with the only Quebec daily that claims to reflect on things, at least occasionally, who spoke of Quebec writers saying:

Our writers

putting the word

our

in quotes.

There's a novelist friend who, invited to meet with students in a CEGEP, I think, was asked:

Who do you think you are, writing novels?

It's happened to me many a time:

You really think you're something, dontcha buster?

And there probably isn't a single poet in Quebec who hasn't heard that at some point.

There's another friend, a few days ago, a poet himself, struggling with the lack of legitimacy that comes with being a poet from a nation that wants to stop feeling, who said to me:

Why are you organizing this event anyway, you know it won't change a thing.

Listen. I'm going to dance.

If, as I believe, we are in the process of disappearing, from wanting so badly to stop feeling, the pain is so great,

If, as I believe, each and every one of us has to make a superhuman effort just to hear another's joy and pain, we're so afraid of one another,

If, as I believe, our memory is in the process of rotting, relegated to the closet of fancy accessories, because we're a country of opportunists scared to death of life,

Opportunists who don't want to see a single knick-knack disturbed in their beautiful livingroom, because that might awaken something in our memory,

Though our memory, and only our memory, gives us the right to call ourselves, human

I am still that seven-year-old child standing in the snow
And that eight-year-old who understands perfectly why we want to disappear into the television set:
So we don't notice that three feet away someone is talking to an ashtray
because there's no one else on earth to talk to!
But now, tonight, I can talk to the child I was and ease his terror, I can take him by the shoulder, that's all he needs,
and I'm the only one who can do it
and say
Shhhhh
And explain to him, gently, try at least to explain to him that ice balls won't make it hurt any less
Math won't either
I can, I must, talk to him. I have no choice. Either
I'm willing to take an honest look at what I'm made of,
or I'll die.

If, as I believe, each and every one of us is convinced of the illegitimacy of memory and of art in Quebec, this illegitimacy which is the reflection of the fundamental, essential illegitimacy of being, simply being, individually, or collectively, the illegitimacy which I believe haunts us all,

And even if, as I also believe, the prayer which I am addressing at this very moment to whom I'm not sure, or what, or where,
If this prayer were to be heard as the complaint of a spoiled baby whining to get some more Pablum to stick in his belly button,
Which is what all of us think about poets, somewhere way down inside,
Even if you were to think that,
As you listen to me scream out the share of memory that was allotted me
As I scream in the face of the nothingness of my people, and myself among them
The nothingness we are in the process of becoming,
A nothingness where there'll be no place for memory, and no one to care about it,

Even if all that must come to pass,
And even when all that has come to pass,
I will go on writing.
Even if it's only to have my words fall into the nothingness of forgetting
But I will write about revolt
Not about the victory of self-contempt and the victory of forgetting
Because the cynical society we have become, that's not, life.

Translated by Linda Gaboriau

DANIEL LATOUCHE

Daniel Latouche is a research professor of Political Science and Urban Affairs at the Institut national de la recherche scientifique and is a former constitutional adviser to the late premier René Lévesque. The following is excerpted from the Gazette *(October 31, 1991).*

10 REASONS FOR SOVEREIGNTY

THERE ARE MANY REASONS WHY A NUMBER OF QUEBECERS SUPPORT THE IDEA OF independence for their province. But somewhere, buried among the political calculus and the desire to get even, is an attitude similar to a mountain-climber's. Why independence for Quebec? "Because it has never been done," will be the answer. The suggestion that it is a dangerous venture and that the view is not so great from the top of the sovereignty mountain will only convince them that it is worth working for.

"What do societies do?" they'll ask you in return. "They build sovereign nation-states," they'll be quick to answer. "Those who were once, if only briefly and hesitantly, nation-states in their own right – the Baltic Republics for example – never seem to have abandoned the hope of regaining this status."

In the end we all suspect Jacques Parizeau to be right when he asks somewhat rhetorically: "Do you think Quebecers will ever be satisfied within the Canadian realm?" The mountain-climbing analogy certainly does not apply to him, but his greatest strength lies in the belief that maybe not this time, or the next, but one day, the mountain will be climbed. His other strength is to know that we share, sometimes grudgingly, his suspicion.

Twenty years ago, the motives of the first generation of Quebec separatists were most primitive. It had to do with the English, with Ottawa, with the status of French and with money. Ghana, Malaysia and Pakistan were independent nations. Why not Quebec? Today the reasons are both more complex and more simple. The belief that it is the normal thing to do, the last item on the agenda, indicates that there is even emerging a non-nationalist set of reasons for wanting to become a sovereign state. Some of us even believe that the only way to get rid of the nationalist obsession is to get on to something else. I have 10 such reasons:

1. The distinct-society clause officially recognizes the status of Quebec as an ethnic society. This is both dangerous and backward-looking. If we were to move further down this road in order to satisfy Robert Bourassa, it could be a catastrophe. What we need to do is to start building a nation-state and not an ethnic society as soon as possible.

2. The Quebec "way-of-doing-things," part concertation, part networking and part government muscle-flexing has to grow out of its provincial boundaries and begin operating in the big leagues. Otherwise it is in danger of turning inward and of becoming an enterprise of collective gossiping.

3. Until Quebec becomes a sovereign state there is not a chance in the world that non-francophones will be able to join Quebec, Inc. Afterwards, they will become indispensable partners. The French will probably not like it one bit, but they will have little choice.

4. Independence for Quebec should be looked upon as just another case of political deregulation. After years of trying unsuccessfully to tone down the size of both the federal and provincial governments, there is only one way left: get rid in one stroke of most of the legislative responsibilities of at least one of them. On a cost-benefit basis, this is surely the best way to achieve positive results on this front for both Quebec and Canada. Quebec as a whole has to be "privatized."

5. Sovereignty is also the best way – which does not mean it is a sure way – to bring down to size the Quebec government itself. One usually has visions of thousands of new civil servants and dozens of additional government departments being added to the payroll of an independent Quebec. For years this has been the favorite line of Jean Chrétien with his condescending remarks on the Cadillacs of the new Quebec ambassadors. But sovereignty will also offer the opportunity to eliminate all those provincial departments whose only raison d'être is to balance the federal ones. The Department of Science and Technology and Radio-Québec will be the first to go.

6. On the other end, if the new federal plan of Brian Mulroney and Joe Clark gets implemented, not only will Quebec get to keep all of its existing departments, but it will also gain a few others to meet its added responsibilities. And if Quebec gets them, so will Ontario and Alberta. Surely, this is no way to run a country.

7. If we believe the new federal proposals, the whole country, and not just Quebec, will be burdened with new layers of bureaucratic regulations and decision-making infrastructures in order to get at this dream of an asymmetric, decentralized and regionalized country. As a minimum, we will get a new and much bigger Senate, a new Council of the Federation, new consultative bodies, not to mention new regional entities and a completely distinct justice system for native people. The Justice Committees of the U.S. Senate and House of Representatives have 4,000 staffers working for them. Do we want this for Canada? Is this the way to reduce our deficit?

8. As a province, Quebec can well afford to live beyond its fiscal means. To some extent, it has no choice but to do so in order to keep up with the Jones in Ottawa and Toronto. Without the financial support of Canada, it will no longer be able to do so. And the same applies to the other nine Canadian provinces. By sticking together they only succeed in pushing up their respective debts.

9. Until Quebec becomes sovereign, there is no chance for the province to seriously consider giving significant powers to its own local and regional governments. Everything has to be decided in Quebec City and has to be uniform from Rouyn to Rimouski in case of a federal intrusion. Until sovereignty there can be no territorial-based language solutions in Quebec.

10. Nationalism is like a toothache. It never gets any better on its own. Its excesses come from the length of time it takes for it to run its natural course towards its equally natural goal – sovereignty.

Nobody will agree with all 10 points. Advocates of a federal solution will probably disagree with all of them. Separatists, on the other hand, will probably be distressed by most of these statements.

Good! But can we all start thinking again instead of keeping on with the same arguments over and over again? If we are going to discuss the respective merits of independence and federalism for the next 10 years – and in all likelihood we are condemned to do so – maybe we could use new arguments.

Anne Hébert

Anne Hébert was born at Sainte Catherine de Fossambault, Quebec. A poet, novelist, short story writer, and dramatist, she is perhaps best known for her novel, Kamouraska, *which was turned into an award-winning movie by Claude Jutra. Her latest novel,* L'Enfant chargé de songes *(1992), is a celebration of the country of her childhood. Her writing is as well known in French-speaking Europe as it is in Quebec. The following essay is abridged from* Century 1867-1967 *(published by Southam Press, 1967).*

Quebec: The Core of First Time

This province is a country within a country. Quebec the original heart. The hardest and deepest kernel. The core of first time. All around, nine other provinces form the flesh of this still-bitter fruit called Canada.

The creation of the world took place on the rock of Quebec. Face to the river. Adam and Eve were Louis Hébert and Marie Rollet. The first dwelling. The first land tilled. The first sheaf of grain reaped. The first bit of bread. The first child brought into life. The first body laid in earth.

The first written word. It was in 1534: "In the name of God and of the King of France." A cross planted at Gaspé by Jacques Cartier. The vocation of writing begun in the wilderness wind.

And then we were surrendered to time. Time followed its course. By turns we were shaken or lulled by time. Like logs drifting down rivers, we slipped by. A defeat in the heart. A rosary between the fingers. Like the dead. Musing on the song of Lazarus. But see the thought give way to the word. The word becomes flesh. To possess the world. To seize and name the earth. Four and a half centuries of roots. The tree, no longer subterranean, admittedly in the light. Erect. Confronting the world. The Tree of Knowledge. Not in the centre of the garden. Those soft prenatal limbs outside of paradise, in the accursed open land. At the hour of birth, a gate opens upon the round and total world.

"In Quebec nothing changes." Once this was truth. Immobile, peasant-like. Beneath the snow, or the summer sun. Yet no Sleeping Beauty can pass unchanged the test of slumber. Beneath so many dreams and sorrows a duty is discerned. Take up thy bed and walk. The heaped-up treasure-board cracks and splits. Reclaim the heritage from foreign imposts.

The river is salt like the sea. Waves beat upon seaweed-laden shores. Here the wind blows free for ten leagues around. The adventure is boundless. Who can merely tell of it? One must shout it, hands forming a loud-hailer.

The two banks narrowing together are thickly black with trees. It is on no human scale. Here we may labour only. Whoever speaks will speak savagely. With a voice of earth and water mixed.

Helter skelter land of wood and sea. North bank. South bank. Kamouraska, Saint-Vallier, Cap à l'Aigle, Saint-Jean-Port-Joli, Île aux Lièvres, Rimouski, Father Point, Sainte-Luce, Anse Pleureuse, Coin du Banc, Pic de l'Aurore, Gros Morne, Cloridorme, Île Bonaventure.

Sea birds by thousands encrust the rock. Lift. Wheel. Raucous cries on the swell of the sea. Gannets, grebes, cormorants, gulls. Beneath the wind the rock seems to shake itself, like a wild beast attacked by superbly fantastic swarms of bees. Above, the sky.

A hundred thousand lakes. Streams with the strength of a river. Forests entangled by deadfalls. An axe in the hand like a cane. The tracks are those of caribou. Mosquitoes smoke upon your body like your own breath.

Burnt-over land as far as the eye can see. New growth of birch on the green moss. Long tendrils of moss, drawn from the soil, like garlands with fine sandy roots. Gathering blueberries. The barrens laden with blue fruit. That silvery mist clouding the fresh berries. That was when I was a child. Now the reign of the birches is threatened. The face of Charlebois is pitted by dead birches. Sad little white bones against the green of the forest.

Calm lakes, like water in the hollow of a hand. Lake Edward. We children were forbidden to go near the water. "Your hair the colour of the fallow deer, your body of peacocks" – hunters might fire in error. The midges, the blackflies ambushed us. Thousands of needles. Was that the sound of a moose? It crosses the lake, swimming. As if it ploughed a mirror. Deer! A deer in the hayfield! A prodigy of a leap! There it is, out of range. Sheltering in the black spruce.

Sainte-Catherine. Each summer's end a brown bear ventured from the forest. Prowled the edges of the fields. While the golden hay assumed the colour of fresh-baked bread. Children saw enormous tracks in the sand of the little strawberry woods. Games were erased. Sand castles crushed. The children gravely enchanted. As if in the night an heraldic beast had come from the high plains of the Countess de Segur, née Rostopchine, claiming her tribute in Canadian land.

Sainte-Foy. Named for a bitter victory. There where the city, the new university city, now expands. During my childhood it was a little wood. A whole summer of holidays. A brook. Green grass-snakes. Symphonies of tree-frogs. Strawberries bordering the fields. Orchards. Apples succeeding apples – the green, the white, the transparents, the Fameuses. Four houses thick-shelled with white brick. Each with its garden and its orchard. The road was called the Avenue of the Four Bourgeois. It was the country.

Quebec. That city where my parents were born. Where my ancestors prospered and were undone. The city is lived in. Above. Below. The city is ours. We need only plainly speak its name, this city. City on a crag. City of the New World. Upper Town. Lower Town. The secret province. Homogeneous. Certain of its identity. Dreaming behind its jalousies. Taking its time. Sauntering through the narrow streets. Through the summer evenings. Releasing in full bloom the beauty of its daughters.

The long length of Dufferin Terrace. Rue Saint-Louis, rue de la Fabrique, Esplanade, rue des Grissons, rue des Glaçis, ruelle du Trésor, côte à Coton, côte de la Négresse, Latin Quarter, rue Dauphine, Jardin du Fort, Jardin du Gouverneur, rue sous le Cap, Petit Champlain. Little by little the aristocratic quarters move from the old city. A whole floating population camps within the walls. The tall dwellings divide into rented pigeonholes. They sell souvenirs. The port overflows with shipping. Whirlpools of gulls. Vast gates of the water. The sea begins. Clerical bands and coifs. A city of terraces and convents.

Sugar and syrup from the Beauce. Honey from Saint-Pierre-les-Becquets. Mushrooms from Waterloo. Cider from Saint-Hilaire. Brome Lake duck. Valcartier turkey. Real geography is learned at the table, in the breaking of bread.

Boucherville, Varennes, Verchères, Contrecœur, Saint-Antoine-de-Tilly, Sorel, Saint-Jean-sur-Richelieu. Old villages of the French régime. Fine stone houses in the style of manors. Elms, of all trees the most civilized; maples; an amiable river. A domesticated landscape. Ripe and reassuring age.

Rapid, rugged ice hockey. The log drive, perilous leap without a net, on rivers in full flood. Twenty-five thousand white geese alight on Cap Tourmente. Take to the sky. Perfect formations. Passing above Quebec. Their faraway raucous yelping, solid, unhearing, almost unreal, dominating the whole autumnal night sky – if you have never heard it, you have never felt the strange sensation of physical envelopment in a dream, never escaped above the earth.

Once this city was called Hochelaga. François-Xavier Garneau wrote of it, "a half-hundred wooden habitations, fifty paces long and twelve to fifteen wide. In each house, walls hung with skins skilfully sewn together, several rooms opened upon a square room containing the hearth. The settlement was surrounded by a triple palisade." This city was called Ville-Marie. There mass was celebrated by the light of fireflies. "Should every tree on Montreal Island become an Iroquois, it is my duty there to found a colony, and I will go." Thus spoke Maisonneuve. This city is called Montreal. More than two million inhabitants. A vigorous, enterprising life. Creates. Defies. Struggles, gains, loses, rejoices in its destiny. Multiplies. Becomes complex. Accepts or rejects. Melting pot. Cultural broth. Constructs. Demolishes. Reconstructs. A perpetual factory. A city which had no age. Which burns its past. Of which its present pride is its future. At the high heat of its energy. At the peak of its endeavours. Victorian Sherbrooke Street is earth-bound. Vive Dorchester Boulevard and its proud, fine sky-scrapers. The calm of Westmount's little streets: Mount Stephen, Oliver, Kensington. Men, ideas, politics, commerce; business, the arts and daily life assert themselves, confront each other. With the rhythm of the neon. Flashing in the immense city. By day as by night.

Country of water. Of the tumultuous strength of water. Untamed water harnessed. Like a hot-blooded team. Proud water tamed and mastered. The powerhouse of La Gabelle. The Beauharnois dam. Manicouagan. The greatest workshop in the world. Man's all-powerful hand set over the energy of the water.

Asbestos. Noranda. Bourlamaque. Gagnon. Arvida. Matagami. The darkness of the earth opened. The black heart of the earth delivers up its treasures. Asbestos, copper, gold, zinc, aluminum, iron. The shadows are heavy. The miner's lamp scarcely lights the depths of the workings. The patient slow efforts of the young master of the premises. Claiming his entire share.

To seize this land in *flagrante delicto*, in the very act of existence. To understand. To do it justice. To put it into words. The task of a poet. The honour of living.

Léon Dion

Léon Dion is professor of Political Science at Laval University in Ste. Foy, Quebec, and one of Quebec's most respected constitutional authorities. The following is reprinted by permission of Dædalus, Journal of the American Academy of Arts and Sciences, *from the issue entitled "In Search of Canada" (Fall 1988, vol. 177, no. 4).*

Quebec: The Homeland

Our homeland! For most Quebecers, this is the land of their fore-fathers, the land of their own flesh and blood; for others, it is only a land of adoption, which they gradually learn to love to the point that they no longer feel any affinity for their home country. It is clearly those of French descent who most strongly feel Quebec to be their homeland, but many Anglophones and speakers of other languages see it in similar terms, especially those whose ancestors have been here several generations.

My own feelings are ambivalent. When I think of Quebec, my homeland, my heart beats fast; when I think of Canada, my country, reason takes over. Yet in a sense Canada too is my homeland: my ancestors discovered, explored, and partially occupied it as far as the foothills of the Rockies, but they were somehow robbed of their great inheritance and gradually pushed back to Quebec, which they clung to and which they multiplied in. My emotional ties with Canada are thus weaker than they are with Quebec.

Among the many incarnations of the Quebecer – trapper, explorer, lumberjack, habitant, settler, sharecropper, farmer, bourgeois – it is the habitant, or the one who clings to his land, who until today has stood out. The habitant of former times, whose memory lives on for our poets and singers, had a great dream: to conquer the forest, to build a country, to preserve it and extend it to all points of the compass.

Clinging to the earth was one way of ensuring the survival of Quebec as a nation. Small wonder, then, that it was in novels about the earth that the main themes of the Quebec homeland were laid down for posterity. As Giuseppe Turi writes, "Quebecers feel an almost visceral need to identify with the soil of Quebec."

As a nation, we still owe much to this conception of ourselves as rural and peasantlike. Neither the crisis of the 1930s nor World War II seems to have done much to alter the wisdom of tradition. Until the early 1960s, neither the representatives of the working class nor those of the bourgeoisie were able to formulate a conception of Quebec as an urban, industrial nation. Workers and bourgeoisie alike were inculcated with the same traditional values that had enabled the people to survive through years of tribulation.

Until now, urban and industrial culture has done little to reinvigorate and enrich Quebecers' conception of their homeland. Popular singers such as Georges Dor, Félix Leclerc, Gilles Vigneault, Claude Léveillée, and Jean-Pierre Ferland, poets like Paul Chamberland and Gaston Miron, dramatists and film directors such as Marcel Dubé, Michel Tremblay, Gilles Carle, Denis Héroux, and Denys Arcand, and novelists like Roger Lemelin and Gabrielle Roy – all these creative artists sing, describe, and speak of the city, yet still usually only to reaffirm traditional values inherited from the land. Few of them, moreover, venture inside the city itself in search of a conception of their homeland that would be more in tune with contemporary social structures and ways of thinking.

A language is far more than just a combination of words. For those who speak it, it represents both the most public and the most private expression of their personalities. The words a person uses generally relate to that person's self-image, projects, and goals. As for language as a whole, the collective is at least as important as the individual, perhaps more so. If a language is primarily a tool of communication for human beings, it also reveals what is most fundamental to them: their mental structure. Language expresses not only a person's identity but also that of the collectivity to which he or she belongs. In short, a language is inextricably linked with the particularity of a culture.

If Quebec were not French-speaking and did not retain certain elements of French culture (albeit elements that have been adapted with time to conditions in the New World), then the question of Quebec would be no different from that of Ontario or Manitoba. It is in this sense, first of all, that Quebec's problem is above all a linguistic one; but this is also the case in another sense. Like other Western societies, Quebec is currently in the grip of a major cultural crisis. It would be wrong to suggest that our main concern today lies in the economic domain, however important a role it plays in ensuring the well-being of a culture. All great cultures in the past have been built on a solid economic base.

French-speaking Quebecers have to contend not only with a soil that lies frozen and unproductive for long months each year but also with the fact that they account for no more than two percent of the population of the North American continent. In addition, Quebec's society has become extremely diversified.

In human, intellectual, and economic terms, people pay a heavy price for expressing themselves in French in North America. One might even ask if, after two centuries of coexistence with the far more powerful and invasive language of English, the French language is still capable of expressing with accuracy and certainty who we are, what we think, what we are doing, and where we are going. Writers here in Quebec are well aware that French is living on borrowed time and that it is gradually degenerating.

How could any well-informed person deny that we live immersed in an English-speaking, North American world that may turn us, partially or completely, into Americans, without our being aware of the change? It was the realization that this threat is hanging over our heads that once prompted Jean Lemoyne, an essayist who reached prominence in the 1950s and the early 1960s, to write: "I must confess that I think we are no longer capable of giving an adequate account of ourselves in French."

For us Quebecers, it is above all the linguistic aspect of French culture that is its most elementary – not to mention its most dramatic – aspect. Since a people's language is by definition the main form of expression of its thought and mentality, those of us who are aware of this primordial function have good reason to wonder whether the French language could become foreign, secondary, or alienating for us. Yet if we do hold onto our language, how accurately does it reflect our continent's social reality, even at the most everyday level? It is as if we lived simultaneously in two worlds out of phase with each other. One is the world of our language, which is turning increasingly in on itself, is often unable to articulate the social realities it must deal with, and requires all possible forms of protection if it is to survive at all. The other is the world of our culture, our institutions, our social realities, which are generally North American in origin. These two worlds coexist within us and around us. We seek a way of reconciling the French language, which has most deeply shaped our individual and collective development since 1608, with the North American culture, which invades us through the medium of English. Such, then, are the most important issues posed by the problem of the present and future of French in Quebec. All other considerations fade into abstractions that have no bearing on our everyday lives or on the anxieties of our poets, novelists, popular singers, businesspeople, and scientists.

In a recent study of young people's attitudes toward French, the Conseil de la langue française reached an alarming conclusion: "The values of young people show a marked divergence from the cultural and lingusitic evolution of Quebec." A large proportion of their culture comes from the United States. Over 25 per cent feel that "living through the medium of French is not essential to their personal development. . . . Moreover, they do not feel any sense of linguistic insecurity."

One should not, nevertheless, be unduly pessimistic about the future of French among young people today. Although a certain number feel detached from it, the vast majority still lives exclusively through the medium of French, notwithstanding its fascination with American popular culture. This fascination is not unique to Quebecers; it is universal. Given the instability of the French language in Quebec, however, it is clearly more damaging here than elsewhere. The greatest problem facing French in Quebec is the standard of teaching in its elementary and high schools. Extensive research by the Conseil de la langue française has revealed, thirty years after teachers first set the alarm bells ringing, that the standard of written and spoken French among schoolchildren verges on the catastrophic. Another study shows that the tyranny of American popular culture has reached such a point that not only French but all foreign languages in Canada are "in a state of crisis" and that there is a sort of "martyrdom of modern languages." Moreover, in the United States also, "the standard of English is in a state of collapse" for the same reasons as elsewhere. As might be expected, the linguistic decline accompanies a crisis in culture everywhere.

If we can be selective in the values we adopt and if we can preserve the best of our heritage, then we need have no worry or guilt about appropriating everything our continent has to offer that is culturally and materially enriching to us. Our loyalty to our ancestors, our duty to ourselves, and our responsibility to our young people, however, all demand that we strive to appropriate it through the medium of French, even if this means sacrificing economic and intellectual efficiency. We will facilitate the task if we remain committed to preserving as large and as stimulating a French-speaking environment as possible in Quebec so that our poets, novelists, scientists, popular singers, and businesspeople can feel happy and relaxed working in their native language.

D AVID H OMEL

David Homel is the author of two novels, Electrical Storms *and* Rat Palms. *He has translated works by many Quebec authors, including Réjean Ducharme, Dany Laferrière, and Jacques Renaud. The following essay is from* Mapping Literature: The Art and Politics of Translation, *edited by David Homel and Sherry Simon and published by Véhicule Press (Montreal, 1988)*

THE WAY THEY TALK IN *BROKE CITY*

IN THE SUMMER OF 1963, AN ANGRY, DEPRESSED YOUNG MAN NAMED JACQUES Renaud checked into a furnished room on the rue Cherrier in Montreal and, after three days of writing at white heat, produced a short novel entitled *Le Cassé. Broke City,* the English version, appeared twenty years later. There isn't much to the *Broke City* plot: a young lumpen named Johnny tries to hold onto his equally down-and-out girlfriend Mena, loses her to a rival (so he thinks), kills the rival, and continues his wanderings through a Montreal that is truly *cassé.* What was outstanding about the book, besides its out-and-out violence and nihilism, was the language in which it was written. Renaud chose to write in *joual,* the working-class French dialect of East End Montreal, and in so doing, along with writers like André Major and Claude Jasmin, helped launch the *joual* movement that was to pave the way for Michel Tremblay and a whole new literary identity for Quebec. Finally, it seemed, Quebec was to have its own distinct literary language. (*Joual,* by the way, is *joual* for the French word *cheval,* meaning "horse.") This movement set off a debate about whether dialect can be a literary language. And, in the Canadian context, translators had to face the problem of how to put that language into English.

With the energies developing during the unquiet era of the Quiet Revolution, it was *joual* that would burst upon the scene as a literary language, if only because of the censorship it had always been subjected to. *Joual* had been considered an inferior dialect, a sub-language, a stigma of a people going nowhere, and it was attacked by religious and civil authorities (who were more often than not one and the same in Quebec). There were *campagnes de bien parler* (good-grammar campaigns), and the slogan *Bien parler, c'est se respecter* (speaking well is a sign of self-respect) was concocted. With the rise of leftist nationalist sentiments in the late 1950s and the 1960s, it was no surprise that certain writers would want to celebrate *joual* as a literary language by dint of creating works in it.

First, a few words about *joual.* It is a simple recipe. Take standard

Quebec French, increase the dipthongization, make the grammar remarkably flexible, and add a healthy dose of Anglicisms – or better, Americanisms. It's this latter addition that gives *joual* its special savour and creates monumental problems for those brave and foolish souls who try to put a *joual*-izing work into English. For not only does *joual* accept English words into its lexicon, it also distorts them once they are inside, in a kind of sabotage action against a linguistic occupying force. *Pushing* in *joual* is not "pushing" in English; *stépines* (step-ins) becomes the word for "panties"; such strange and wonderful cases abound.

But this linguistic sabotage, though amusing for collectors of odd morphemes, is not the heart of the Anglicism problem in *joual.* Take a simple Renaud sentence: *Il s'est assis sur le tchesteurfilde.* He sat on the sofa. Yet this straightforward (and perfectly correct) English rendering does not and cannot render the socio-linguistic complex present in this short sentence. Why is Renaud saying *tchesteurfilde* instead of the standard French *divan*? And what does it mean when he does? What is the difference of meaning between these two terms that both refer to something you sit on? And what do we do with this state of affairs when we want to translate into English?

In Quebec, since the 1760s, English has been the dominant language and, until recently, the language of domination. Nowhere is this clearer than in *joual*, in a sense the linguistic nerve centre of Quebec society. English invades French, not the other way around. The fact that we speakers of English say *tête-à-tête* or *crêpes suzette* or, on an etymological level, "government," is nothing compared to the density of the foreign influence in *joual.* Speakers of *joual* will say *Il a pogné un flatte* or *Elle l'a pitché dehors* or *Il est sur le chômage, il bomme*, not because French words for these English terms don't exist, but because the English words better betray the domination, both economic and linguistic, under which these people live. And, in passing, it is no accident that most Anglicisms refer to actions of violence or desperation.

What does the translator do when he or she decides to put *joual* into English? The first thing to realize is that the act is impossible. English influences and alters French in North America, not the other way around. Domination is a one-way street. There is no adequate translation for the domination and linguistic and economic poverty lurking in the simple sentence *Il s'est assis sur le tchesteurfilde.* Of course, translating *joual* may be only slightly more impossible than translating any other work of literature, and with that rationale firmly in mind, I decided to take a stab, so to speak, at Renaud's *Le Cassé* (*Broke City*, Guernica Editions, Montreal,

1984). As the southern United States writer Bob Houston has said, we don't write dialect, we represent it. Like the writer, the translator has to make a choice of dialects to stand for *joual*, and unfortunately none of the pre-existent choices seemed to work. The main character named Johnny in *Broke City* is a northern white, and his ancestors have been in the country for over three hundred years, so black, southern U.S., rural, immigrant, and Atlantic dialects are out of the question. So are many other ones you can name. I ended up opting for a generalized big-city, working-class, northern white dialect, the speech of people who have a lot of emotions to express and no words to express them in, whose frustrations predictably lead to anti-social expressions. As I was preparing to work on *Broke City*, I remembered a grade-school teacher who chastized us when we used "ain't" or some other equally guilty ungrammatical expression: "If you can't speak well, you shouldn't speak at all." It is to her that I should have dedicated my translation.

Along the way I discarded the other possibility of creating a new English dialect that would have been the geographical and social equivalent of *joual.* I could have gone down to the taverns along Wellington Street in Point St. Charles and Verdun on a Saturday night, kept my mouth shut and my ears open, and built a dialect around what English-speaking people, the equivalents of Renaud's Ti-Jean in the East End, would say. But I rejected this option precisely because it was *research*, a concocted language, and I wanted to get as close as possible to the white-heat conditions under which Jacques Renaud wrote the work. But whatever way a translator chooses, *Il s'est assis sur le tchesteurfilde* is still "He sat down on the sofa"; there's not much more that can be done to capture the domination and despair in that simple phrase.

In 1967, Renaud said of the language he used, "*Joual* is the language both of submission and revolt, of anger and impotence. It's a non-language, a denunciation." *Joual* is language against itself. In that contradiction is contained the paradox of *joual* and, indeed, that of other similar dialects, like *el pocho*, spoken along the Mexican-American border. (*Pocho*, interestingly enough, means "faded" in Mexican Spanish, as if speakers of this English-flavoured dialect have somehow lost their original colour.) How much can anyone say using the language of people who have traditionally had nothing to say, who have been too far down the social ladder and too weighted with frustrations to make works of art? How much elbow room does the writer have when he or she decides to inhabit the universe of *joual*? Is it even fair to use the language of a group of people for whom this very language is a sign of humiliation and poverty and isolation? Renaud himself became aware of this problem in the years that followed. Like all good paradoxes, there is no clear solution. It probably is true that once the liberating effect of *joual* was felt, once this language, so typically *québécois* in its contradictions, was celebrated and moved closer to the mainstream, it became less imperative to write in it.

Michel Tremblay's use of *joual* in the 1980s is anything but shocking and revolutionary, and Jacques Renaud has since abandoned that extremist language for something more meditative, which is not necessarily a progression in the moral or aesthetic sense, but more like an inevitability. This seems to be the lesson of recent Quebec literary history: *joual* was the manifestation of a key historical moment for Quebec writing, but at present, no one would turn any heads by writing in it. It has truly become a literary language. Is this the banalization or the apotheosis of *joual*? Probably neither. It is more like a society accepting itself and making literature out of its own speech.

LISE BISSONNETTE

Lise Bissonnette is the publisher of Le Devoir, *Quebec's most influential newspaper. The following excerpt is from the CBC's 1990 Graham Spry Lecture, which she gave at the Canadian Centre for Architecture in Montreal.*

CULTURE, POLITICS AND SOCIETY IN QUEBEC

ANY SELF-RESPECTING POLITICIAN IN THIS COUNTRY IS PREPARED TO SWEAR TO HIS OR her gods that Quebec must preserve its language and culture. The misunderstanding simply revolves around the means which must be taken to achieve this noble objective.

But exactly what culture are we talking about? Attempting to answer this question frankly means facing the cultural complexity of Quebec. . . . The paradox, and in some ways the tragedy, of Quebec culture is that it must constantly survive the indifference of those who claim to have its interests at heart.

For the culture people talk about, which tails Quebec like a shadow, is no more than a vague anthropological notion. What is being referred to, for better or for worse, is little more than an ethnic heritage. In the eyes of the Americans who still believe in the "melting pot," Québécois culture appears to be a remarkably resistant strain, a bizarre throwback rooted in the precious relics and memories of the French regime. In the eyes of English Canadians, who like to believe that they practice the canons of multiculturalism, Québécois culture is just one stem in the great and colourful cultural bouquet which blossoms from coast to coast. Those who ardently profess great respect for Quebec, for its language and culture, are usually thinking of its historical heritage. Be it General Montcalm or Maria Chapdelaine, everyone is happy to see us nurture a vivid memory of these lingering traces of Old France in America.

It would be interesting to compare all the political speeches on Quebec and its future given, for example, between 1980 and 1990, a particularly prolific decade. I am convinced that the references to Quebec culture would be abundant. I am equally convinced that the word would never be used in the contemporary sense, that it would never, or rarely, refer to "la culture vivante," living culture, the culture currently being produced – in other words, the work of contemporary artists in Québec. This is how the prevailing political debate locks the notion of Québécois culture into a nostalgic framework. Seen this way, culture is essentially an historical heritage which must be lovingly enshrined, preserved and protected from all threats.

Translated by Linda Gaboriau

Boundaries of Identity

The Gender of Sovereignty

Critics since the Quiet Revolution period have automatically assumed that the tragedy, the wandering, the blackness, and the frustrated mysticism that recur in Quebec men's writing from the poetry of Émile Nelligan to the present are the reflection of a national search for identity, condemned to unending circularity or paralysis by the ambivalence of Quebec's situation within Canada. But what if this alienation were also a gender-based phenomenon? And what if, existing alongside 'his story,' there were an 'other' story, offering a different perspective not only on the national dilemma, but on reality in a more general sense?

Patricia Smart, scholar
From *Writing in the Father's House*, 1988

JAN NOEL

Jan Noel teaches history at the University of Toronto and is now doing extensive research on Quebec women's history (1800-1850). This is a new version of her essay "New France: Les femmes favorisées," which appeared in Atlantis, *vol. 6, no. 2 (Spring 1981) and in* Rethinking Canada: The Promise of Women's History *(1986).*

NEW FRANCE: WOMEN WITHOUT WALLS

THE NOTION OF "WOMEN'S PLACE" OR "WOMEN'S ROLE," POPULAR WITH NINETEENTH century commentators, suggests a degree of homogeneity inappropriate to the seventeenth century. It is true that on a formal, ideological level men enjoyed the dominant position. This can be seen in the marriage laws, which everywhere made it a wife's duty to follow her husband to whatever dwelling place he chose. In 1650, the men of Montreal were advised by Governor Maisonneuve that they were in fact responsible for the misdemeanours of their wives since "the law establishes their dominion over their wives." Under ordinary circumstances the father was captain of the family hierarchy. Yet, it is clear that this formal male authority in both economic and domestic life was not always exercised.

The idea of separate male and female spheres lacked the clear definition it later acquired. This is in part related to the lack of communication and standardization characteristic of the *ancien régime* – along sexual lines or any other. One generalization, however, applies to all women of the *ancien régime*. They were not relegated to the private, domestic sphere of human activity because that sphere did not exist. Western Europeans had not yet learned to separate public and private life. As Phillipe Ariès pointed out in his classic study, the private home, in which parents and children constitute a distinct unit, is a relatively recent development. In early modern Europe most of domestic life was lived in the company of all sorts of outsiders. Manor houses, where all the rooms interconnect with one another, show the lack of emphasis on privacy. Here, as in peasant dwellings, there were often no specialized rooms for sleeping, eating, working, or receiving visitors; all were more or less public activities performed with a throng of servants, children, relatives, clerics, apprentices, and clients in attendance. Molière's comedies illustrate the familiarity of servants with their masters. Masters, maids, and valets slept in the same room and servants discussed their masters' lives quite openly.

Though familiar with their servants, people were less so with their children. They did not dote on infants to the extent that parents do today. It may have been, as some writers have suggested, that there was little point in growing attached to a fragile being so very apt, in those centuries, to be borne away by accident or disease. These unsentimental families of all ranks sent their children out to apprentice or serve in other people's homes. This was considered important as a basic education. It has been estimated that the majority of Western European children passed part of their childhood living in some household other than their natal one. Mothers of these children – reaching down, in the town, as far as the artisan class – might send their infants out to nursemaids and have very little to do with their physical maintenance.

This lack of a clearly defined "private" realm relates vitally to the history of women, since this was precisely the sphere they later were to inhabit. Therefore it is important to focus on their place in the pre-private world. To understand women in New France one first must pass through the antechamber which historian Peter Laslett appropriately calls "the world we have lost."

In this public world people had not yet learned to be private about their bodily functions, especially about their sexuality. For aid with their toilette, noblewomen did not blush to employ *hommes de chambre* rather than maids. The door of the bed-chamber stood ajar, if not absolutely open. Its inhabitants, proud of their fecundity, grinned out from under the bedclothes at their visitors. Newlyweds customarily received bedside guests. There was not the same uneasiness in relations between the sexes which later, more puritanical, centuries saw, and which, judging by the withdrawal of women from public life in many of these societies, probably worked to their detriment.

Part of the reason these unsqueamish, rather public people were not possessive about their bodies was that they did not see themselves so much as individuals but as part of a larger, more important unit – the family. In this world the family was the basic organization for most social and economic purposes. As such it claimed the individual's first loyalty. A much higher proportion of the population married than does today. Studies of peasant societies suggest that, for most, marriage was an economic necessity.

The family was able to serve as the basic economic unit in preindustrial societies because the business of earning a living generally occurred at home. Just as public and private life were undifferentiated, so too were home and workplace. Agricultural and commercial pursuits were all generally "domestic" industries. The idea of man as breadwinner and woman as homemaker was not clearly developed. Women's range of economic activity was still nearly as wide as that of their husbands.

In New France, wives of artisans took advantage of their urban situation to attract customers into the taverns they set up alongside the workshop, which was often also their home. On the farms where most of the population lived, "work" and "home" differed least of all. Both sexes toiled in the fields together. In this period and for generations afterward it was reported that rural couples conferred before making financial decisions.

Given the economic importance of both spouses, it is not surprising to see marriage taking on some aspects of a business deal. We see this in the provisions of the law that protected the property rights of both parties contracting a match. The fact that wives often brought considerable family property to the marriage, and retained rights to it, placed them in a better position than their nineteenth-century descendants were to enjoy.

In New France the family's importance was intensified even beyond its usual role in *ancien régime* societies. Colonization required the work of both spouses, and there was an exceptionally high annual marriage rate. The importance of the family as a social institution was compounded because other social institutions, such as guilds and villages, were underdeveloped. This probably enhanced women's position, for in the family women tended to serve as equal partners with their husbands, whereas women were gradually losing their position in the guilds and professions in Europe.

Law reinforced family relations. The outstanding characteristic of the legal system in New France – *the Coutume de Paris* – is its concern to protect the rights of all members of the family. The *Coutume* reinforced the family, for example, by the penalties it levied on those transferring family property to non-kin. It took care to protect the property of children of a first marriage when a widow or widower remarried. It protected a woman's rights by ensuring that the husband did not have unilateral authority to alienate the family property (in contrast to eighteenth-century British law).

The law valorized families in other ways too. In a colony starved for manpower, reproduction was considered a matter of particularly vital public concern – a concern well demonstrated in the rewards for large families and the extremely harsh punishments meted out to women who concealed pregnancy. We see a positive side of this intervention in the care the Crown took of foundlings, employing nurses at a good salary to care for them and making attempts to protect these children from stigma. Midwives too were paid by the Crown. This, and the training they received, helps account for an unusually low rate of female mortality in the childbearing years. (Up to age 60, women had a one-to-three year longer life expectancy than men.)

State regulation of the family was balanced by family regulation of the State. Families had an input into the political system, playing an important role in the running of the State. Women's political participation was favoured by the large role of entertaining in political life. For the courtier's role, women were as well trained as men, and there seems to have been no stigma attached to the woman who participated independently of her husband. Six women, Mesdames Daine, Péan, Lotbinière, de Repentigny, Marin, and St. Simon, along with six male officers, were chosen by the Intendant to accompany him to Montreal in 1753. Rural women had elections to select parish midwives. Women were also part of what historians have called the "preindustrial crowd." Along with their menfolk, they were full-fledged members of the old "moral economy" whose members rioted and took what was traditionally their rightful share (and no more) when prices were too high or when speculators were hoarding grain. The four hundred women who rioted for bread in the hungry Quebec winter of 1759 illustrate this aspect of the old polity.

Demographic Advantages

Demography favoured the women of New France in two ways. First, those who went there were a highly select group of immigrants. Second, gender imbalance in the early years of the colony's development also worked in their favour. Most of the female immigrants to New France fall into two categories. The first was a group of well-connected and highly dedicated religious figures. They began to arrive in 1639, and a trickle of French nuns continued to cross the ocean over the course of the next century. The second distinct group was the *filles du roi,* government-sponsored female migrants who arrived between 1663 and 1673. These immigrants, though not as outstanding as the *dévotes,* were nevertheless privileged compared to the average immigrant to New France, who arrived more or less threadbare. The vast majority came from Île-de-France and the northwestern parts of France, where women enjoyed fuller legal rights, were better educated and more involved in commerce than those in southern France. When they set foot on colonial soil, the immigrants would find themselves prized as a scarce resource.

The great religious revival of the seventeenth century endowed New France with several exceptionally capable, well-funded, determined leaders imbued with an activist approach to charity and with that particular mixture of spiritual ardour and worldly *savoir-faire* that typified the mystics of that period. The praises of Marie de l'Incarnation, Jeanne Mance, and Marguerite Bourgeoys have been sung so often as to be tiresome. Perhaps, though, a useful vantage point is gained if one assesses them neither as saints nor heroines, but simply as leaders. In this capacity, the nuns supplied much-needed money, publicity, skills, and settlers to the struggling colony.

Marie de l'Incarnation, a competent businesswoman from Tours, founded the Ursuline Monastery at Quebec in 1639. Turning to the study of Indian languages, she and her colleagues helped implement the policy of assimilating the young Indians. Then, gradually abandoning the futile policy, they turned to the education of the French colonists. Marie de l'Incarnation developed the farm on the Ursuline seigneurie and served as an unofficial adviser to the colonial administrators. She also helped draw attention and money to the colony by writing over the course of thirty years some 12,000 letters, many to admirers in court circles.

An even more prodigious fund-raiser in those straitened times was Jeanne Mance, who had a remarkable knack for making friends in high places. They enabled her to supply money and colonists for the original French settlement on the island of Montreal, and to take a place beside Maisonneuve as co-founder of the town. The hospital she established there had the legendary wealth of the de Bullion family – and the revenues of three Norman domains – behind it. From this endowment she made the crucial grant to Governor Maisonneuve in 1651 that secured vitally needed troops from France, thus saving Montreal. Mance and her Montreal colleague Marguerite Bourgeoys both made several voyages to France to recruit settlers. They were particularly successful in securing the female immigrants necessary to establish a permanent colony.

Besides contributing to the colony's sheer physical survival, the nuns also raised its living standard. They conducted the schools attended by girls of all classes and from both races. Other nuns established hospitals in each of the three towns. The hospitals provided high-quality care to both rich and poor, care that compared favourably with that of similar institutions in France. Thus, the *dévotes* played an important role in supplying leadership, funding, publicity, recruits, and social services. They may even have tipped the balance toward survival in the 1650s, when retention of the colony was still in doubt.

In the longer run, they established an educational heritage, which survived and shaped social life long after the initial heroic piety had grown cold. Admittedly, women never shared men's access to the Jesuit College, the training schools for artisans and river pilots. The schools that the *dévotes* founded did, however, prevent a situation such as developed in France, where education of women increasingly lagged behind that of men. The opinion-setters in France sought to justify this neglect in the eighteenth century and a controversy began over whether girls should be educated outside the home at all. Girls in Montreal escaped all this. Indeed, in 1663

Montrealers had a school for their girls but none for their boys. The result was that for a time Montreal women surpassed men in literacy, a reversal of the usual *ancien régime* pattern. The unusually good education of women that Charlevoix extolled in 1744 continued to be noted by travellers long after the fall of New France. Late in the seventeenth century literacy was roughly double the 14 per cent rate in the mother country. Marguerite Bourgeoys' congregational nuns provided free schooling in Louisburg, and in the Montreal District, while the urban elite paid to send their daughters to Ursuline schools. The Ursulines were traditionally rather weak in teaching housekeeping (which perhaps accounts for Swedish traveller Pieter Kalm's famous castigation of Canadian housewifery). Nevertheless they specialized in needlework, an important skill since articles of clothing were a major trade good sought by the Indians. Moreover, the Ursulines taught the daughters of the elite the requisite skills for administering a house and a fortune – skills which many were to exercise.

Apart from the nuns, the famous *filles du roi* were women sent out by the French government as brides in order to boost the colony's permanent settlement. Over 800 arrived between 1663 and 1673. If less impressive than the *dévotes,* they, too, appeared to have arrived with more than the average immigrant's store of education and capital. The majority of the *filles du roi* (and for that matter, of seventeenth-century female immigrants generally) were urban dwellers, a group that enjoyed better access to education than the peasantry did. Over one-third were educated at the Paris Hôpital Général. Students at this institution learned writing and such a wide variety of skills that in France they were much sought after for service in the homes of the wealthy. Six per cent were of noble or bourgeois origin. The *filles* brought with them a 50-100 *livres* dowry provided by the King and in many cases supplemented this with personal or family funds ranging from 200-450 *livres.* These two major immigrant groups, the *filles du roi* and particularly the nuns, account for the superior education and "cultivation" travellers attributed to the colony's women.

The other demographic consideration, the much greater emigration of men to the colony, might lead one to expect that the needed group would receive favoured treatment. The facility of marriage and remarriage, as well as the leniency of the courts and the administrators toward women, suggests that this hypothesis is correct. Women had a wider choice in marriage than did men in the colony's early days. There were, for example, eight marriageable men for every marriageable woman in Montreal in 1663. Widows grieved, briefly, then remarried within an average of 8.8 months after their bereavement. In those early days the laws of supply and demand operated to women's economic advantage, as well. Rarely did these first Montreal women bother to match their husband's wedding present by offering a dowry.

Economic opportunities

Even more than demographic forces, the colonial economy served to enhance the position of women. In relation to the varied activities found in many regions of France, New France possessed a primitive economy. Other than subsistence farming, the habitants engaged in two major pursuits. The first was military activity, which included not only actual fighting but building and maintaining the imperial forts and provisioning the troops. The second activity was the fur trade. Fighting and fur trading channelled men's ambitions and at times removed them physically from the colony. This helped open up the full range of opportunities to women. Many adapted themselves to life in a military society. A few actually fought. Others made a good living by providing goods and services to the ever-present armies. Still others left military activity aside and concentrated on civilian economic pursuits – pursuits that were often neglected by men. For many this simply meant managing the family farm as best as one could during the trading season, when husbands were away. Other women assumed direction of commercial enterprises, a neglected area in this society that preferred military honours to commercial prizes. Others acted as sort of home-office partners for fur-trading husbands working far afield. Still others, having lost husbands to raids, rapids, or other hazards of forest life assumed a widow's position at the helm of the family business.

New France has been convincingly presented by the historian William Eccles as a military society. The argument is based on the fact that a very large proportion of its population was under arms, its government had a semi-military character, its economy relied heavily on military expenditure and manpower, and a military ethos prevailed among the elite. In some cases, women joined their menfolk in these martial pursuits. The seventeenth century occasionally saw them in direct combat.

The most famous of these seventeenth-century *guerrières* was, of course, Madeleine de Verchères. At the age of fourteen she escaped from a band of Iroquois attackers, rushed back to the fort on her parents' seigneurie, and fired a cannon shot in time to warn all the surrounding settlers of the danger. Legend and history have portrayed de Verchères as a lamb who was able, under siege, to summon up a lion's heart. Powdered and demure in a pink dress, she smiles very sweetly out at the world in a charming vignette in Arthur Doughty's *A Daughter of New France, being a story of the life and times of Madeleine de Verchères,* published in 1916. Perhaps the late twentieth century is ready for her as a musket-toting braggart who extended the magnitude of her deed with each telling and who boasted that she never in her life shed a tear, a contentious thorn in the side of the local *curé* (whom she slandered) and of her *censitaires* (whom she constantly battled in the courts). She strutted through life like an officer of the *campagnard* nobility to which her family belonged. One wonders how many more there were like her.

By the eighteenth century, women had withdrawn from hand-to-hand combat, but many remained an integral part of the military elite as it closed in to become a caste. In this system, both sexes shared the responsibility of marrying properly and maintaining those cohesive family ties which lay at the heart of military society. What is more surprising is that a number of women accompanied their husbands to military posts in the wilderness. Wives of officers, particularly of corporals, traditionally helped manage the canteens in the French armies. Almost all Canadian officers were involved in some sort of trading activity, and a wife at the post could mind the store when the husband had to mind the war, as did the imperious Madame Lusignan who created a state of near-mutiny at Fort St. Frédéric in the 1750s by monopolizing the trade there, with her husband, the Commandant, helping to enforce it. The nuns, too, marched in step with this military society. They were, quite literally, one of its lifelines, since they cared for the wounded. A majority of the invalids at the Montreal Hôtel-Dieu were soldiers, and the Ursuline institution at Trois-Rivières was referred to simply as a *hôpital militaire*. Humbler folk also played a part in military society. In the towns female pub-owners conducted a booming business with troops. Other women served as laundresses, accompanying armies on campaigns. At Quebec City, prostitutes plied their trade as early as 1667.

While warfare provided a number of women with a living, it was in commerce that the *Canadiennes* really flourished. Here a number of women moved beyond supporting roles to occupy centre stage. This happened for several reasons. The first was that the military ethos diverted men from commercial activity. Second, many men who entered the woods to fight or trade were gone for years. Others, drowned or killed in battle, never returned. This left many widows who had to earn a livelihood. This happened so often, in fact, that when women, around the turn of the eighteenth century overcame their numerical disadvantage, the tables turned quickly. They soon outnumbered the men and remained a majority through to the Conquest. Generally speaking, life was more hazardous for men than for women – so much so that the next revolution of the historiographic wheel may turn up the men of New France (at least in relation to its women) as an oppressed group.

The geographically mobile male population projected a number of women into forms of activity more typically performed by males. Feminine enterprise was certainly not unknown in France. Absent husbands in New France made it particularly likely that female relatives would cover home base, and it was not unusual for men heading west to delegate powers of attorney to their wives. Some procured supplies or kept accounts or made trade goods. Canoes were built by women and girls at Trois-Rivières under government contract. In the colony's first days Jeanne Enard was an important though unscrupulous trader at Trois-Rivières while Mesdames de la Tour and Joybert shipped furs from Acadia. In the eighteenth-century Mesdames Couagne and Lamothe were substantial merchants at Montreal as were the Desaulniers sisters whose Indian trading post was a front for a Montreal-Albany smuggling operation.

The final reason for women's extensive business activity was the direct result of the hazards men faced in fighting and fur-trading. A high proportion of women were widowed; and as widows, they enjoyed special commercial privileges. In traditional French society, these privileges were so extensive that craftsmen's widows sometimes inherited full guild-master's rights. More generally, widows acquired the right to manage the family assets until the children reached the age of twenty-five (and sometimes beyond that time). In some instances they also received the right to choose which child could receive the succession.

Thus, in New France, both military and commercial activities that required a great deal of travelling over vast distances were usually carried out by men. In their absence, their wives played a large role in the day-to-day economic direction of the colony. Even when the men remained in the colony, military careers often absorbed their energies. In these situations, it was not uncommon for a wife to assume direction of the family interests. Others waited to do so until their widowhood, which – given the fact that the seventeenth-century wife was about eight years younger than her husband and that his activities were often more dangerous – frequently came early.

New France had been founded at a time in Europe's history in which the roles of women were neither clearly nor rigidly defined. In this fluid situation, the colony received an unusually capable group of female immigrants during its formative stage. Long remaining in short supply, these women appear to have been relatively privileged within marriage, at school, in the courts, and in social and political life. Circumstances enabled the women of New France to play many parts: wife and mother, but also *dévote,* trader, warrior, landowner, smuggler, politician, educator and entrepreneur. For us to understand them, we have to overcome our own era's demarcation of private and public life.

DIANE LAMOUREUX
Diane Lamoureux is a professor of Political Science at Laval University. The following is abridged from "Nationalism and Feminism in Quebec: An Impossible Attraction," an essay published in Feminism and Political Economy, *edited by Meg Luxton and Heather Jon Maroney (Methuen, 1987).*

NATIONALISM AND MISOGYNY

THE CORNERSTONE OF THE IDEOLOGY OF SURVIVAL IS THE MYTH OF NATIONAL origin. New France was seen as an era of French cultural expansion wiped out by the hideous misfortune of the British conquest, which temporarily coerced French Canadian people into a state of submission. The darkness of the present was forgotten as traditional nationalism rewrote the past in glorious terms, offering it as a guarantee of a resplendent future. A direct link was posited between the past and the future: the present was obliterated, and along with it the political dimension of the national question was reduced to a mere cultural matter.

A bright future depended on two conditions: first, the maintenance of the specificity of the Québécois nation (which implied a group large enough to resist the pressures of external encroachment), and second, a system to pass culture and tradition from one generation to the next so that this specificity could withstand the test of time. Traditional nationalism identified the family as the institution that could best fulfill these two roles:

> All the same, the French Canadian family assumes an even more glorious apanage, the result of its faithful spirit, the chastity of our morals: the French Canadian family begets the future. (Lionel Groulx, 1919)

Once the central role of the family had been established, with its implications of a precise role for women, the stage was set for the entire discourse of "la revanche des berceaux" – revenge of the cradle. The French Canadian elite, faced with the dilemma of being a minority in a country that it did not control, chose to adopt a pronatalist policy rather than to formulate a political strategy that would allow it to resolve the national question. The phenomenon of high fertility, "la revanche des berceaux," cannot be interpreted in solely economic or demographic terms, although these factors were influential.

After 1763, when local elites deserted the cities and returned to France, Quebec became a patchwork of isolated rural communities, a process that became even more pronounced with the defeat of 1837–38. Agriculture developed on a small scale and in an autarchical manner outside the networks of commercial exchange. This form of agricultural production required a large labour force; the availability of greater numbers of people would seem to lead to higher productivity and thus decrease the likelihood of entering into relations of external dependence. This observation has led some writers to emphasize the economic importance of the family:

> One can see without difficulty that the pronatalist political and religious discourse which encourages a high birthrate for moral and ideological reasons . . . only further rationalizes a process of reproduction whose primary logic lies in population policies compatible with the organization of agriculture. (Laurin-Frenette, 1979)

But this kind of economic interpretation neglects the fact that Quebec land was not as fertile as Quebec mothers. A high birthrate combined with poor agricultural output and shortages of arable land led first to emigration and ultimately to assimilation for francophones who left their rural communities for the Canadian west and the U.S.A.

Rather, the ideological role of the family was of greater importance than its economic role in sustaining birthrates. It was seen as the only institution that was under the nation's complete control, that refused all compromise with foreign domination; it was the key to the future. The revenge of the cradle was both a defensive response to the large influx of immigrants and an assertive policy designed to regenerate the national group. In this context, no societal project was complete without a coherent family policy.

In *Notre maître le passé*, Lionel Groulx emphasized that the vocation of "old maid" was outlawed in New France in 1669. A refusal to marry or to procreate was met with fines, while those who complied were financially rewarded. A good French Canadian family was a large one, incomplete without the constant chatter of children. These legal and ideological constraints help explain why New France sustained the highest birthrate of any country of European origin right up to the 1960s.

> In a country whose very survival seemed to depend upon keeping up a frantic birthrate, women were "called upon" to produce French Catholic children, and to bring them up to adulthood, where, if they were not happy with the system, they could consecrate themselves to the service of God,

> caring for the sick, orphans, school children, and the poor, secular celibacy being taxed with egoism and individualism. (Michèle Jean, 1977)

Indeed, the revenge of the cradle proved to be so durable that in the 1960s demographers were still calculating the number of children each francophone family should have to maintain or increase their weight within Quebec and Canada. Many members of the Parti Québécois also saw a high birthrate in a positive light. Jacques Grand'Maison was quite explicit: "This much decried demographic expansion has played a most positive role in our collective future."

Nationalists saw the family not only as the basic unit of society; it was also the microcosm of the nation. Although the nation was oppressed in all other domains, within the structure of the family it could flourish. The maintenance of the family thus became the *sine qua non* of national survival. This connection serves to explain, in part, why nationalists frequently adopted very reactionary positions on issues affecting women, including, for example, the right to vote and the right to gainful employment. It also explains the nationalist outcry against the federal government's 1925 law legalizing divorce. Even the Fédération Nationale St. Jean Baptiste (the women's branch of the Société St. Jean Baptiste), pioneers of the suffrage movement, abandoned their struggle when pressured by religious and nationalist elites. After the Second World War, these same elites campaigned to get women out of the workforce and back to their kitchens, relegating them to the role of full-time housewives.

The overwhelming importance of the family's socializing role went hand in hand with the weakness of Quebec's educational system. As Yolande Pinard has pointed out, "The clerico-nationalist ideology assigns women a supplementary function: they are the guardians of the Christian faith, language, and tradition." Language, culture, and tradition, the seeds from which nationalist ideology was cultivated, are all learned first in the family. The ideological importance accorded to women's role as educators, and the periodic absence of husbands who left the homestead to find work, has led some observers to speak of a matriarchy in Quebec.

The idea of a matriarchy is a myth at several levels. Since their prestige was directly proportional to the number of children they produced, women had no value in their own right, but only as mothers. Even as mothers, however, their labour had no intrinsic value, but was seen as instrumental in achieving the greater goal, national survival. The contemporary heritage of this prescription was vividly sketched in Denise Boucher's portrait of the alienation of a woman who, having undergone repeated pregnancies, could only feel emptiness once deprived of her children.

In a context where the family is perceived as the microcosm of the nation, the mother's role of bearing and rearing children takes on special significance:

> In oppressed nations such as Quebec, Ireland, and Euskadi, nationalist arguments are used by the dominant classes to keep women "in their place," thereby strengthening Catholic ideology. Religious puritanism is thus appended by the myth of the woman/mother, as the only source of social, emotional, and political stability. (League ouvrière révolutionnaire, 1978)

To be "in the family way" – preferably year after year – was the patriotic duty of Québécois womanhood. The Société St. Jean Baptiste had constant praise for this kind of patriotism:

> The heroism of the French Canadian mother is no less than any other and . . . she herself is superior to most. Strong in her Catholic faith, she has provided the Church and the Fatherland with as many valiant sons and vigorous daughters that Providence has seen fit to ask of her in gratitude of the most sacred causes. (Frechette, 1943)

But such acts of faith in the procreative will of the French Canadian mother and her seemingly important role in the family should not lead to the conclusion that there was a matriarchy in Quebec. On the contrary, she was deprived of her most basic rights:

> The immobility of French Canadian society for three generations was certainly not going to provoke legislators into reforming the legal structures of the family or marriage. The double principle of matrimonial and paternal power was well established, and its main result was the total legal incapacity of the married woman. (Dumont-Johnson, 1968)

As for the maternal role in the transmission of national values, it was a profoundly dominated one. The words of women were of importance only when they echoed the discourse of the church and the educational system which were, and still are, for all intents and purposes, the same. Women did indeed play a vital role in the transmission of ideology, but they had no input into what they taught. They merely repeated and amplified in the home a discourse defined by clerical nationalists. Just as she "kept" her husband's house, she "kept" an ideology that was not her own:

> It seems to us, however, that the specific authority of women in the family comes from the fact that her position there assures the structural articulation of the family to the Church as the general apparatus of control and reproduction. The discourse of the mother is really that of the priest, which explains how this discourse is imposed on the family, including the father. This link between the family and the Church is, incidentally, all that allowed women to read and write. (Laurin-Frenette, 1979)

The notion of the Quebec matriarchy is also inadequate precisely because its limited perspective on women in the family failed to consider either their situation outside the family or the place of the domestic sphere in the hierarchy of social values. Nationalist ideology was founded upon a strict separation of powers which originated with the distinction between the Kingdom of Caesar and the Kingdom of God in the Catholic interpretation of the New Testament. . . .

This strict separation of spheres of activity found its most systematic expression in Henri Bourassa's ideological definition of difference. In his view, even if the two spheres were complementary, one must in any case provide leadership for the other. Just as the Kingdom of God is ultimately paramount to that of Caesar, the world of men dominates the world of women. Thus, even when the father is absent, he remains head of the household:

> Should the truth be known, the only real function of the father is authority. He does nothing other than act as the official breadwinner, and, although the education of the children is out of his hands, he directs it all the same. (Gagnon, 1974)

[Quotations appearing in the above text have been translated by Diane Lamoureux.]

Notes:

Boucher, Denise. 1979. *Les Fées ont soif.* Montréal: Intermède.

Dumont-Johnson, Micheline. 1968. *Histoire de la condition de la femme dans la province de Québec.* (Étude pour la Commission Royale d'enquête sur le statut de la femme au Canada.) Ottawa. Imprimeur de la reine.

Frechette, Louis-Albert. 1943. "Hommage à la mère canadienne." *L'action nationale* 21, no. 2.

Gagon, Mona-José. 1974a. Les femmes vues par le Québec des hommes. Montreal: Le Jour, Editeur.

Grand'maison, Jacques. 1970. *Nationalisme et religion*, Vol. 2. Montreal: Beauchemin.

Groulx, Lionel. 1919. *La naissance d'une race*. Montreal: Bibliothèque de l'action française.

Groulx, Lionel. 1924. *Notre maître le passé*. Montreal: Bibliothèque de l'action française.

Henripin, Jacques, et al. 1981. *Les Enfants qu'on n'a plus au Québec*. Montreal: Presses de l'Université de Montréal.

Jean, Michèle, ed. 1977. *Québécoises de 20e siècle*. Montreal: Quinze.

Laurin-Frenette, Nicole. 1979. Production de l'État et forme de la nation. Montreal: Nouvelle Optique.

Lavigne, Marie, Yolande Pinard, and Jennifer Stoddart. 1979. "The Fédération nationale St. Jean Baptiste and the Women's Movement in Quebec." In *A Not Unreasonable Claim*, ed. Linda Kealey. Toronto. Women's Press.

Pinard, Yolande. 1977. "Les débuts du mouvement des femmes." In *Les femmes dans la société québécoise*, ed. Marie Lavigne and Yoland Pinard. Montreal: Boréal Express.

JANET BAGNALL

Janet Bagnall is a Montreal journalist who writes on social issues.

The following is abridged from the Montreal Gazette *(January 18 and January 22, 1992).*

YOUR FAMILY?

• There are 50 per cent more single-parent families in Quebec than in the rest of Canada. One in five Quebec families is headed by a single parent, in the vast majority of cases by a woman.

• There are more unmarried couples in Quebec than any other province. Although Quebecers account for only 25 per cent of Canada's population, 40 per cent of the country's 500,000 unmarried couples live in Quebec.

• The rate of child poverty is higher. Across Canada, nearly a million children lack adequate food, shelter and clothing. That's one in six Canadian children. In the region of Montreal, it's one in four children.

• Where the divorce rate in Canada has stabilized at 40 per cent, the rate in Quebec appears to be still growing. It reached a historic high of 46.6 per cent in 1988.

Driven by the fear that Quebec's political weight might decline with its population base, the Quebec government has designed its support system for families of three or more children. Yet families of three or more children make up fewer than a fifth of Quebec families, according to Renée Dandurand, an anthropologist with the Institut Québécois de Recherche sur la Culture who has been studying the family for nearly 20 years. This means Quebec is failing to provide real support for the work and responsibilities of the majority of Quebec's 1.75 million families.

Among single mothers, in 1990, the rates of labor-force participation were 64 per cent for those with children under 16 and 50.4 per cent for those with children younger than 6. A huge gap in family income has developed between two-parent and single-parent families in Quebec.

In 1988, a two-parent family with one child under the age of 7 earned $45,744. A single parent in the same situation earned $16,487.

Micheline de Sève

Micheline de Sève is a professor of Political Science at the Université du Québec à Montréal. Her interest in feminism, at first personal, became political in 1979 when a group of students asked her to give a course on women and politics at the Université Laval. She published Pour un féminisme libertaire *(Montreal, Boréal) in 1985 and, ever since, she has tried to link feminism with social movements, both in her practice and in her writings. Her most recent book,* L'échappée vers l'Ouest *(Montreal, CIDIHCA: 1991), presents the life histories of refugees from Central Europe. In her words, the book permitted her "to combine feminist methodology and reflection with a continuing desire to study how political life can be transformed to meet the needs of people." The following excerpt is from* Le féminisme en revue *(vol. 4, no. 1, November 1990).*

The Quebec Federation of Women

With the failure to ratify the Meech Lake Accord, Canada has flatly refused to recognize Quebec as a distinct society. Its national identity denied, the Quebec community now faces the urgent need to define, according to its own terms, the political expression of its collective aspirations. Could it be that such a fundamental debate does not concern us as women and as feminists?

Recently, we celebrated the fiftieth anniversary of the right of Quebec women to vote. In 1940, many considered this a useless whim. After all, couldn't women trust the men in the family to represent them? And since married women "generally" shared their spouse's beliefs, what purpose could be served by doubling the vote of married men or, worse still, causing husband and wife to squabble? Fortunately, attitudes have changed; it is no longer necessary to justify the right of women, married or not, to hold their own opinions and to express those opinions themselves. We know very well that to get something done, you have to do it yourself. Although in numbers, the presence of women in public life is still too low, women have shed new light on old issues; most of all, they have enlarged the political field to include questions once relegated to the isolation of private life. Violence to women and children, for example, is no longer considered a family affair, just as women do not accept that their ability to bear children should result in the loss of control over their own bodies.

But are we sure today that the legitimacy of female participation in political life is a widely accepted fact? If this were the case, wouldn't we have received equal representation at the constitutional table discussing the future of the Quebec nation? It is troubling to note the ease with which the

Bélanger-Campeau Commission ignored the existence of organized women's groups while supposedly forming an assembly representative of the nation as a whole. With only eight women on its board of 37 members, the Commission has tried to hide its discrimination by pointing to the absence of women holding managerial positions in the major organizations called to its meetings. And we thought we had left behind the days when serious matters were discussed man-to-man, as though the male sex had exclusive rights to citizenship.

But if there is to be a decisive moment in our collective orientation, this is it. Quebecers, both men and women alike, now face a situation that is untenable in any democratic state: our community is governed by a constitution we have not signed. Partisan allegiances aside, this is a fundamental political concern which can leave none of us indifferent. How can we abdicate our right to make decisions on an equal footing with the men of Quebec when the rules that are to be made will apply just as much to us as to them? How can we abstain from participating at a moment when men and women are being called to rise above partisan considerations to draw up a new social plan? Feminism is not an abstract ideology, it is the concrete expression of an identity.

Feminism begins with the claim to autonomy of every woman, but it doesn't stop there. Acquiring one by one the right to speak, we have quickly recognized in each other our affinities, our shared experiences, and common culture. So long as men do not join forces with women in providing direct child care, so long as sexism continues in education, so long as violence taints relations between the sexes and the equality of pay or representation goes unrealized, women must above all stick together and remain vigilant. Discussing our experiences and expectations with other women has shown us an even more positive dimension to feminism: the pleasure of joining together in the specifically political sphere of speech and of discovering the collective meaning of lived experiences which are more than personal.

At this time, when we are striving to pinpoint what brings us together as well as what distinguishes us, our identity as feminists and Québécoises is indivisible. Without a common history and a common language, how could we communicate? How could we, as women, say who we are or share our experiences without the Ariadne's thread of culture tying us one to the other? Acknowledgement of our collective identity is an essential condition for establishing a productive political dialogue. Some Quebec males want to define the parameters of our common experience without us; in doing so, they are depriving themselves of access to a part of the labyrinth which so far only we have explored.

Some Canadian men and women do not recognize that we belong to a distinct society; they are denying themselves entrance to this space where a common language and culture have forged entirely different links to the past and the present. As Quebec women, we refuse the marginality and exclusion to which this ignorance of our specific identity condemns us. Just as we would be unable to content ourselves with living by proxy in the framework of silence and reserve which was once the lot of the housewife, so we could not agree to efface ourselves in the centralism of Canadian federalism. We want to speak for ourselves in a space where our voice can express its own intonations. Opting for sovereignty means not allowing anyone else to assume the right to say on our behalf what we are, or to decide our future for us. It means trying to establish a dialogue between Quebec and the exterior based on a genuine recognition of our specific needs in the real world; it means asserting our will to overcome our status as minorities in the public sphere – as female citizens – as well as in the private sphere – as women.

The moment at hand is too serious for us to think only of our immediate interests as a lobby group or to content ourselves with merely reciting our grocery list of demands, however essential it may be. What is required at this unique moment in history is a willingness to move beyond sector-based considerations by elaborating, as fully-fledged female citizens, our overall vision of the social plan to be carried out. On the individual level, every woman knows that opting for sovereignty does not mean shutting oneself in but rather determining to master one's own destiny with the tolerance and respect of one's peers. The same process awaits us at the collective level: that of marshalling our energies in order to replace the frustration of cultural and political marginalization, with new possibilities for action and dialogue among equals.

Translated by Christopher Korchin

Susanne de Lotbinière-Harwood

A translator who teaches at Concordia University in Montreal, Susanne de Lotbinière-Harwood has won the John Glassco and the Felix Antoine Savard translation awards. She has published her own work, in English and French, in different literary reviews. The following is excerpted from "Crashing the Language Line," published in Re-Belle et Infidèle: La traduction comme pratique de réécriture au féminin / The Body Bilingual: Translation as a Rewriting in the Feminine, *published by Les éditions du remue-ménage/Women's Press (Montreal, Toronto, 1991).*

Crashing the Language Line

No matter which native tongue we speak, all women are bilingual. We use the dominant man-made code we learn as children. We also communicate in a predominantly unrecorded women's way, where oral expression and body language play a major part. Anthropoligist Edwin Ardener developed his "dominant/muted" model to help represent such language situations. There are many ways of visualizing that model. For simplicity's sake, I rewrite it:

DOMINANT	=	male semantic space (public)
	=	the language line: "reality" line: line of repression
MUTED	=	female semantic space (private)

Obviously, the Ardener model does not apply only to women in relation to men. "All language is the language of the dominant order," writes Elaine Showalter in *Writing and Sexual Difference,* therefore the muted semantic space is occupied by people of every class, race, religion, condition and category who have a lesser voice in society. Since gender is an organizing category of language and of society, women are the most universal representatives of a muted group.

The idea that translation is familiar to women because the only language available is man-made (male-made, to be precise) often comes up in women's texts. Women, writes Gail Scott, are "excellent at translation / women are skilled at stepping into spaces (forms) created by the patriarchal superego and cleverly subverting them." African-American writer Donna Kate Rushin reiterates this point: "I've got to explain myself / To everybody / I do more translating / Than the Gawdamn U.N." For French writer Marguerite Duras, "the writing of women is really translated from the unknown, like a new way of communicating rather than an already formed language."

Language is never neutral. A voice comes through a body which is situated in time and space. The subject is always speaking from a place. The "I"s point of view is critical when translating. As a first example, consider the following: three different English translations exist of French feminist psychoanalyst Luce Irigary's *Ce sexe qui n'en est pas un.* Both translations signed by women are titled *This Sex Which Is Not One.* The one signed by a team of two men reads *That Sex Which Is Not One. This*: the one close to, nearest in place, time or thought. *That*: the one farther away or less immediately under discussion. It would be interesting to see what the distancing did to the rest of *that* translation.

Feminism disturbs the patriarchal scheme of things. Our infidelity is to the code of silence imposed on women since pre-"historical" times, and to the way the story traditionally is told. In speaking out, feminists have moved beyond "a woman's place" and have made our alien language heard for the first time. Like writing in the feminine, feminist translation collaborates in this subversion by crashing the language line and voicing what was muted.

NICOLE BROSSARD

Born in Montreal, Nicole Brossard is one of Quebec's most innovative writers. Co-founder of the reviews la Barre du Jour *(1965) and* la Nouvelle Barre du Jour *(1977), she is the author of nineteen collections of poetry, seven novels, a play, essays, and several radio works. She is also a co-director of the film* "Some American Feminists" *(1986). Brossard is an active participant in international conferences on literature and feminism and has twice won the Governor General's Award for poetry in French. The following is abridged from "December 6, 1989 Among the Centuries," a text written to commemorate the fourteen women killed at the Université de Montréal. (From* The Montreal Massacre, *published by gynergy books, 1991.)*

DECEMBER 6, 1989 AMONG THE CENTURIES

ON THIS SIXTH OF DECEMBER IN 1989, I AM SLOWLY DRIFTING THROUGH BLUE luminous Paris, rue des Archives between the grey stones, rue des Blancs-Manteaux, and I am not thinking of what it's like in Montreal. I am on Paris time, no jet lag, and headed for a rendezvous with a Lebanese woman who is a student. She will be talking to me about a horror that is inconceivable to anyone who comes from such a peaceful place it is not yet called a country. Yes, I come from a place where the blood and clabbering noises made by humans in the pain of mass death haven't yet entered the site where words are formed.

That day I was walking slowly, following my usual habit of looking only at women as if to reassure myself about humanity. I walk in the full light of day. I have no reason to think of death. I have no intention of thinking of death. Paris is blue. Montreal is far away and covered with snow. I walk in absolute reality.

On December 7, 1989, I learn that a man has just killed fourteen women. The man, they say, separated the men and the women into two groups. The man called the women feminists; he voiced his hatred toward them. The man fired. The women dropped. The other men ran away.

Suddenly,
I/they are dead
felled by a
break in meaning.

Sexist Quebec Tragedy

The question is delicate, and nothing is less certain than our ability to answer it properly. Yet a large part of our incredulity, our stupor before the fact, and our shame at the Polytechnique massacre can be related to this question: how could such a thing happen in Quebec? Are Quebec men more sexist than the rest, do they feel more threatened, more ripped off, or rejected by feminism? Has Quebec feminism known such success that we must now speak of a "suppressed" sexist misogyny? To these questions, I cannot respond. I can only note that in no other population with Roman Catholic traditions has feminism so rapidly influenced people's private lives and social and cultural reality, in no other *French language* population has feminism been able to fight publicly, and with a certain success, sexism in language and advertising. But, it will be said no doubt, men here are able to listen to what feminists say. Yes, it is true there is a certain audience, but what is more important is that Quebec society has had to acquire in thirty years all the important currents of thought founded on principles of liberation (the ideology of decolonization, secularization, the counter-culture, Marxism, feminism), all the while educating itself in order to be transformed and to conquer its identity. In other words, Quebec feminism was able to develop and take its place in the public sphere more easily because it was part of an immense liberation movement, because it happened at the strategic moment of Quebec's arrival on the world scene as a modern *North American* society.

Young Women and Vertigo

This permanent hostility men have toward women, this is what we forget about when the sky is blue, that is what those survivors – who were so quick to declare they weren't feminists – had forgotten. What, in fact, did they actually mean to say? Did they want to disassociate themselves from women who fight against unjust laws, against violence against women, against the degradation of women's image? Did they want to make it clear they were not lesbians, that they were not against men? Did they think, as the media would have us believe, that feminists are a category of undesirable women whose perspective is narrow and partisan, whose words are bitter and excessive, and whose bad will does enormous harm to the "women's rights" the majority of women would be interested in? Did they think that feminists threaten the "harmonious" relations between men and women? But what can a woman be thinking of when she says, "I'm not a feminist"? What hasn't she thought of? Whom hasn't she thought of?

Translated by Marlene Wildeman

Louky Bersianik

Since her arrival on the Quebec literary scene in 1976 with her best-selling triptych novel, L'Euguélionne, *Louky Bersianik has been one of the major feminist voices in Quebec literature. Born Lucile Durand in Montreal, she decided to adopt a name that was neither inherited from her father nor conferred on her by marriage. After receiving an M.A. in literature and pursuing her Ph.D. course work at the Université de Montréal, she studied for five years at the Sorbonne and later at the Centre d'études de radio et de télévision. Her academic credentials include diplomas in music, library science, and applied linguisitics. Among her other works are* Maternative; Le Pique-nique sur l'Acropole; Karameikos; *and* La Théorie, un dimanche. *The following text is from* The Montreal Massacre, *edited by Louise Malette and Marie Chalouh and published by gynergy books, 1991.*

Bloody Quadrille

As a woman conscious of living in a world still dominated by men, I refuse to endorse the power imbalance which allows patriarchal society to make decisions about my body, my desires and my needs, through laws which criminalize abortion or usurp my reproductive power with new technology. Above all, I refuse to consider the daily violence against women, in whatever form, a natural, isolated or commonplace phenomenon.

This violence throws itself in my path day after day and weighs heavily on my life and my writing. It makes me frustrated and angry, for it is the vulgar expression of a universal misogyny which permeates all cultures with its poison, made from a formula no one can decipher. What is unbearable is that this misogyny passes from one generation to the next in the form of knowledge, in works of art and literary masterpieces, in history, rituals and the customs of every country, from the beginning of time. This is a fierce misogyny, whose deleterious action takes place as much within religious, legal, medical, athletic and financial institutions as it does within the work world, families, the private life of each couple, and the organization of each social group. Upon this misogyny we have very little purchase, for it is not written under its real name in legal documents, good conscience and Christian doctrine. And even though it is not an aspect of human nature, it has become an unavoidable aspect of the human condition in all eras and throughout the latitudes.

WHAT IS MISOGYNY? A monstrous parasite with an archaic cortex which has slowly worn away the human brain since the beginning of time. A violent emotion, it steers a course straight for the rape and murder of human females, all the while abusing them and using them as doormats or stepping stones.

Misogyny has nothing to do with an unhappy childhood, the absence of a father, too much or not enough love from the mother. It has nothing to do with the standard excuses that are always dredged up to exonerate men for their crimes against women. It has nothing to do with generalized violence.

Misogyny is a characteristic of civilization, a leftover barbarism that each generation believes it has definitively eliminated, but which reappears like ancient script on a palimpsest, at the slightest contrariness felt by any little backyard prince. Twenty-five centuries of hatred will not be ruled out by a simple initial at the bottom of a chart.

Misogyny is there when a child is born, when he or she grows up, gets married, dies. It is always there, latent or newly re-constituted, favouring boys and endangering girls. It accompanies the life of each human being, and fosters close ties with it, sometimes to the point of suffocation.

MISOGYNY IS HATRED, hatred pure and simple; hereditary hatred; irrational, illogical, murderous hatred.

Law courts resound with voices full of hatred and contempt for women, and it is from the judges' bench that these remarks emanate: "As we say, laws are like women, meant to be broken"; "It's no crime to beat your wife, it's chickenshit"; "The causes of conjugal violence can be traced back to the Department of Agriculture." And elsewhere, "Men have a right to beat their wives; women deserve it." One would believe that the judges are in agreement with the old Muslim proverb: "Beat your wife every day; if you do not know why, she will." For these men, this is not a simple sexist joke but an order heeded by all batterers.

Women too have had unhappy childhoods, they too have been sexually assaulted by a male parent (and much more often than their brothers), they too have been unloved children, they too have suffered due to the absence of their father or their mother. But we don't see women taking it out on men and little boys, subjecting them to all manner of atrocities, even murder; we don't see women arm themselves with a hunting rifle and only fire on men.

"I am a woman but I am not a human," says Euguélionne [the main character in a novel by Bersianik], "for nothing is more human than to be inhuman." This violence directed toward the female of the species is specific to humans. Unless we renounce our humanity, all human beings must inevitably become conscious of the fact that misogyny is cultural and institutional, and that it insidiously affects the grey matter and the behaviour of each man and woman on this planet. I challenge the integrity of every patriarchal culture. In my eyes they've lost all credibility. I have no respect for them because ALL OF THEM are violent toward women, in a way which is not isolated, nor accidental, nor due to the odd mind afflicted with madness, but in a way which encourages systematic and daily violence, physical and psychological violence.

I cannot consider myself human under a banner of violence. I am the object of hatred but I am not indifferent to hatred. Is it love that men want to destroy? When they themselves were nothing we gave our physical hospitality to these men who hate us enough to kill us.

Societies which call themselves democratic must recognize in ordinary violence the root of evil eating away at them. They must examine the omnipresence of this particular violence aimed only at women, like the bullets of the killer at the University of Montreal in December 1989. Throughout the centuries, in all eras and in all social milieux, we witness this *bloody quadrille* which separates human beings into two categories, whether they are white, black, Jewish, Christian, Arabic, Muslim, whether they live in modest conditions or in wealth: WOMEN ON ONE SIDE, MEN ON THE OTHER, so that, among the human beings present, there will be no mistake about who can be massacred, wiped out, mutilated, beaten to death, or reduced to nothingness with impunity.

The greatest violence that can be inflicted upon a group is to deny the existence of violence, and to make the group's reaction the "real" problem. In other words, to frame their protest as the real violence. For example: "Let's not talk about violence against women; let's talk about how women are violent!" Or: "the victim inflicts violence upon the killer, for she makes him do her a big favour. The power of the victim, know what I mean?"

It is common knowledge that the most effective way for the oppressor to justify himself is to place blame on the person he oppresses. This phenomenon has been apparent for a very long time in the courts: it's the fault of the victim if she allows herself to be beaten, raped, harassed or sexually assaulted. This is Freudian discourse *par excellence* with regard to women, turning the facts around, distorting reality. In incest cases, it is little girls who do the seducing, mothers who are to blame for it. This discourse coincides perfectly with that of the Bible: Eve committed Adam's sin.

At the end of her book *La Porte du fond*, Christiane Rochefort quotes Françoise Dolto: "In father-daughter incest, the daughter adores her father and is very pleased to be able to thumb her nose at her mother! Question: So, the little girl is always consenting? Dolto: Precisely. Question: But after all, there are plenty of cases of rape, no? Dolto: There is no rape at all. They consent to it."

And Rochefort, in the body of the text, writes: "And who would believe you? People don't believe children. Guard dogs, always on duty, will continue to bark at kids caught in the parental trap, 'They all consent to it.' That's what kills me; that's the coup de grâce." Freud and his unconditional followers are the spokesmen for the patriarchy, and the judges base themselves on Freud and the Bible, in order to condone violence against women and girls.

Recently, newspapers reported a case of incest involving a little girl three years of age. The judge declared that this girl had contributed to the incest because she had been sexually aggressive! Clearly, fathers need protection from their little girls. What next? An ombudsman for men who are sexually assaulted by their children?

We could well ask why men continue to hound us when they have all the power, when the world was made for them and by them, and when this world continues to function à la masculine? Why do they still need to crush us with violence, why do they always have to put us "in our place" by force, when contempt alone is not enough? Why are judges misogynists and full of prejudice toward women? Why is the man who murders his wife, the father who rapes his daughter, considered mentally ill and not a criminal?

There are men who are starting to be clairvoyant and who dare to speak out: "All men are guilty," writes Dorval Brunelle, professor and sociologist at the University of Quebec in Montreal. "Feminists have every reason to rise up; all these crimes are political, and the latest, the one at the Polytechnique, is supremely so. The affidavit is clear and proof is at hand: in the present state of affairs, men are incapable of establishing equality between the sexes. What they give with one hand, in charters or laws, they swiftly take away with the other, when they desecrate certain values and destroy lives."

"In masculine fantasies," says Robbe-Grillet, "woman's body is the ideal site for the crime." Only in fantasies? Well, thank you, good apostle! Fantasies like this selective mass murder at the Polytechnique (winter 1989), like this odious injunction against the body of Chantal Daigle (summer 1989), like this gang rape at McGill University (1988), like the murder of Hélène Lizotte by her husband (August 1987)! Fantasies like the women who are battered every day; like the women murdered by the Love of their Life; like the women raped, tortured, burned alive for not having a dowry; like the women who are for sale, prostituted! Fantasies like the little girls forced into incest, pornographied, clitoridectomized, murdered, infibulated, assassinated, dismembered, cut into pieces, thrown out with the garbage! Miscellaneous fantasies such as those worthy of publication in *Allô Police!* "Leave our fantasies alone," bawl the Robbe-Grillets of freedom of speech, "They don't hurt anyone." !!!

Our democracies are so hypocritical, they would take the breath away from each and every one of us. ENOUGH IS ENOUGH!

Translated by Marlene Wildeman

Boundaries of Identity

Marks of Identity: Immigrants and 'Other' Citizens

Nor is the black fact to be compared with le fait français. *In spite of everything by which they differ – the catalyst of the future, the heritage of history, the ties of church and family, above all the colour of their skin – there are those among the disaffected of French Canada who see themselves and Afro-North Americans as struggling in a common cause, as united in a common enterprise. It is one thing for black militants to reach out to the people of a tenuously defined third world. They need all the help that they can get. Who would deny them what psychological support – there'll be no foreign aid – may come from Africa, China, Cuba, and other 'liberated areas'? But this does not excuse French-speaking radicals in their self-deception. To imagine, as some do, that their hang-ups with the English are in any way akin to the monumental injustices befalling Negro Americans is a symptom not of persecution but of persecution mania. It is a failure of the historical imagination.*

James Eayrs, historian
From the *Toronto Daily Star,* February 28, 1991

Dorothy Williams

Born and raised in the Little Burgundy community of Montreal, Dorothy Williams attended the School of Community and Public Affairs at Concordia University. In her final year, she was approached by the Quebec Human Rights Commission to write an internal document on the mobility of blacks in Montreal. The culmination of three years of research, her fascinating study was published by the commission. The following is abridged from Blacks in Montreal 1628–1986: An Urban Demography, *published by Les Éditions Yvon Blais Inc., 1989.*

Slavery 1628–1834

In 1606, Samuel de Champlain reached Canada. It was on this third trip that Matthew da Costa, a Black man, accompanied Champlain. He was chosen by Champlain because of his linguistic ability – he knew the language of the Acadian Micmacs. This was obviously not da Costa's first trip to Canada,[1] but this was the first record of a Black man in Canada.[2]

The subsequent history of Black immigration to Canada was one of enslavement. African slavery began slowly in New France from 1628 onward.[3] Oliver Lejeune was the first slave to be imported. He came from the island of Madagascar.[4] Though this was the beginning of the institution of slavery, it was not till 1685 with the introduction of the "Code Noir," that it attained some legal status.[5] The status of slaves was regulated by this code, which though never officially proclaimed, was used as a customary law in New France for slave ownership.

May 1, 1689, is considered the official birth date of African slavery in Canada. On that day Louis XIV, King of France, "reluctantly" gave permission to his subjects of New France to import African slaves. After 1689 the practice of slave owning by the French merchant class and clergy became common.

No exact census of the slave population in Quebec can be found, however local records revealed 3,604 separate slaves by 1759; of these 1,132 were Negroes.[6] Most of the African slaves were domestic servants who lived in or near Montreal, where 52.3 per cent of the known total lived. In fact, unlike the American colonies, the majority of slaves in Quebec (77.2%) resided in towns.

The slave owners' mentality and religious attitudes in New France were said to have differed greatly from those of British colonies to the south. Those Canadian historians that have even chosen to mention slavery in Canada, often describe a romantic, or an idealized, slave regime in New France.[7]

The very nature of Roman Catholicism and its doctrine, "which held that the spiritual nature of the slave transcended this temporary status and that to give a man his freedom was to please God" (Winks, 1971: 12), supposedly created a "tolerant benevolence" and more humane laws in New France. Thus, even though the Church in New France tended to soften the effects of slavery, this religious justification allowed it to condone the institution – even when slaves were tortured and killed.[8]

One recorded example is that of Marie Joseph Angelique, who in her bid for freedom destroyed almost half of Montreal by fire in 1734. Forty-six buildings including the convent, the church, and the hospital were consumed (*Silent Minority,* n.d.: 12).

Yet despite this incendiary disaster there is no mention of this event in the recent literature on the story of Montreal. Is this because Montreal's early historians believed that the destruction of about half of the city had no impact on its social and economic development? Could it be that the actions of a recalcitrant slave were not worth noting? Angelique's hideous punishment is a testament to the fact that Montreal's citizens felt otherwise.

On the day of her execution Angelique was first tortured until she confessed her crime. Then she was driven through the streets in the scavenger's wagon . . . A burning torch had been placed in her hand. At the main door of the parish church in Place d'Armes she was made to kneel . . . and her hand was cut off. Then, once again, she was placed in the scavenger's wagon and taken to the place of public execution and hanged. After her body was burnt at the stake, her ashes were scattered in the wind.[9]

"Slavery is slavery in whatever form it takes."[10] The veracity of this statement was underscored in New France. Those enslaved were not content. Many tried to escape – some repeatedly. Slave owners fought back in the courts and in the Church to protect their right to own human property. The strongest deterrent against escape, the Code Noir, though not always enforced in the colony, gives an indication of the colonists' benign view of slavery:

> Si le Noir s'évade, on lui coupe les oreilles et on le marque au fer rouge d'une fleur dy lys à l'épaule; s'il récidive, on lui coupe les jarrets. S'il ose recommencer une troisième fois, c'est la mort. (Marcil, 1981: 75)
> [If a Black tries to escape, we cut off his ears and we brand a fleur de lys on his shoulder with a hot iron; if he repeats the crime, we cut the hamstrings on the back of his legs. If he dares to try a third time, the penalty is death.]

In reality, the "benevolence" exhibited by slave owners in New France towards their African slaves was due to economic and social factors rather than any humanistic tendency. Panis, or Indian slaves, were a cheap source of labour for agricultural and hard manual work, whereas the African represented a superior type of slave labour in the towns and the cities. African slaves were to be found in the houses of government officials, or of wealthy merchants and seigneurs.

Not only were the expensive African slaves used as "labour saving devices" (Winks, 1971), but they were also considered valuable property that functioned as symbols of social status amongst the elite. Considering their domestic work status, their high price, and the degree of difficulty in obtaining them, most African slaves were "benevolently" treated simply because longevity of service was desired.

Official slavery survived in New France for seventy-one years, and only briefly during this time did conditions favour the potential growth of slavery. Between 1663 and 1704, in an expanding New France, slave labour might have been used to considerable advantage; but slavery was not given full legal support until 1709, well after the colony had developed its mercantilist base. And after 1713, when New France fell into decline, the institution declined with it.

The decline of slavery in New France can be understood as an economic development. The chief reason slavery gained little hold in New France arose from the fact that the economy was almost exclusively based on the fur trade. Unlike the mass-production gang labour economies to the south, free entrepreneurial labour was far more advantageous for the beaver trade in the north. As long as the colony was so dependent on the fur trade, there was little demand for either domestic servants or manual labourers. The decline in slavery, like the treatment of slaves, was not due to a particularly humane French regime, but rather, it was a circumstance of geography and political economy.

However, not all Blacks in the colony were slaves. Manumission was practiced and encouraged by the clergy. Freed Black men were entrepreneurs, such as fur traders and fishermen. Many also had valuable and prestigious roles as mediators between the Indians and the French.[11] Trudel (1960) estimates that in 1759, just prior to the defeat of New France, 962 households had slaves. Though the economic structure had placed relatively little importance on the acquisition of slaves, slavery was part of the accepted social order in New France.

Revival: 1760

With the Conquest and the introduction of British laws and institutions into

Lower Canada, slavery grew in importance and obtained greater legal status. African slavery, which was a dying institution under the French, was revived in two stages: under the British, slavery continued for another seventy-four years.

First, General Amherst in September 1760 officially agreed to the requests of the conquered French that both the Black and Indian slaves would remain enslaved. This policy was supported by the British government.[12]

Later, during and after the War of Independence of 1776-88, Loyalists, Black and White, slave and free, streamed into Canada. Twelve percent of the registered forty-two thousand United Empire Loyalists that entered Canada were of African descent. However, most of the free Black loyalists went to the Maritimes.

Seven thousand Loyalists came to Lower Canada. Many brought "their more valuable slaves with them as they hastily fled the United States" (Walker, 1980). In spite of this influx, more French citizens (97%) continued to own slaves than the English in Lower Canada.[13] Those Loyalists who had entered Canada without slaves considered slavery a symbol of the "republicanism" they had just fled. Later on, many of these Loyalists became staunch abolitionists.

Approximately three hundred new slaves were brought into Lower Canada by Loyalists. Although it is not possible to establish a figure for the exact number of slaves brought into Montreal, the number living there increased substantially (Bartolo, 1976). Negro slaves virtually supplanted Panis slaves in Montreal. Also, because many of the slaves came from larger plantations where they had been trained to do specific jobs, the variety of work done by Blacks in Montreal's labour market was greatly expanded. Free Blacks and slaves were sawyers, carpenters, blacksmiths, and candle-makers. In the early days of Montreal, Blacks held important roles in the city's economy.

However, unlike the Maritimes and Upper Canada, the majority of the Blacks that entered Quebec were slaves (Winks, 1971). The reasons for this were two-fold. First, this was probably due to the unavailability of fertile land in southern Quebec. Other than the slaves of Loyalists, free Blacks could not settle in Quebec as easily as in the less densely populated regions of Canada, for much of the cultivated land was already held through the seigneurial system and was meted out through family and kinship ties.

Secondly, the center of colonial economic power in Canada resided in Lower Canada. Here, the new colonial administrators favoured the expansion of slavery in order to alter the mercantilist base of production. The British in Europe were in the forefront of the capitalist mode of economy.

The previous experience of the British showed that a slave economy increased the chances of capitalist production, while at the same time it extended the notion of private property which was essential to the development of capitalism.

From the correspondence of military governor General James Murray, it was apparent that the British administrators stationed in the Canadas were anxious to develop such an attitude in Quebec. In 1763, he wrote to a colleague in New York: "Without servants nothing can be done and (French) Canadians will work for nobody but themselves . . . Black slaves are certainly the only people to be depended upon."[14]

Subsequent British laws attempted to confirm and strengthen the rights of White property owners. For example: "In legislation passed to encourage immigration to British North America, one article specifically allowed the importation of 'Negroes,' household furniture, utensils of husbandry or clothing. The same law discouraged the immigration of free Blacks" (Warner 1983: 4; Case 1977: 9).

The entrenching of such a political attitude led to more hardship for the "human chattel" in the colonies. This was felt throughout the North American colonies so much so that slaves in the Canadian provinces under British rule increased their efforts to escape. A southbound underground railroad was established, and between 1788 and 1792 slaves held in Canada fled to the slave-free northern states under the Americans (Thomson, 1979). Contrary to popular belief, the first underground railroad between the U.S. and Canada existed to free slaves held on Canadian territory (Walker, 1980).

Abolition 1789–1834

The actual fight to abolish slavery in Quebec began in 1789 when Chief Justice, Sir James Monk of the Court of King's Bench, released two slaves on a two hundred year-old technicality, and went on to say that therefore "slavery did not exist in the province" (Winks, 1971: 100). This dictum was upheld through court decisions in subsequent years by other judges. These decisions led to "fear among slave owners in Montreal that the courts could no longer be counted on to regard their slaves as chattels. The value of slaves deteriorated," and slaves escaped more and more frequently.[15] As the owners lost their legal right to purchase and sell human property, the right to own such property became tenuous.

Moreover, about 1790, the press headed by A. Brown and J. Nelson, owner-editors of the *Quebec-Gazette,* spearheaded the attack on the institution of slavery in the province. That same year Joseph Papineau, on behalf of the citizens of Montreal, presented a petition to provincial authorities to abolish slavery. Though nothing was done immediately, in 1801 and 1803 two abolitionist bills were presented in the provincial legislature (Israel, 1928: 65). Both bills were defeated, but the simple tabling of the bills kept the abolition issue alive in Lower Canada.

Elsewhere, abolitionist forces met with greater success. In Upper Canada, Lieutenant Governor Simcoe guided an anti-slavery bill through the Upper Canada legislature. This bill "encouraged slaves to escape into the free areas of the Northwest territories of the U.S. and into Vermont and New York" (Bartolo, 1976). This combination of judicial and legislative manipulation and media influence, created an anti-slavery attitude. By 1820 this attitude helped to effectively end "legal" slavery in Quebec.[16]

For 125 years, a total of 5,400 people had been enslaved in the province: one thousand of whom were of African descent (Trudel, 1960). On August 1, 1834, when the Imperial Act freed nearly eight hundred thousand slaves in the British colonies, there were "probably fewer than half a hundred" left in all of British North America (Winks, 1971: 111).

Conclusion

Canada was not created for the equality of all its citizens. As a colony its existence was maintained for the wealth of its owners and as a nation it continues to maintain this goal. Class and race, like language and religion, are issues used by different elite groups at different times to keep people divided; such divisions maintain the status quo. Still, human beings are very adaptable. One can learn another language, change religion or win a lottery. For the vast majority of people there is "chance" or opportunity to move up or down the vertical ladder.

But race is a very different issue from these other three. The reason is socio-cultural. There is a prevailing belief among the general populace that Blacks are Canada's newest immigrants. This assumption remains despite the burden of proof to the contrary. There has been an obvious and systematic obfuscation of the historical Black presence in this country.

Systemic racism (one that does not acknowledge the existence of Blacks) is a two-sided issue. Against Blacks it maintains the illusion that they are foreigners to this soil, while it clearly sets up the assumption that Canada was, and is, a White country. One consequence of these lies is the day-to-day struggle for acceptance by Blacks, and the "polite" racism of tolerant Canadians.

When a White individual sees a Black person they see first and foremost that the individual is Black. A Black man is a "no good" man. No, it does not matter whether he speaks Bantu, Creole or French. It matters not whether he lives in a hovel or the finest home in Westmount. It does not even matter whether his ancestry in this country goes back to 1825 or even 1659. Generation after generation, his Blackness is a visible sign of his difference from all that is "Canadian."

It is this social reality that continues to dictate, consciously or unconsciously, much of the social interaction for Blacks in this province.

Today, Montreal's Black population is a multi-cultural, multi-lingual community consisting of Blacks from Africa, Europe, Canada (further divided between the Maritime Blacks and the rest), the Caribbean, and Latin America. On the whole, though they have tended to concentrate in certain neighbourhoods, (anglophone Blacks in the west and francophone Blacks in the east) residency has not been prescribed solely by linguistic convention. For the presence of great socio-economic diversity within Montreal's Black population has also fuelled Black mobility. This pattern is evident within all class groupings, even amongst the disadvantaged and working classes in the inner-city whose mobility aspirations mirror those of the middle and upper classes in the off-island and metropolitan suburbs.

Notwithstanding the above elements, i.e. those which played a role in the dispersal of the community, there were other counterbalancing factors conducive to the formation of residential clusters. Foremost, we see that the historical pattern of Black mobility in Montreal was clearly influenced by the racist response of Montreal's property owners to the Black householder. For though Blacks came to Montreal with many different national, cultural and socio-economic frameworks, all too quickly these immigrants came to realize that their unique social and national identities mattered little in a society that put a much greater emphasis on their racial characteristics than on their socio-economic status.

It was not long ago in Montreal, when Blacks in their search for housing were often confronted with signs that read, "No niggers, dogs or Jews allowed." Today signs like this may not be the fashion, but in many instances they have only been replaced with more subtle ways and means of denying access.

Notes:

[1] Historians speculate that da Costa had previously visited as a crew member of Portuguese vessels that had fished off Newfoundland. See: "Silent Minority" (n.d.); L. Bertley (1977) *Canada and Its People of African Descent* (Pierrefonds: Bilongo Pub.). See also E. Thornhill (1982: 2), "Race and Class in Canada: The Case of Blacks in Quebec" (Seminar paper, Montreal), who states that Matthew served in the Poutrincourt-Champlain expedition of 1606. And J. Bertley (1982: 7) in "The Role of the Community in Educating Blacks in Montreal from 1910 to 1940 with

Special Reference to Reverend Dr. Charles Humphrey Este" M.A. Thesis (Montreal: McGill University), says that Matthew settled at the Port Royal Habitation on the bank of the Annapolis River in Nova Scotia, where he died and was buried.

[2] According to Bertley (1977: 11-13), and J. Bertley (1982: 7) there is earlier documented proof that Africans *discovered* the "New World" in the 14th century, thus predating Columbus. See: The *Montreal Star* (1975, 9 April) "Ancient Stones Bear Witness: Libyans Visited Quebec in 500 B.C., Archeologist Says."

[3] Other accounts such as R. Winks (1971), "The Blacks in Canada: A History" (Montreal: McGill-Queen's University Press), refer to earlier dates: 1501 in Newfoundland by Gaspar Corte Real, and 1608 in Acadia by Sieur Du Gua de Monts; both were slaveowners of Indians and Africans. See: n.a. "Black Days in the North: Sad Roots" in *Canadian Heritage* (1979, December).

[4] C. Marcil (1981) "Les communautés noires au Québec" in *Éducation Québec* (vol. II no. 6) says Lejeune was from Guinea rather than from Madagascar. Both places are cited as possible in "Silent Minority."

[5] "The Code was designed to protect owners from slaves' violence and escape." Colin Thomson (1979: 17) *Blacks in Deep Snow: Black Pioneers in Canada* (Ontario: J.M. Dent & Sons Ltd.).

[6] According to Winks (1971: 9), no exact census of the slave population in Quebec can be found. See Paul Dejean (1978: 95) *Les Haïtiens au Québec* (Montréal: Les Presses de l'Université du Québec). See also: Dr. G. Hill (1983) "Black History in Early Ontario," Paper presented to Fairweather Lecture Series, University of Ottawa.

[7] F.X. Garneau, in *Histoire du Canada Français depuis sa Découverte,* claimed that "the peculiar institution never sullied the skies of Canada." And T. Watson Smith, in *The Slave In Canada* mentioned that the prominent Canadian historians in 1889 had neglected this "sombre and unattractive chapter." Not much in Canadian historiography has changed since then. A sampling of contemporary college and university textbooks still confirms that the deliberate obfuscation of slavery within Canadian history continues. See: W. L. Morton (1963) *The Kingdom of Canada*; E. McInnis (1969) *Canada: A Political and Social History* ; R.C. Harris & J. Warkenton (1974) *Canada Before Confederation.* This attitude at the national level contrasts with the writing of Montreal's earliest historians many of whom have included the slave chronology in their texts. See: Teril, *A Chronology of Montreal and of Canada A.D.* 1752. Hector Berthelet, *Montréal le Bon Vieux Temps*; Atherton, Montreal 1535–1914.

[8] For an account of this and other punitive measures taken against slaves, see: "Negro Slavery in Montreal," (n.d.); M. Trudel (1960) L'esclavage au Canada Français: histoire et conditions de l'esclavage (Québec: Presses de l'Université Laval); Wilfred Israel (1928: 66-67) "Montreal Negro Community" M.A. Thesis (Montreal: McGill University); L Bertley (1976) "Slavery" in *Focus Umoja Montreal*, no. 16; Bertley

(1977); Thomson (1979); D. Williams (1983) "The Black Presence in Montreal: A Multi-Cultural Community"; L. Warner (1983) "Profile of the English-Speaking Black Community in Quebec" (Montréal: Comité d'implantation du plan d'action à l'intention des communautés culturelles); "Silent Minority" (n.d.); Marcil (1981).

[9] For an account of the role of the Church in her death see: Thornhill (1982: 3).

[10] Case (1977: 10). Other historians have ignored this fact. With one breath they describe Canadian slavery as benevolent. "The evidence, on the whole, would indicate that the conditions of slaves were not hard." *Negro Slavery* (n.d.). "As a rule, it appears that the slaves were not badly treated..." Bortolo (1976: n.p.) "Blacks in Canada: 1608 to Now" in A *Key to Canada* Part II (Toronto: National Black Coalition of Canada). "Black slaves in Canada had it easier than their cousins in the States and the West Indies" (Heritage, 1979: 43). One of the more recent perspectives found in *Quebec Women: A History*, The Clio Collective (1987: 97), published by The Women's Press (Toronto) even goes so far as to present a picture of Black slaves as being uneducatable and therefore responsible for their harsh treatment. The writers, while acknowledging that "the death rate amongst these slaves was high" go on to explain that it was because "adapting to white society was difficult." Thus, they conclude, slaves "did not always make ideal servants, even if they did not have to be paid for their work."

[11] For a discussion of the varied occupations of free Blacks in the colony see: *Silent Minority* (n.d.: 5-8); Winks (1971); Marcil (1981).

[12] After the Conquest, colonial officials "sent instructions to promote the establishment of 'plantations' in Canada," similar to those of the South (*Negro Slavery*, n.d.). While this plantation system was not instituted, these official edicts served to clarify and re-establish the right of slave-owning in the colony.

[13] See Bartolo (1976: n.p.). For a list of prominent slaveowners see: J. Walker (1980: 12) *A History of Blacks in Canada: A Study Guide for Teachers and Students* (Hull: Minister of State); Bertley (1977); "Negro Slavery"; Marcil (1981); Winks (1971); Thornhill (1982); W. R. Riddell (1919) "The Slave in Upper Canada" in *The Journal of Negro History*, ed. G. Woodson (Lancaster: The Association for the Study of Negro Life and History Inc.) vol. II.

[14] Ida Greaves (1930: 11) "The Negro in Canada," *Economic Studies* No. 16, (Montreal: McGill University).

[15] Israel (1928: 65) Chief Justice Osgood, in 1803 decided at Montreal that "slavery was incompatible with the laws of the country."

[16] Israel (1928: 64). In fact this eradication would seem to have occurred even earlier. The last slave had the distinction of being overthrown by judicial interference. See also: Borthwick (1891) *History of Montreal*; Greaves (1930); "Negro Slavery"; Marcil (1981).

Nantha Kumar

A journalist with The Star *in Malaysia, Nantha Kumar moved to Montreal in 1982. He writes about issues of concern to Montreal's ethnic communities for the* Mirror, *Montreal's leading English-language newsweekly. He is also a regular contributor to* Now *magazine in Toronto. The following article is from the* Mirror, *(December 26, 1991–January 9, 1992).*

No End to Racism in the Force

STANDING AT THE CORNER OF ST. JACQUES AND GEORGE VANIER ON NOVEMBER 14th, looking at a pool of blood on the lawn of a newly-built condominium, I felt uneasy. Osmond Seymour Fletcher's body was on its way to the mortuary, but the atmosphere was still tense. Earlier in the day, MUC (Montreal Urban Community) cops spotted him and gave chase, but it ended in tragedy. An all-black crowd was milling around, and they were angry.

Sûreté du Québec (SQ) officers were on the scene to investigate the incident. Less than an hour after the shooting, they released statements to the press indicating Fletcher had shot himself. Their final report arrived at the same conclusion. But residents in Little Burgundy don't believe the police version of what happened.

Why do the people of Little Burgundy think otherwise? Why do blacks, not just in this district, but all over the city distrust the police? Most feel the police are racist, and feel harassed by them for nothing.

Police say they are only doing their job, cleaning out crack houses and fighting crime in the neighbourhoods. And according to the Police Brotherhood, their job is getting more and more dangerous every day. So much so that the union says it is getting too dangerous for their members. What is even more frightening is that the head of the homicide squad says his department is having difficulties solving murders in the Montreal Urban Community (MUC) because the killings are carried out by highly sophisticated killers. They think they have a problem. But the problem is ours.

The black community has legitimate reasons to fear the police. It's their boys that are getting killed. Remember Anthony Griffin, Leslie Presley, and Marcellus François? All three were killed by MUC policemen. Griffin was shot in the parking lot of Station 15 in 1987, Presley in a downtown nightclub in 1990, and François in the summer of 1991. A public inquiry into the death of Osmond Fletcher is much needed to clear doubts in the minds of the community. Perhaps this would clear up some of the questions raised by the inquest into François' death, among them the illegal conduct of one police officer, and, at the very least, poor judgement on the part of officers who conducted the operation and who shot the unarmed man in his car.

Community leaders are under pressure to find ways to make the police more accountable to the public. Lack of accountability is one thing the MUC police are used to, as their internal investigations and disciplinary actions against officers are never made public.

Public security minister Claude Ryan has rejected the need for an inquiry into police activities in Little Burgundy saying it would be inappropriate in view of complaints before the police ethics commission. But the commission, which is responsible for investigating public complaints against MUC police, SQ, and other municipal police departments in the province, has also become a farce. Until it begins to impose harsh disciplinary action on irresponsible officers, the public cannot take the commission seriously. What is needed here is an inquiry similar to the one set up in Nova Scotia after race riots broke out in Halifax on July 19th. Do we have to wait for race riots to break out here for this to happen?

Racism is a problem within the police force. But both the MUC and the provincial government don't seem to be taking the problem very seriously, and their lack of action seems to condone the actions of trigger-happy cops. Part of the problem lies in the structure of the MUC police: 94% of its 4,454 employees are white and francophone. The MUC has a meager 0.6% visible minority representation in its police force, 26 people of black, Asian, Indo-Pakistani, Arab, or Latino background. This does not even begin to reflect the make up of our society. And there doesn't seem to be much effort to improve the situation either. In 1988 there were only 17 members from visible minorities and today there are 26, an increase of nine people in three years.

Increasing ethnic minority representation in the police force would be a step in the right direction, but in itself is not sufficient. One of the MUC's proposed solutions to racism in the force was multicultural awareness training. Between 1987 and 1988, close to 5,000 police and civilian employees of the MUC police attended awareness sessions, which were intended to show them how "to cope with diversity." The idea was that people on the police force were no different from the average Joe, and they had to be taught to accept the fact that immigrants were coming to Canada, and that they are here to stay.

I was one of 34 active resource persons from different cultural communities who took part in the sessions that dealt with different ethnic communities. What struck me immediately was the cultural ignorance of some of the police officers. Some did not know the difference between a Sikh and a Rastafarian. I was appalled, but should I have been? After all, what does the average Canadian/Québécois know about these two groups or any other ethnic group? The MUC had made it mandatory for their employees to participate in these sessions, and not surprisingly most came with the idea "let's do it and get it over with." Some were interested, but most looked bored. One particular incident during a session at Station 24 comes to mind. In the middle of a break, a police officer took the opportunity to express her feeling about the workshop, which probably reflected the views of the majority. She did a drawing of a black taxi driver being pulled over by a cop, with the taxi driver exclaiming to the cop that he was stopped because he was black. Her colleagues were amused. But for me, it was a message to those conducting the multicultural awareness training that it was going to be an almost impossible task to change long-held attitudes.

Tensions between blacks and the police were already high at that time. Griffin had just been shot by Alan Gosset of Station 15, and the police were on the offensive after the black community labelled the shooting a racist incident. Griffin was shot as he attempted to run away from police. He was unarmed. Four days later, an officer from Station 15 used a photograph of a black child for target practice "as a joke." A black police officer, who was also working at the station, reported the incident. He is now behind a desk at the MUC's human resources department.

Since then we have had more than our share of "racist" incidents, including one in October in the Snowdon Metro where a police officer pointed his revolver at the neck of a 15-year-old black youth assuming he had started a fight. It was later found out that the incident had been sparked by three white men who had accosted the youth as he was leaving the subway.

Relations between the police and the black community have never been good, and so far all efforts to improve the situation have failed. Responses from highly-placed bureaucrats haven't helped in diffusing the situation. Statements made by Yves Lafontaine, president of the Quebec Human Rights Commission, implied that the black community's problems were played-up by the community itself and by the anglophone media. And Alain St. Germain, head of the MUC police, didn't help either when he defended his officers, who have called blacks "niggers," by stating in a television interview that such terms were "commonly used" in society. What kind of message does this send to his officers?

So what should we do? Do we just hope that goodwill will prevail and that the police will try to do better next time? That seems unlikely. It is up to the provincial government to order a commission to look into police racism, not just in Montreal, but throughout the province. Racism is a disease which has to be eradicated at its source, and we cannot adopt a wait-and-see attitude. A racist civilian can shout abuses at you, but a racist police officer can shoot you. It's time we started putting pressure on all levels of government to implement recommendations put forward by Jacques Bellemare, who presided over a Quebec Human Rights Commission inquiry into Griffin's death. He made over 70 recommendations to improve relations between the police and the visible minority communities, the most important being affirmative action to hire minorities. How long must we wait for this to happen?

Note: On February 13, 1992, a month after this article about racism on the police force was written, more than 2,000 Montreal police officers belonging to the MUC Police Brotherhood marched through the city to protest against an internal report made public by their police chief, Alain St. Germain. The report concerned the death of Marcellus François, 24, an unarmed black man who was shot in the head by a SWAT team after they intercepted his car. The report criticized the officers involved who had mistaken François for another suspect.

Paul-André Linteau

Paul-André Linteau is a professor of History at the Université du Québec à Montréal. He is the author of L'histoire de Montréal depuis la Confédération *and one of the co-authors of the two-volume* Histoire de Québec contemporain. *The following essay is abridged from* Arrangiarsi: The Italian Immigration Experience in Canada, *an anthology edited by Roberto Perin and Franc Sturino and published by Guernica Editions, 1989.*

The Italians of Quebec

In 1968, in the small Montreal suburb of Saint-Leonard, the language question sparked violent incidents between Italians and French Canadians. The issue was the following: should the municipality's Italian immigrants be forced to send their children to French schools or should they be free to choose their languge of instruction? The conflict stirred passionate debate, turbulent meetings and street battles between members of the two groups.

The episode marks an important stage in the Quebec political and language debates of the sixties and seventies. The issues extend beyond the situation in Saint-Leonard, reflecting the larger context of changes in Quebec society during this period: the rise on the one hand of the new Quebec nationalism and the affirmation on the other of the "allophone" groups – those that are neither French nor British in origin. Italians are the largest of these groups. They were drawn into the centuries-old struggle between French and English Canadians in Quebec. They became the focus of a conflict which at first was not of their own making, but in which they came to play an active role by defending their own positions with respect to the new Quebec nationalism.

Despite the diverse origins of the allophones who arrived after the War, the group is still composed – as it was since the beginning of the century – of two major categories. More than half are either Jewish or Italian in origin. The majority of immigrants during the first half of the twentieth century were Jews; after the War they were Italians, making it the largest ethnic group neither French nor British in origin. By 1971, Italians accounted for about 3% of the Quebec population, almost 6% of the Greater Montreal area and 7.6% of the Island of Montreal. Given these figures, it is not surprising that Italians should have been at the heart of the ethnic and linguistic debate in Quebec over the past decades.

Strategies for Managing Ethnic Relations

Ethnic relations for many decades in Quebec were basically a dialogue between English and French. Only late in the twentieth century did these relations become diversified. The long history of ethnic relations in Quebec therefore tells a very distinctive story – that of a land where, for over a century, two groups of European descent shared majority status, even if their numbers were far from equal.

Quebec became characterized by a multitude of separate and parallel institutions. The most extreme fragmentation occurred in charitable and other private institutions; the public education system, however, retained a relatively simple structure. The system was officially divided into two sectors but in practice there were three: the Anglo-Protestant and the Catholic which in turn, was subdivided into a main branch for French Canadians and a secondary branch in English for the Irish. These ethnic separations were complicated by an additional, unofficial, separation based on social class. Within each network, institutions intended for the mass of the population were distinct from those which served the elite.

This strategy is a far cry from the American melting pot. The ethnic partitioning of Quebec was in fact a kind of anti-melting pot, without declared aims of assimilation. The system sought to minimize friction between groups by reducing points of contact between them. It aimed to ensure that each group could, if it so wished, remain safe from outside influences and develop according to its own norms.

Could a system based on separation and discrimination survive the arrival of new groups? During the first half of the twentieth century it adapted quite well. The newcomers were mainly Jews and Italians. Out of their long experience of persecution, the Jews rebuilt in Montreal a series of institutions brought from Europe. The Italians, although not as well structured, could count on the Church to provide them with specific services including priests of their nationality. Synagogues and Italian Catholic parishes dispensed specific social and cultural services, adding to Montreal's institutional diversity.

For the public educational system, however, this ethnic diversification posed a particular problem. Should new school systems be created, even though the constitution offered guarantees only for Catholics and Protestants? The problem was most pressing for the Jews. But after lengthy debate they were integrated into the Protestant school system which turned into a *de facto* non-Catholic system. The Jewish people of Quebec gradually learned English, but this of course did not mean that they were integrated or assimilated into the British minority. They formed a very distinct cultural group in the city, subject to discrimination in the school system which took various subtle forms. It was only after the Second World War that the barriers of discrimination were definitely eliminated.

The old strategy of ethnic separation continued to function until the War. It was bolstered by further social distinctions between new and established immigrants. Montreal was a city of ethnic isolation, a multitude of separate cultural universes.

The Development of Italian Community Institutions

The initial integration of Italians into Quebec life was coloured by two major factors: the well-established pattern of separate ethnic institutions and the intense community life of the Italians. Both of these elements were profoundly affected by the new Quebec nationalism of the 1960s and by the new attitudes of post-war Italian immigrants. The new wave was not very different from the first. As a rule the newcomers came as part of a network based on kinship and neighbourhood. In Montreal they were met by relatives or friends, and their integration into the new city and milieu was relatively easy.

Despite these similarities, it did not take long for tensions to develop between the two groups. . . . The older Italian settlers had little education; they had come to Montreal during a period of economic uncertainty and hard work and had been severely affected by the difficulties of the Depression and the War. The newcomers were generally more educated and more dynamic; they were able to take advantage of post-war prosperity. During the 1950s there was a general rise in the standard of living in Montreal, and the situation of the Italians improved as well, even if they continued to hold low-skilled jobs in construction work and in factories.

Ethnic groups not defined as either Anglophone or Francophone seemed at first to be outsiders in the debate over Quebec nationalism. Anglo-Quebec leaders quickly saw that the integration of allophone ethnic communities into the English-language school system would strengthen the British minority whose numbers were in relative decline. They saw that it was in their interest to forget the discriminatory attitudes of the past and to accept the transformation of the Anglo-Protestant and Anglo-Catholic school systems into English-language multi-ethnic systems. That way they could preserve and strengthen their own institutions, at least in Montreal.

For their part, the French-speaking community had always counted on the strength of numbers. With the dramatic drop in the French-Canadian birthrate at the end of the sixties, this strength was increasingly fragile.

Many analysts and intellectuals realized that the future growth of the Quebec population would depend on immigration and that in the medium term the proportion of French Canadians in Quebec might decrease.

For many observers, the future of French Quebec depended on making the allophones French speaking and it became essential that immigrants join the Francophone group. Two complementary strategies were envisaged. The first consisted in attempting to modify immigration patterns by recruiting immigrants principally from French-speaking countries. But this reorientation came at a time when the overall rate of immigration to Quebec was considerably reduced. So strategists turned to the second option – that of making immigrants already settled in Quebec and especially their children French-speaking. The language battle had begun.

The Language Battle

The Italians of Quebec were at the centre of this battle for several reasons. First, as we have seen, they were the largest ethnic group after the French and the British. Their numbers, their visibility, and their geographic concentration made them the symbol of all the allophone groups. What is more, the many immigrants among them were perceived as less acculturated to the British group than the Ashkenazi Jews, for example. In addition, French Canadians traditionally had closer contacts with the Italians of Quebec. The fact that most Italians chose to attend English schools was a recent phenomenon. Many French Canadians were shocked when they learned how many Italians preferred English schools. There had also been something of an aggressive side to relations between French Canadians and Italians among the lower classes because the two groups competed in the same job market. Through their community structures Italians were organized and had leaders able to engage in public debate – in French – with French Canadians.

The language battle began in 1968 in Saint-Leonard, a new Montreal suburb whose population was then mainly French Canadian but with a very strong minority of Italian origin. The Saint-Leonard conflict, however, was just the spark which led to a heightened awareness of the importance of linguistic questions and of the language of instruction for all ethnic groups in Quebec.

Italians had their own positions to defend. They entered the debate on the basis of what they considered to be their own interests and they became important participants in it. But it must be recognized that Italians also became pawns in a battle between French and English Canadians and that they were used in a conflict which was not necessarily their own.

Beginning in 1968 the Quebec government, under pressure from Francophone groups, brought in legislation to regulate language use in Quebec. At first, this intervention concerned the language of instruction only, but gradually the objective became making all areas of society French-speaking.

Before 1968 the language of instruction was determined by what was called free choice. Whatever their ethnic origins, parents could choose to send their children to French or English schools, the only criterion being religion. Catholics, whether English or French-speaking, were served by the Catholic system. All the others used the Protestant system which was overwhelmingly English, although there were a few French schools.

The first legislative act, Bill 63, was passed in 1968. It sanctioned the existing principle of free choice but sought to promote the teaching of French in the English school system and to ensure that all the peoples of Quebec, whatever their origin, be able to speak French. Because it maintained the principle of free choice, Bill 63 was received with indignation by many Francophone nationalist groups. Their opposition contributed to the fall of the *Union nationale* government which passed the law.

Following the report of the Gendron Commission on the status of French in Quebec, the Liberal government adopted Bill 22 in 1974 which went much further in establishing the priority of French in Quebec society. It made an important new change concerning the language of instruction: the English system was to remain intact for the population of British origin, but immigrant children were to enter the French school system.

Only those who could pass a test proving competence in English were allowed to enter English schools: all the others were obliged to register in French schools. Bill 22 was intended to increase the prestige of the French language and extend its use to all sectors of activity. The act was greeted with cries of protest not only by Anglophone groups, traditional supporters of the Liberals, but also by the Italian community which was directly affected. It also received negative reactions from the most nationalist Francophone groups and from those favouring independence, who considered that it did not go far enough.

In 1976, as soon as it came into power, the *Parti Québécois* began preparations for a new law, Bill 101, called the "Charter of the French language," which was passed in 1977. It strengthened measures already provided for in Bill 22, considerably restricting access to English-language schools. Only children with at least one parent who had studied in an English-language primary school in Quebec were allowed to attend. It also added greater rigour and compulsion to measures in Bill 22 dealing with making Quebec society French-speaking. The intention of the Charter of the

French language was not only to give schools and other public institutions a French character, but to make the entire society French-speaking.

As a result of the many changes which occurred between 1968 and 1977, the management of ethnic relations was entirely transformed, particularly with respect to language issues. The Quebec state openly became the government of French Canadians and implemented a number of measures intended to make English less attractive to both allophones and some Francophones. In the period of a few short years, the rules of the game had changed completely.

How did Italians react to these changes? It is important here not to overgeneralize. Just as Francophone nationalism had different tendencies, the reactions of the Italian community were diverse. The media only presented the most extreme positions. While there was clearly a majority tendency within the Italian population, there was also a diversity of positions.

The Italian community of Montreal had never been perfectly united. It had always been marked by the tensions and oppositions that are normal in any group of that size. From the early years, there existed regional divisions. More recently there was the distinction between older and newer immigrants. Language choices also created separations: those who studied in French became integrated into different networks from their compatriots educated in English. Social milieux, business interests, and political options were also divisive factors.

It is clear nonetheless that a majority of Italians reacted very negatively to the language laws. These laws jeopardized the choices they had made for their children and changed their perceptions of Quebec and Canadian society.

Some chose open resistance: rejection of the policy of "francisation," organization of clandestine classes, illegal registration of children in English schools. This resistance was led by the *Consiglio educativo italo-canadese*. It was actively supported by the English-language press and by the administrators and teachers of the Anglo-Catholic school system.

Other leaders opted for negotiation and conciliation. Some tried to get concessions through the political parties. They put their hopes in the Liberals and felt deceived by Bill 22. In 1976 they fell back on the *Union nationale* and in 1981 turned again to the Liberal Party.

Except for a few extremist groups, the majority of Italian leaders did not officially object to the increased use of French in Quebec. They were however opposed to unilingualism and favoured the idea of a bilingual Quebec. This stand made them supporters of the federal Liberal anti-nationalist position of Pierre Elliot Trudeau and opponents of the nationalist Liberals and advocates of independence.

The majority of Italians were for the status quo – free choice – which in practice meant the right to educate their children in English. They were convinced that English was essential for socio-economic advancement and necessary to ensure that their children could move out of Quebec if they wished.

There is another aspect to the Italian reaction that many French-speaking analysts tend to neglect but which from the Italian point of view was absolutely fundamental. Spokespersons for Italian organizations considered that the language laws were discriminatory because they protected the acquired educational rights of Anglo-Quebecers but neglected those of immigrants by making French obligatory for children of immigrants. The following argument was heard on several occasions: if you wish to make the school system French, impose French on everyone, even Anglo-Quebecers; then we will accept it as well. These arguments had no effect on Quebec governments. . . .

Italians and a Decade of Change in Quebec 1970–1980

Beyond the conflicts and the language question itself, Quebec has become undeniably more French since 1960, and this process was accelerated in the second half of the 1970s. Members of this generation took advantage first of the rapid growth in the public sector, especially in education, medical and social services, and in the government administration. They were given positions of responsibility which were still hard to obtain in the private sector.

This trend spread during the 1970s to the private sector. The decade saw the emergence of new large-scale enterprises under Francophone control. At the beginning of the 1980s the language situation in the private sector in Quebec was very different from what had prevailed ten years earlier. For example, some large Anglo-Canadian banks now have Francophone vice-presidents heading their Quebec activities, a situation which would have been unthinkable in the mid-1960s. These changes therefore contributed to the intensified French character of Quebec.

What has happened to the Italians in all this? The young Italian children who received an English education in view of a job market which in the 1960s was strongly English now find themselves in a society where the job market favours people who are French-speaking.

Recent language tensions seem to have had the effect of strengthening the Italian sense of identity in Montreal. Italian is used much more for family and neighbourhood communication than it is in Toronto, for instance. The tensions resulted in a new political awareness, the emergence of a new leadership and the creation of new organizations, in particular the

Congrès national des Italo-Canadiens (Québec). The system of separate institutions became even stronger.

According to sociologists, these developments worked primarily to the advantage of the new Italian bourgeoisie, which arose out of the ethnic economy and the Italian labour market. These businessmen succeeded in replacing the old elites and took over the leadership of the official organizations of the Italian community.

Perhaps the developments of the last few years have accentuated the "ghettoization" of the Italians. But it is possible to imagine the beginnings of a medium-term solution: a process which would put an end to ethnic isolation without imposing assimilation or denying cultural specificity. Such tendencies have surfaced over the last few years. When their phase of linguistic imperialism ended in the late 1970s, supporters of the independence option began to show more openness toward the ethnic and cultural diversity of Quebec. *Cultural communities* is now the term used; a Ministry has been created, and it promotes programmes to teach heritage languages. The idea of a melting pot *à la québécoise* is losing ground. Academics are falling into step: research on ethnic groups is now one of the most dynamic fields in the Quebec social sciences.

As for the Italians, they too are undergoing changes. A recent study shows more acceptance of the French fact. Although they still wish to maintain their cultural autonomy, a growing number of Italian intellectuals are seeking stronger links with Francophones.

We are now on the threshold of a new era in the history of Quebec. The two communities must develop new, more open means of communication and a path to mutual acceptance. This is the challenge of the future, the history of a future which has yet to be written.

Translated by Sherry Simon

S H E R R Y   S I M O N

Sherry Simon teaches in the Département d'études françaises at Concordia University in Montreal. She has translated essays by Michel Foucault and Suzanne Lamy. The following is abridged from her essay in Marco Micone: Two Plays, *published by Guernica Editions (Montreal, 1988).*

SPEAKING WITH AUTHORITY: THE THEATRE OF MARCO MICONE

THE EXISTENCE OF A MINORITY OR ETHNIC VOICE AT THE HEART OF QUÉBÉCOIS LITerature is rather new. Until recently, the fundamental cleavage between *nous autres* and *les autres* seemed to preclude the possibility of defining the Quebec population and its consciousness in other than dualist terms. Quebec literature, like Quebec scholarly writing, saw only French versus English and hardly recognized the specific existence of the ethnic communities.

If for a very long time the only immigrant culture in Quebec to have produced a significant body of literature was the Jewish community (and it was written in English), this situation is now changing. The Italian and Haitian communities especially, but other groups as well, are beginning to produce works in French which define themselves explicitly within the context of Quebec literature and Quebec society. This process of self-definition accompanies a sudden spurt of interest on the part of Quebec academics (principally sociologists) in the *third constituency* of Quebec society. Such a new perspective will perhaps mark a shift in the role which the *other* communities of Quebec have traditionally been asked to play politically: to neutralize their specificity in aligning themselves with one or the other major group in the province. For many, the increasing visibility and prominence of Quebec's cultural communities promises an end to what has become a sterile stand-off between majority (Francophone) and minority (Anglophone) populations.

Italian writers in Quebec are currently the most visible and active community to emerge during this new phase of cultural readjustment. The recent publication of an anthology of Italian writing in French (*Quêtes*, Guernica Editions, 1983) and the dynamic trans-cultural review *Vice Versa* (a trilingual cultural magazine edited by Italian writers) are indicators of the significant activity of *Italo-québécois* writers in the cultural life of Quebec.

The work of Marco Micone, playwright and essayist, is of particular interest in this context because of its very explicit social and political focus. Most other *Italo-québécois* writers stay away from explicit references to social and national questions, but Micone shares the concern for language which characterizes much contemporary Québécois writing. Micone, however, formulates his concern for language within a political universe, a dramatic world informed at all levels by power relationships. Language becomes an instrument and a manifestation of authority. To master language, and this involves mastering particular languages, is to be able to impose one's interpretation of reality.

Micone has written two plays, *Gens du Silence* (translated into English as *Voiceless People*) and *Addolorata*. Both have been successfully produced for Montreal audiences and these plays – along with several essays on immigrant culture – have made Micone a spokesperson on *minority issues* for the Quebec writer's community.

Certainly one of the principal characteristics of ethnic writing is the sense of linguistic relativity which Daphne Marlatt describes as being characteristic of the world of immigrant or outsider:

> The sensation of having your world turned upside down or inverted also, I think, leads to a sense of the relativity of both language and reality, as much as it leads to a curiosity about other people's realities. . . . It leads to an interest in and curiosity about language, a sense of how language shapes the reality you live in, an understanding of how language is both idiosyncratic (private) and shared (public), and the essential duplicity of language, its capacity to mean several things at once, its figurative and transformative powers. [from "Entering in the Immigrant Imagination," in *Canadian Literature*.]

In Micone's plays, this kind of sensitivity is linked, on the one hand, to the status of specific languages (French, English, Italian) within Quebec society and, on the other hand, with the question of the authority of personal expression. Who has the right to speak, and what authority will his/her words have?

Language Choice and Authorship

All writers must choose from among the various vernaculars or literary idioms which are offered by their mother tongue. Some writers – members of minority groups or of "minor literatures" – will, however, opt for a natural language which is not their own, often because this second language will give them access to a greater readership. Multilingualism has always been treated as a deviation by institutions of criticism, generally formed along national lines. The few odd deviants who have transgressed national barriers and written in second languages (Nabokov, Beckett, Conrad) are treated as singular linguistic acrobats, capable of feats of prowess totally inaccessible to ordinary writers. The writer is expected to define what linguistic "mastery" is; or how can he or she dare attempt to dominate in more than one field?

Writers themselves have been important in reinforcing the notion that there is an exlusive allegiance to the mother tongue. Psychoanalysis, psycho and sociolinguistics have investigated and documented the extremely emotional and exclusive bond between the speaker and their native tongue. But the idea that there is necessarily a mystical union between the writer and a single, native language is false. We have only to consider the huge gap which often existed between the literary language and the vernacular in many cultures. Certain historical eras have sometimes demanded multilingualism for writers: Leonard Forster in *The Poet's Tongues: Multilingualism in Literature* (Cambridge University Press, 1970) suggests that during the Renaissance, for example, multilingualism for writers was the rule rather than the exception. Some subjects, for instance, were treated only in specific languages (i.e. love poems in Italian).

For the *Italo-québécois*, Italian is the language of a country and a culture with which he or she is only partially familiar. English is the language of a continent, a powerful and omnipresent trading language. And French, the language of a people whose relationship to the Outsider has yet to be defined. In choosing one of these three languages for literary expression, the writer makes a choice which carries social implications.

In the prefaces to his plays, in the various essays he has written, and in his plays themselves, Micone has stated the reasons which led him to choose French as his language of expression. His reasons were political: French is the language which opposes the economic power of *les Anglais,* and French is the language which will be understood by those who count: "You can write what you wish, but only if you write in French will we have a chance of being understood and respected for what we are. It's now or never."

Micone was then confronted with an unusual problem: How to represent the French spoken by Italians when there is no existing, general model to imitate? Micone explains in an interview (*Vice Versa*, February 1984) that after rejecting the idea of a standard international French and having decided that a popular idiom would not necessarily make his characters ridiculous, he opted for a hybrid language. This language, he suggests, represents the street language which Italians will speak in about twenty years from now in Quebec. It is a popular language and includes words like

"Sacraminte," the Italian version of the popular Quebec swear-word *"Sacrament."*

The talking matches in Micone's plays are jousts, conflicting versions of reality which confront one another in mutual incomprehension. There are basically three voices in these discussions: that of the dominant male (Antonio, Giovanni) who represents the traditional, conservative view; that of the subordinate but lucid female (Anna, Nancy, Adolorata) perhaps on her way to emancipation; that of the symbolic character, Zio in *Voiceless People* and the announcer in *Addolorata*. The male-female voices confront one another in dialectic; the symbolic characters introduce a third voice, a synthesis giving the play larger dimensions. We see language operating as an instrument of power within the family (who speaks, what authority do his/her words have) and also as an indicator of social status. Because languages in Quebec are identified with different social constituencies, we are given through the characters in the plays an often humorous version of the immigrant's perception of these associations.

For Antonio, English is the language of the bosses and therefore the language which inspires respect. Antonio insists therefore that his children go to school in English. Antonio's son, Mario, who was born in Quebec and who did indeed go to English school, speaks half-French and half-English and copiously punctuates the resulting mixture with *fucks*. Antonio is proud that Mario can speak three languages, but Mario's unsure grip on language is a reflection of his inability to obtain social advancement, he will go to work in the same factory as his father. He is consoled by the marvellous roar of his Trans-Am.

Lolita, the young fiancée in *Addolorata*, sees only advantages in multilingualism. Her "four languages" are a precious asset for *marriageability* and the good life. Satire here reveals the link between the profusion of languages and cultural poverty. Possessing language is not only manipulating a code correctly – in many cases of multilingualism, especially among immigrants, this level of mastery is often not attained. Language and culture are the means through which individuals interpret their past and their present.

The incapacity to master language becomes, in *Voiceless People,* the inability to understand one's reality. Nancy: "I teach adolescents who have Italian names and whose only culture is that of silence. Silence on the peasant origins of their parents. Silence on the reasons which led their parents to emigrate. Silence on the manipulations of which they are victims. Silence on the country in which they live and on the reasons for this silence."

In Micone's plays, male rhetoric is an active agent in the oppression of women. In the dialectic of power/powerlessness which characterizes the particular situation of the male immigrant (source of authority within the family, powerless outside the home), rhetoric – whether it be from the right or the left – becomes an almost concrete manifestation of selfhood.

If Micone the playwright can choose among various languages of expression the one most appropriate to his needs, his characters have little choice. This indeed seems to be the dialectic he presents: the language of authenticity is accessible only to those excluded from the possibilities of both power (economic power) and authority (the limited power exercised by the head of the family). Because they are *doubly immigrant*, women have no stake in and no access to the rhetoric of authority.

By adopting the family as his particular area of investigation, by shattering questions of language and power into a dynamic configuration of interrelated fragments, Micone shows finally that the "immigrant question" is simply a variant of the theme of powerlessness. Here is a subject, suggests Micone, on which women speak with authority.

Mordecai Richler

Mordecai Richler's novels include The Apprenticeship of Duddy Kravitz, Cocksure, St. Urbain's Horseman, Joshua Then and Now, *and the recently acclaimed* Solomon Gursky Was Here. *He has written two popular children's books, produced three collections of essays, and is the editor of two anthologies, including the recently published* Writers on World War II. *After living in London for twenty years, he returned to Montreal with his famly in 1972. His work has been translated into many languages and has established him as one of Montreal's most respected international writers. The author's latest book,* Oh Canada! Oh Quebec! Requiem for a Divided Country *ridicules Quebec's language laws and discusses the history of anti-Semitism in Quebec. When an excerpt from the then-unpublished book appeared in a September 1991 issue of the* New Yorker, *it created an instant uproar. The hostile response of many French Quebecers to the article was perhaps best characterized by the prominent co-chairman of the Commission on the Political and Constitutional Future of Quebec, Michel Bélanger. Although he had not read the article, he expressed the following opinion. "Foreigner is not the right expression," for Montreal-born Richler, he told the press. "I think the right expression is he doesn't belong." The excerpt that appears here is from the author's passionate response (published in the* Gazette, *September 28, 1991) to critics of the* New Yorker *excerpt.*

"Je Me Souviens" ["I Remember"]

Let me cite chapter and verse:

1. On June 20, 1906, Henri Bourassa, founder of *Le Devoir*, told the House of Commons that he was not bound by anti-racial motives. However, he did offer our parliamentarians the benefit of the following *pensée:* "Simply given the experience of every civilized country . . . the Jews are the most undesirable class of people any country can have. . . . They are vampires on a community instead of being contributors to the general welfare of the people. . . ."

2. In the 1930s, *Le Devoir* advised its flock to avoid Jewish shopkeepers, who had "cheating and corrupting in their bloodstreams." In those halcyon days the newspaper – according to Esther Delisle's thesis, *Antisémitisme et nationalisme d'extreme droite dans la province du Québec, 1929-30* – assumed the following editorial position: Jews should be deported; Canadian nationality should be denied Jewish immigrants; Jews should not have the right to vote.

3. Although André Laurendeau, another nationalist hero, did not become editor of *Le Devoir* until 1958, he possibly qualified by writing in *Les*

Cahiers des Jeunes – Canada, in 1933: "Everybody in the world knows that the Jews aspire to that happy day when they will dominate the world."

Laurendeau changed his mind about the Jews after a two-year sojourn in Europe, including a passage through Hitler's Germany. However, in 1964, he upbraided the *Montreal Star* in his Diary for pronouncing Abbé Lionel Groulx, author of *L'Appel de la Race*, a racist.

"It is unjust to attack him for things he is not guilty of," Laurendeau wrote. This in defence of a cleric of severely limited intelligence, who wrote, in 1954, that the Jew's passion for money left them without any scruples, and that they were behind every pornographic enterprise, "livres, cinéma, théâtres, etc."

As good at injustice-collecting as anybody else in Canada, I could go on and on, but I have already been charged, here, there, and everywhere of brooding on events long past, that is to say, outrages that occurred in the 1930s and '40s. This, astonishingly, from a people who have had "Je me souviens" stamped into every license plate in the province – a motto evoking events that happened more than two centuries ago.

Jean-François Lisée

Jean-François Lisée is one of Quebec's most respected journalists and the author of In the Eye of the Eagle, *a best-selling book on the relationship between the Lévesque government and the Americans. The following is abridged from* L'actualité *(December 1991).*

Interview with Pierre Anctil

If you read the excerpt from Mordecai Richler's recent book, *Oh Canada! Oh Quebec! Requiem for a Divided Country* which was published in the *New Yorker*, Quebec came across as remarkable on two scores: for its oppression of its anglophone minority, and for its anti-semitism. We asked Pierre Anctil, the author of two books on the subject, *Le Rendez-vous manqué [A Missed Opportunity*] and *Le Devoir, les Juifs et l'immigration [Le Devoir, Jews and Immigration]*, for his opinion. He is also a co-editor of a collection of essays on Yiddish culture in Montreal called *An Everyday Miracle*, published by Véhicule Press. In the interview that follows, from which no one emerges unscathed, Anctil sets the record straight, denouncing Richler's exaggerations, blasting some Quebec media for their latent anti-semitism, and taking a strip off certain Jewish leaders and intellectuals along the way. Anctil, who has degrees in geography and social anthropology, has been studying the place of Jews in Quebec for ten years now. His interest has led him to learn Yiddish and to collaborate with Goldie Morgentaler on a Yiddish translation of Michel Tremblay's *Les Belles Soeurs*.

Lisée: Are today's Québécois anti-semitic?

Anctil: Under the most rigorous definition, anti-semitism refers to a country with laws that are hostile to Jews, which is not the case in Quebec. Another definition refers to job discrimination. Here too, the answer is no. The third criterion: a desire to eliminate any Jewish reference from the national culture. No again. But if you expand the definition to include suspicion and hostility, the answer could be yes. For example, when a headline in *La Presse* two years ago read "Jewish Problem in Outremont," that was an act of hostility and suspicion.

Lisée: An act of anti-semitism?

Anctil: The anti-semitism wasn't radical or aggressive, it was latent because there is no "Jewish problem" in Outremont. The problem has to do with the co-existence of two communities. The description of the Jews in the article was offensive, as was the paper's reply to the criticisms it received. The entire episode was one of the most remarkable acts of anti-semitism during the past decade in Quebec. Then there was the case of graffiti in a Jewish cemetery outside Quebec City. But that's the extent of outright anti-semitic acts.

Lisée: A recent list published by the B'nai Brith League of Human Rights showed thirty-six incidents of vandalism or harassment in Quebec in 1990 . . .

Anctil: . . . compared with 106 in Ontario. And the number of incidents of vandalism and harassment is declining in Quebec and increasing in the rest of Canada. Thirty-six incidents in a year for a population of six million is not insignificant – I deplore them, and I believe we must act to reduce the number. But it amounts to three per month; that's not serious, and it includes things like drawing a swastika on the wall of the Jewish Studies Department at McGill. In my opinion these acts aren't the work of an organized campaign; they don't result from a will to act against the Jewish community. If they did, it would be serious. There was a case of some young people beating up orthodox Jews in Outremont last year. They were xenophobes, who could just as well have attacked a black person or a woman in a sari. Hideous though it was, their behaviour wasn't *specifically* anti-semitic.

Lisée: How does anti-semitism in Quebec compare with that in other western societies?

Anctil: I was in Montpellier, France, recently, where a bomb went off outside a synagogue. That's a hell of a lot worse than anything that has happened here. Some Jewish graves were violated in Carpentras, raising the possibility of a deliberately organized campaign, a specifically ideological gesture. What's important is not the anti-semitic act itself, or its gravity, but whether the acts are repeated, whether they express an organized will.

Lisée: But groups like the Ku Klux Klan can be found in Quebec now, to say nothing of skinheads?

Anctil: Some copies of *The Klansman* were distributed last summer in the Eastern Townships and Dorval. It's an English-language publication from the U.S., which accuses the Jews among other things of being behind the Quebec independence movement! Does that represent francophone anti-semitism? Get serious! As for the vandalism in the cemetery at Sainte Foy, outside Quebec City, what was painted on the tombstones were the letters "ZOG." They stand for Zionist Occupational Government, an expression used by American fascists to designate the Israeli government. How many average suburban francophones know that code?

The most disgusting recent cases of anti-semitism in the country have occurred not in Quebec but in English Canada. It's significant that when one David Irving, who denies the existence of the concentration camps, wanted to make a cross-country tour, he left out Montreal.

Lisée: Still, polls show Québécois as having more anti-semitic reactions than other Canadians.

Anctil: What polls showing Québécois as having more anti-semitic reactions than other Canadians measure is a barrier of perception, a lack of contact. After ten years of observation I can say that Montreal francophones have very few contacts with Jews – and vice versa. Without being malicious, I'd like to see what a similar poll would show about Jewish attitudes towards French Canadians. They might be very negative. I myself speak English well enough to pass for anglophone, and I've heard hostile remarks in Montreal Jewish circles, such as: "Francophones are anti-democratic, anti-human rights, willing to violate basic democratic rules." Those opinions are based on deep historic gulfs.

Lisée: In a speech to a Jewish audience on the eve of the election of the Parti Québécois in 1976, Charles Bronfman called the Péquistes "a bunch of bandits who are out to destroy us." Was his opinion widely shared in the community?

Anctil: If "anti-quebecism" were to be measured on a scale like anti-semitism, Bronfman would rank very high, but still that speech represented perceptions, not acts. Just as after the PQ was elected, some Jews were convinced that a song sung at the victory rally was the French version of a Nazi song. There were even some Jewish intellectuals who published an article about it in an American periodical. Obviously that was completely false. I think it came about because of the inability of some anglophone Jews to understand the language, the context, where the nationalists were coming from. That's typical of the lack of contact. The rumour was responding to a sense of anxiety.

Nowadays, I wouldn't go so far as to say that such perceptions are very widespread. But *The Suburban* [a free weekly paper distributed in the west end of Montreal] said recently that the present situation in Quebec was comparable to that in Germany in 1934. The statement, which was denounced by the Canadian Jewish Congress, didn't represent the position of the majority. Still, sometimes when I've spoken in synagogues or to private groups, I've been asked in all seriousness, by educated Jews, "Why did no one in French Quebec speak out against Bill 178?" [a law that places strict limits on the use of English on commercial signs]. When I tell them it was denounced in both *Le Devoir* and *l'Actualité,* they're flabbergasted. They don't know, they don't read, they don't understand. That's a major problem.

Lisée: Who is to blame?

Anctil: Nobody! The underlying reason for all the misunderstandings is that when Jews started arriving here, in 1905, the educational and institutional networks were closed to them. The fault lies in the version of Canadian history that's based on the notion of two founding peoples. For the Jews, that binary system was ridiculous; for the francophones, the Jews didn't count, and so they were excluded. The Protestants eventually made room for them – very reluctantly, as the documents show.

Lisée: The Jews would have chosen English schools in any case?

Anctil: Because of the situation that prevailed here before the Quiet Revolution. Put yourself in the shoes of a new immigrant who sees a mass of uneducated French Canadians at the bottom of the economic ladder – which was still the case in 1969.

Lisée: Has it been established that during the 1930s and until the Second World War, anti-semitism was predominant in Quebec?

Anctil: Anti-semitism originated with the Catholic church, where Jews had been perceived as Christ-killers since the fourth century. According to Church teachings, the Jew was condemned to poverty and exile because he refused God; Christians were at the top of the pyramid, and the Jews were the dregs of history.

Lisée: How long did such teaching continue in Quebec?

Anctil: It wasn't until 1965 that the Vatican stopped holding the Jewish people responsible for the death of Christ. How long would it take for that change to reach here? If certain intellectuals of the Quiet Revolution were honest with themselves, they'd admit that their own perception of Jews stems from those teachings. The second source of Québécois anti-semitism in the 1930s was France. It was staple intellectual fodder at the time, as Henri Bourassa (founder of *Le Devoir* and a nationalist leader) admitted himself. The final source was fascism, which appeared later. That's a substantial legacy.

Lisée: During that pre-war period, was there more anti-semitism in Quebec than elsewhere in North America?

Anctil: In the United States during the pre-war period, the industrialist Henry Ford was a notorious anti-semite who financed an anti-semitic newspaper. There were American priests who led anti-Jewish crusades. Here, we had Adrien Arcand and his Christian National Socialist party, but the equivalent existed in English Canada. If you examine the data, you'll see there was no major difference between the two.

Lisée: Was there discrimination against Jews by francophones during that period?

Anctil: There was a strike at Notre Dame Hospital in 1934, one of the most serious anti-semitic incidents in Quebec history. Five hospitals were shut down for several days to force a Jewish intern to resign. Aside from that, my research in the archives of the Canadian Jewish Congress, which are very reliable, shows there was no significant violence aside from some rioting in Jewish neighbourhoods by Arcand's followers during the conscription crisis. In fact, Montreal anglophones were probably guilty of a lot more anti-semitism than francophones.

Lisée: You talk about widespread practices?

Anctil: At McGill, generally speaking from 1930 to the late 1940s, the percentage of Jewish students was cut from 25 percent to 12 percent, and in medicine to less than 10 percent, depriving many young Jews of promising careers. That didn't happen at the Université de Montréal because in general, Jews wanted to be educated in English.

Of course Jews were excluded from the Montreal Stock Exchange, as were francophones and women. They couldn't get jobs with anglophone banks – not even as tellers – and they were almost systematically excluded from big business, corporations, business and social clubs. It wasn't francophones from east-end Montreal who could prevent Jews from getting jobs in banks! But it's important to remember that as of 1933, there was a total ban on Jewish immigration to Canada – at the time of their greatest need. There was a "gentlemen's agreement" between the anglophone and francophone elites.

Lisée: Is it true to say that *Le Devoir* was anti-semitic during the 1930s and to add, as Richler does, that the newspaper has "a long and disgraceful history of anti-semitism"?

Anctil: No, it's false. In the research for my book on *Le Devoir,* I found only twelve editorials in ten years that were hostile to Jews, within a very precise historic context. That's not enough to declare a newspaper "anti-semitic." *Le Devoir* is a newspaper of ideas, so if it had really had an anti-semitic bias, it would have been expressed much more systematically. What you can find there is hostility and contempt. But even that kind of editorial disappeared in 1939, because of censorship, and beginning in 1945 there wasn't another word about Jews. Not one. Later, in the early fifties, there was one pro-Jewish editorial. Then, nothing more until the relatively positive pieces that have appeared in recent years. Richler's remark is unfair and unacceptable, and the editor of *Le Devoir* was quite right to defend her paper.

Lisée: Whose responsibility is it today to build bridges between the two communities?

Anctil: The francophone majority must become sensitive to differences and start opening doors. The Jewish community, for its part, has a duty to start opening its cultural institutions, its libraries and schools, as it is beginning to do. But you can't just open a community the way you open an office or a closet, to let in the air.

Translated by Sheila Fischman

MERRILY WEISBORD

Merrily Weisbord lives in the Laurentian mountains, north of Montreal. She is the author of The Strangest Dream: Canadian Communists, the Spy Trials and the Cold War *and* Our Future Selves: Love, Life, Sex and Aging. *She is co-author of* The Valour and The Horror: The Untold Story of Canadians in the Second World War. *The following article, originally written in French, appeared in a special issue of* Liberté *(June 1989) devoted to Quebec's anglo writing community.*

BEING AT HOME

MY COMPANION'S FATHER HAS JUST DIED. HE HAS HARDLY ANY FAMILY LEFT ALIVE. He lies in the tub, soaking and talking out the sadness. His parents who came to Quebec from Poland and Germany via Belgium, France, and Italy lie buried east of Mirabel, past St. François, in the snow-covered fields of Quebec. Far, it seems to him, from where they began. My companion thinks of William Johnson claiming his Quebec roots with the graves of his family buried in the Eastern Townships and the French press asking if it were now necessary to cry over the bones of Mr. Johnson's dead grandmother. And yet, the sanctity of the burial place goes back to Homer, says my friend, searching for his connection to his parents, to his destiny, to life itself.

My father's father was a blacksmith who came to Quebec to avoid conscription in the Czar's army. My great-grandfather, on my mother's side, was the chief Rabbi of Quebec City. My father grew up in St. Sophie and my mother on Bagg Avenue. They joined the Communist Party during the Spanish Civil War, and I had no religious training. I was brought up to believe in the Brotherhood of Man.

The other day I was swimming at the Polyvalent in St. Jerome. A little girl, shivering, grumped and grepsed as her mother rushed to dry her off. Beside us, on the bench, a pregnant woman watched. After much rubbing, the kid, warm enough to look around, said prophetically, "C'est dur d'avoir un enfant."

"Tu as raison," I said to the kid. "Comme tu es intelligente." The kid looked at me, looked at me again and whooped in surprise, "Mama, c'est une anglaise."

My daughter, Anna, 15, sings, loves and perhaps most amazingly, dreams in English and French. She should be fêted but instead she feels like she is on both sides of the fence:

> Having gone to French classical lycée, I was attacked for not understanding the French grammatical accords, and got the genuine French versus English

> line, 'Ah, t'es Anglais!' shot back at me every time the feminine double e came around. I was a bloke.
>
> Now, in English school, I am a pepper. Accused of speaking the Dreaded Language of French and having, uh, French friends. Personally, I think the French can have our precious English slang, and we their French clichés, as long as I get to belong to one side or the other. Being neither a "bloke" or a "pepper," I've been left out in the cold, or should I say froid – the linguistic nightmare of this super cool province.

When my older daughter, Kim, went to Polyvalent St. Jerome, she often overheard, "Fais pas ton juif." She was brave enough to say she was Jewish and to ask her friends to restrain themselves. When she went to her friends' homes for dinner, their parents would say, "Fais pas ton juif" and her friends would spring to her defense with, "Fais pas ça, c'est une juive, elle."

Now, Kim, 25, trained in St. Hyacinthe, a doctor of veterinary medicine, lives with "un Québécois pure laine," and hangs out with her high-school gang of Louise, Claudie, Lorrain and the two Pierres. She works at a clinic in St. Sauveur where she has established close professional ties with many animal lovers. The other day, a woman whose animals she routinely treats, came in with a difficult case. Kim cajoled the dog and reassured the woman. Together, they lifted the dog up on the table. The dog peed, and the woman yelled, "Mon petit juif."

In the 30s, the Anglo establishment had a quota system for the number of Jews they allowed to attend their elite universities. My mother made it in but her brother didn't. Clubs, schools, and resorts were closed to my parents because they were *not* Anglo, English, Canadian Canadians.

Now, in the current reductionist environment, I am an Anglo. Or even worse, an Anglophone, probably one of the least euphonic words in the lexicon of divisionist jargonese. But this is not me. I can't identify with simplistic categories – middle-age, pre-menopausal, old, intellectual, anglophone.

On my wall there is a Wonder Woman sticker, a newsphoto of ninety-two-year-old La Pasionaria, and this Bertrand Russell quote, ". . . in spite of death, man is yet free during his brief years, to examine, to criticize, to know and in imagination to create."

I voted "Oui" in the referendum because I thought that a new Quebec would be committed to social justice, embracing all people as equals. Now, too often, I recall Montreal poet, A.M. Klein's phrase, "the body-odour of race," a phrase representing an attitude not particular to Quebec, but unworthy of it.

Today, Kim tells me she has been accepted to do her postdoctoral residency at Guelph. She sits in the big chair in the living room, her legs apart, remembering Ontario with trepidation: "Nowhere have I felt so Québécois. They don't laugh out loud in movies. They don't drive fast. They don't speak French. They don't kiss in public. They don't sit with their legs apart, not even the men."

Who is Québécois? How big is Quebec's heart and imagination? My children are the flowers of this potentially fecund soil. Yet there is no word to describe them as, I think, no one word can describe me. We live here, in the case of my family, tied to the soil, having, for better or for worse, taken root.

Leonard Cohen

A native Montrealer, Leonard Cohen has won worldwide acclaim as a songwriter. His recent album, I'm Your Man, *inspired an eclectic musical tribute from his peers, entitled* I'm Your Fan. *He is the author of two novels,* The Favourite Game *and* Beautiful Losers, *and many celebrated books of poetry. Offered a Governor General's Award in 1968 for his* Selected Poems, *he declined the honour, saying in a letter that "the poems themselves forbid it absolutely." A new collection of his poems and lyrics has been rumoured to be in the works. The following excerpt is from* Beautiful Losers *(1966). Used by permission of the Canadian Publishers, McClelland & Stewart, Toronto.*

The History of Them All

Arm in arm, we climbed the streets that led to the mountain, Mont Royal, which gives its name to our city. Never before had the shops of Ste. Catherine Street bloomed so brightly, or the noon crowds thronged so gaily. I seemed to see it for the first time, the colours wild as those first splashes of paint on the white skin of the reindeer.

– Let's buy steamed hot dogs in Woolworth's.

– Let's eat them with our arms crossed, taking risks with mustard.

We walked along Sherbrooke Street, west, toward the English section of the city. We felt the tension immediately. At the corner of Parc Lafontaine Park we heard the shouted slogans of a demonstration.

– Québec Libre!

– Québec Oui, Ottawa Non!

– Merde à la reine d'angleterre!

– Elizabeth Go Home!

The newspapers had just announced the intention of Queen Elizabeth to visit Canada, a state visit planned for October.

– This is an ugly crowd, F. Let's walk faster.

– No, it is a beautiful crowd.

– Why?

– Because they think they are Negroes, and that is the best feeling a man can have in this century.

Arm in arm, F. pulled me to the scene of commotion. Many of the demonstrators wore sweatshirts inscribed with QUÉBEC LIBRE. I noticed that everyone had a hard-on, including the women. From the base of a monument, a well-known young film maker addressed the cheering assembly. He wore the scholarly thin beard and violent leather jacket so commonly seen in the corridors of L'Office National du Film. His voice rang out clearly. F.'s judo pressure cautioned me to listen carefully.

– History! the young man called over our heads. What have we to do with History?

The question inflamed them.

– History! they shouted. Give us back our History! The English have stolen our History!

F. pressed deeper into the mass of bodies. They received us automatically, like quicksand swallowing up the laboratory monster. The echoes of the young man's clear voice hung above us like skywriting.

– Booo! Hang the English!

I felt a pleasant sensation at the base of my spine and jiggled ever so slightly against the thin nylon dress of a fanatic, who cheered behind me.

– In 1964 History decrees, no, History commands that the English surrender this land, which they have loved so imperfectly, surrender it to the Frenchman, surrender it to us!

– Bravo! Mon pays malheureux! Québec Libre!

I felt a hand slip down the back of my baggy trousers, a female hand because it had long fingernails smooth and tapered as a fuselage.

– Fuck the English! I shouted unexpectedly.

– That's it, F. whispered.

– History decrees that there are Losers and Winners. History cares nothing for cases, History cares only whose turn it is. I ask you, my friends, I ask you a simple question: whose Turn is it today?

– Our Turn! rose in one deafening answer.

The crowd, of which I was now a joyful particle, pressed even closer about the monument, as if we were a nut on a screw to which the whole city we longed to possess wound us tighter and tighter like a wrench. I loosed my belt to let her hand go deeper. I did not dare turn around to face her. I did not want to know who she was – that seemed to me the highest irrelevance. I could feel her nylon-sheathed breasts squash against my back, making damp sweat circles on my shirt.

– Yesterday it was the Turn of the Anglo-Scottish banker to leave his name on the hills of Montreal. Today it is the Turn of the Québec Nationalist to leave his name on the passport of a new Laurentian Republic!

– Vive la République!

This was too much for us. Almost wordlessly we roared our approval. The cool hand turned so now her palm was cupped around me and had easy access to the hairy creases. Hats were jumping above us like popping corn, and no one cared whose hat he got back because we all owned each others' hats.

– Yesterday it was the Turn of the English to have French maids from our villages in Gaspé. Yesterday it was the Turn of the French to have Aristotle and bad teeth.

– Booo! Shame! To the wall!

I smelled the perfume of her sweat and birthday presents, and that was more thrillingly personal than any exchange of names could be. She herself thrust her pelvic region hard against her own trouser-covered hand to reap, as it were, the by-products of her erotic entry. With my free hand I reached behind the both of us to grab like a football her flowery left cheek, and so we were locked together.

– Today it is the Turn of the English to have dirty houses and French bombs in their mailboxes!

F. had detached himself to get closer to the speaker. I snaked my other hand behind and fastened it on the right cheek. I swear that we were Plastic Man and Plastic Woman, because I seemed to be able to reach her everywhere, and she traveled through my underwear effortlessly. We began our rhythmical movements which corresponded to the very breathing of the mob, which was our family and the incubator of our desire.

– Kant said: If someone makes himself into an earthworm, can he complain if he is stepped on? Sekou Touré said: No matter what you say, Nationalism is psychologically inevitable and we all are nationalists! Napoleon said: A nation has lost everything if it has lost its independence. History chooses whether Napoleon shall speak these words from a throne to a throng, or from the window of a hut to a desolate sea!

This academic virtuosity was a little problematical for the crowd and provoked only a few exclamations. However, at that moment, out of the corner of my eye, I saw F. lifted on the shoulders of some young men. A wildcat cheer went up as he was recognized, and the speaker hastened to incorporate the spontaneous outburst into the intense orthodoxy of the whole crowd.

– We have among us a Patriot! A man the English could not disgrace even in their own Parliament.

F. slid back into the reverent knot which had hoisted him, his clenched fist raised above him like the periscope of a diving sub. And now, as if the presence of this veteran conferred a new mystic urgency, the speaker began to speak, almost to chant. His voice caressed us, just as my fingers her, just as her fingers me, his voice fell over our desire like a stream over a moaning water wheel, and I knew that all of us, not just the girl and me, all of us were going to come together. Our arms were tangled and squashed, and I did not know if it was I who held the root of my cock or she who greased the stiffening of her labia! Every one of us there had the arms of Plastic Man, and we held each other, all naked from the waist, all sealed in a frog jelly of sweat and juice, all bound in the sweetest bursting daisy chain!

– Blood! What does Blood mean to us?

– Blood! Give us back our Blood!

– Rub harder! I shouted, but some angry faces shushed me.

– From the earliest dawn of our race, this Blood, this shadowy stream of life, has been our nourishment and our destiny. Blood is the builder of the body, and Blood is the source of the spirit of the race. In Blood lurks our ancestral inheritance, in Blood is embodied the shape of our History, from Blood blooms the flower of our glory, and Blood is the undercurrent which they can never divert, and which all their stolen money cannot dry up!

– Give us our Blood!

– We demand our History!

– Vive la République!

– Don't stop! I shouted.

– Elizabeth Go Home!

– More! I pleaded. Bis! Bis! Encore!

The meeting began to break up, the daisy chain began to fray. The speaker had disappeared from the pedestal. Suddenly I was facing everyone. They were leaving. I grabbed lapels and hems.

– Don't go! Get him to speak more!

– Patience, citoyen, the Revolution has begun.

– No! Make him speak more! Nobody leave this park!

The throng pushed past me, apparently satisfied. At first the men smiled when I seized their lapels, attributing my imprecations to revolutionary ardour. At first the women laughed when I took their hands and checked them for traces of my pubic hair, because I wanted her, the girl I'd come to the dance with, the girl whose round sweat fossils I still wore on the back of my shirt.

– Don't go. Don't leave! Seal the park!

– Let go of my hand!

– Stop hanging on my lapels!

– We've got to go back to work!

I implored the three big men wearing QUÉBEC LIBRE sweatshirts to hoist me on their shoulders. I tried to get my foot hooked on the top of a pair of trousers so I could scramble up their sweaters and address the disintegrating family from the height of a shoulder.

– Get this creep off me!
– He looks English!
– He looks Jewish!
– But you can't leave! I haven't come yet!
– This man is a sex pervert!
– Let's beat the shit out of him. He's probably a sex pervert.
– He's smelling girls' hands.
– He's smelling his own hands!
– He's an odd one.

Then F. was beside me, big F., certifying my pedigree, and he led me away from the park which was now nothing but an ordinary park with swans and candy wrappers. Arm in arm, he led me down the sunny street.

JACQUES HENRIPIN

A professor at the Université de Montréal and one of Quebec's most respected demographers, Jacques Henripin has been a frequent advisor to the Quebec government on population trends. The following excerpt is from his submission to the Bélanger-Campeau Commission on Quebec's political and constitutional future. This excerpt is reprinted with the permission of Richard Fidler, ed., Canada, Adieu? Quebec Debates its Future, *co-published by Oolichan Books and The Institute for Research on Public Policy, 1991.*

IS THE CONSTITUTION THE PROBLEM?

I SUPPOSE I AM EXPECTED TO DISCUSS QUEBEC'S OUTSTANDING POPULATION PROBLEMS and indicate, to the degree possible, some ways to resolve them. The main problem can be summed up in two words: declining fertility. Two other problems related to migration are the substantial emigration to other provinces and the difficulty integrating a major portion of the immigrants from abroad. Let us take a brief look at each of these.

1. Fertility.

By the end of her childbearing years, a Quebec woman now between the ages of 25 and 30 will probably have given birth to about 1.6 children (and not 1.4 as is often claimed). This is 0.5 children fewer than needed to ensure generational replacement – a deficit of close to 25 per cent.

At this rate, two unwanted consequences will appear:

(a) A *substantial* aging of the population. This will become quite pronounced around the year 2010, and by 2030 about 25 per cent of the population will be 65 and over. The proportion today is about 11 per cent.

The only real remedy is an improvement in fertility.

Note: Contrary to what is often said, immigration does little to rejuvenate the population.

(b) By about 2030 Quebec's population will be well on the way to absolute decline. This decline will begin around the year 2000, then accelerate and reach cruising speed shortly after 2030, resulting in a reduction of about 25 per cent each quarter century. By 2080 Quebec will have about 4,000,000 inhabitants, or six-tenths of its present population.

These are problems faced to varying degrees by the entire industrialized world, including Japan. But they may be considerably more serious in Quebec, for two reasons: (a) the fertility is lower than elsewhere; (b) migratory trends, which are usually unfavourable, could accentuate the decline in population.

2. High emigration to other provinces.
It is mainly the Anglophones who are leaving, with their possessions, that is, with their skills, their capital, and (this is never mentioned) a form of collective wisdom that is a useful complement to that of the French-Canadian majority. Between 1966 and 1986, 20,000 Anglophones and 9,000 Francophones left Quebec each year for some other province. In relative terms, 15 times as many Anglophones (and about 5 times as many allophones) as Francophones are leaving Quebec for the rest of Canada.

Let us also note that Quebec does a rather poor job of retaining its foreign immigrants: 40 per cent leave within 10 years, 50 per cent within 20 years, and 60 per cent within 30 years. Obviously, this makes immigration from abroad a much less effective means to overcome demographic deficiencies. We need to take in close to three immigrants in order to keep one.

3. Difficulty integrating immigrants.
The foregoing is itself an indication of the lack of integration. However, Quebec has a particular problem. Only 30 percent of immigrants whose language is neither English nor French, and who must, therefore, choose between the two dominant languages, adopt French. This does not come close to reflecting the distribution of the two dominant languages in the host population, which is the population not of Quebec but of Montreal, and which is about 70 per cent Francophone (only 60 per cent on Montreal Island). The disproportion is, therefore, less pronounced than is usually suggested. But it is nevertheless quite high, and there is no doubt that English exercises a very strong attraction.

Census figures indicate that in 1986, after nine years of enforcing Law 101, the relative attraction of English and French was about the same as in 1971. This is no cause for surprise, since schoolchildren are the only ones severely constrained by that law.

One might well wonder whether some advantage offered to adults might be more effective than the "stick" applied to the children. What kind of advantage? I think Quebec society as a whole and its public authorities in particular (including civil servants) are rather mediocre in their reception of strangers. We might achieve greater success by recruiting non-Francophone civil servants (provided they are competent, of course) than by prohibiting signs in any language other than French.

No outside jurisdiction prevents the Quebec government from recruiting non-Francophone civil servants or conducting educational campaigns to reduce what indeed should be called chauvinism.

We should mention, as well, that it has never been demonstrated – at least to my knowledge – that the survival of French is threatened by a sign that is one-quarter English or Italian.

Since we have just referred to the survival of French, let me use the opportunity to recall that it was long feared – and not without reason, incidentally – that the proportion of Francophones was diminishing in Quebec, and in Montreal in particular. These fears were belied by the most recent census findings, in 1981 and 1986, and there is no reason to think that things will change over the next decade and a half.

However, if Quebec were to dramatically increase its immigrant population, things might turn out quite differently in a quarter of a century. For example, if fertility were to be maintained at its current level, and we decided to compensate for the vacuum (which would necessarily result) by resorting to immigration from outside, the perspective would be completely different.

If there is any threat to French today, it is from the sorry state of the written and spoken language. And there is no use hiding one's head in the sand; this is not the fault of the English or of the Constitution! No doubt several factors are involved, but we cannot deny the enormous responsibility of the Quebec government and the teachers. I will be told that I am not an expert on the matter. My reply is that perhaps that is good: some experts used to defend *joual*! And in any case I have been in a good position to observe, for more than 35 years. I get the products of our schools, at the end of the line. And I can affirm that, of all the Francophone students I may have known, the French Canadians are those with the least mastery of their language. I would say, in fact, that close to one-fifth of the students in our French-language universities do not have sufficient mastery of their mother tongue to develop a logical thought.

It is this, above all, that threatens the vigour of French in Quebec. . . . And the concern to maintain French should not preclude some concern about the chances for survival of English. At this point I would not say that the English minority faces impending disappearance, but it is certainly heading that way. However, no one will deny that in Montreal (but only in Montreal) the English community is still full of vigour – and is beginning to speak French. So much so that in a few years it will be the Anglophones who are the real bilinguals! The Francophones will have lost this specialty, thanks to the shortsighted distrust of English that is fostered in the French-language school system. This is a fine example of the stupidity produced by protectionist ideology. . . .

Translated by Richard Fidler

South Asian Women's Community Centre

The following brief was presented at public hearings held by the Montreal Catholic School Commission concerning proposed regulations on the use of non-French languages, between students, outside classrooms. The restrictions would have applied to areas within school parameters, such as hallways and schoolyards. The proposals met with strong public protest and were dropped. This brief was prepared by Jennifer Chew and Shree Mulay of the South Asian Women's Community Centre, a support organization for South Asian women in Montreal that operates in English, French, and many South Asian languages. This English version of the brief appeared in Montreal Serai *(April/May 1990), an interdisciplinary magazine devoted to cultural, social, and political issues that affect Montreal's immigrant community.*

The Degeneration of the Language Issue: What's Next?

This brief is being presented on behalf of the South Asian Women's Community Centre. We are a women's organization whose mandate is to help integrate South Asian women and their families, with origins in India, Pakistan, Bangladesh, Nepal and Sri Lanka, into Quebec society. The organization was formed because there was a recognition that immigrant women from the visible ethnic minorities experienced tremendous hardship in the process of integration and adaptation.

We are alarmed by the fact that racial and linguistic tensions have reached such a level that there is a need to hear briefs on the question of linguistic policy in the school yard.

All allophones, our children, attend French schools. Many of us who had a choice because of the grandfather clause in Law 101, chose to send our children to French rather than English schools, because we live in Quebec. For those who came after 1977, this choice was removed and the children were obliged to attend French schools.

Although Law 101 took away the choice of language for allophones, it would be fair to say that the majority of allophones would like their children to be fluent in French, English and possibly their own mother tongue. We do not wish to debate the pros and cons for learning or using two or more languages but only wish to point out there is no need to prove to the allophone community the desirability of learning French. The reality is that the school system and particularly the Catholic School Commission has not done enough to support parents who do not speak

French or English fluently and yet have to deal with the school bureaucracy to follow the progress of their children.

The responsibility of bridging the linguistic gap between parents and teachers does not lie with the parents alone. The school boards have been aware of the demographic changes in Quebec for a long time; they should have made an assessment of the changing needs of their population base and developed resources accordingly. Instead, they have responded to crisis after crisis in an ad hoc fashion with stop gap measures.

In response to English being spoken by allophone students in the school yard, the schools now propose a coercive policy of French-only on school premises. If this policy is a precedent, what is to stop the policy from being extended to the very streets we walk! This may sound absurd but who would have dreamt a year ago that we would be here defending a fundamental human right. Moreover, what signals are the schools giving to young impressionable children? That you can coerce people to "love" a language? That it is all right to trample on the rights and freedom of minorities? Is this how the schools hope to impart respect for others and teach our children about democratic principles?

The schoolyard language policy proposes to remove from school life the richness and experience that exposure to other cultures can bring. It will relegate cultures and languages other than French to a second class position. Enforcement of a language policy will not aid in maintaining discipline in the school. Rather, it will create unnecessary tension in the schools. Authoritarian measures can only encourage resentment and rebellion. Moreover, it makes a mockery of multiculturalism and it will discourage immigration to Quebec. Clearly all studies demonstrate that Quebec needs more immigrants.

On the surface it may appear that this policy will not affect Francophones. However, when any government or its institutions begin to encroach on the rights and freedoms of its minorities it is only a matter of time before other repressive measures are instituted. Measures which may impinge not only on freedom of speech but other fundamental rights guaranteed by the Quebec charter of human rights which affect the entire population.

The root cause of many of the tensions is not the language policy per se but the ingrained racism which exists in society. Instead of weeding out such ideas by reinforcing positive aspects of multiculturalism, the schools have chosen to pander to xenophobia and racial discrimination.

The South Asia Community Centre has always supported the concept that people who live and work in Quebec should make every attempt to learn and speak French. Since its inception, the centre has held French classes for recent arrivals because we see the importance of being able to communicate in the language of the majority of Quebec.

We want to build a harmonious society in Quebec in which there is mutual respect for all cultures, including those of the minorities. We strongly believe enforcement of French-only school policy will have very detrimental effects and should not be adopted by the school commission.

We believe that many measures can be taken to encourage the use of French and improve race relations in schools. In this regard, we propose the following:

1. That the schools should introduce an enrichment linguistic program for all its students including Francophones so that the standard of written and spoken French can be improved;
2. That school boards develop resources to assist parents who do not speak French to communicate with the schools about the progress of their children and also to encourage them to participate in school activities so that positive reinforcement is provided to students;
3. That the school boards sensitize their teachers to cultural differences and encourage them to develop programs in their geography and civic studies which provide positive images instead of negative stereotypes about other cultures and countries;
4. That the educational and awareness programs be developed by a body charged with the responsibility of ensuring that all intercultural and interracial policies are established within a specific period of time and with the participation of community organizations;
5. That school boards publicize the resources that are available to them to redress the problems they face in the education of their children.

Fatima Houda-Pepin

Fatima Houda-Pepin works for the Centre Maghrébin de recherche et d'information, an organization of Francophone ethnic groups originating in North Africa. The following is from her oral testimony presented to the Bélanger-Campeau Commission and is adapted from Richard Fidler, ed., Canada, Adieu? Quebec Debates its Future *(Oolichan Books and The Institute for Research on Public Policy, 1991).*

Give Some Content to Independence

Independence must not be seen as a magic solution that will solve all our problems. If we don't give substance to this independence, it will be difficult to sell it to minority groups. There is an idea (which to my mind has no foundation) which questions the allegiance of the minorities to the Quebec government because the minorities have always been associated with the federal government, with multiculturalism, with a certain view of society. I believe that Quebec society must change this perception, because the minorities have no prejudices about the Quebec government or the political class in Quebec. Minorities are uneasy about ethnocentric nationalism; they fear it because they fear being excluded. If the society of the majority can demonstrate its ability to welcome them and consider them full citizens, the members of the minorities won't hesitate or won't necessarily oppose the plan for Quebec's independence, and in some cases will champion it.

A Quebec identity should be pluralistic; a Quebecer is someone who wants to be one. It's up to us to make this identity happen, but the majority of society must accept it. Let me give you some examples. I received a phone call from a government TV service that was preparing a program about marriages with foreigners. I asked them what they meant by "foreigner," and they told me it was someone who is an immigrant.

As long as you continue to see us as foreigners, there will be a problem in defining what a Quebecer is. I can give you many other examples. I attended a conference on education. One of those attending made a presentation on the problem of francizing the allophones, allophone children, and she made a speech that is completely in line with current thinking: French is in trouble because of the immigrants and allophone children. And, of course, she cited the example of Saint Luc school. [A secondary school in Montreal with 1,650 students, 90% of whom are of non-Quebec ethnic origin. They are made up of 87 ethnic groups, 45 languages and 9 religions, and, although the school is a French-language school operated by the

Catholic school board, the common language many of the students use to communicate is English.] That example makes me furious. At one point, I asked if she could tell me the quality of the French in schools having a high concentration of native-born Francophones. And do you know what I got by way of an answer? Silence, for several minutes. They realized that a fundamental question had just been asked.

It's very easy to blame the immigrants for their inability to speak French, but that doesn't improve the quality of French. If we really want to promote French, we have to promote the quality of French, of French education for all children, with no distinctions but with consideration of the specific needs of allophone children who have particular problems, of course. But the most interesting thing was that a few days later I met one of the people who was seated beside me at that conference, and who is known to be a very congenial nationalist. I asked him: "How did you react to my question?" I felt I'd embarrassed people. And he said to me: "You know, it's a little like having a child with bad manners; when you say it has bad manners, that's fine, but when an outsider says it, that's hard to take. So there we are, it's an automatic reflex, sometimes it isn't even intentional; it's built into us. For us, it stems in part from our idea of the Catholic French Canadian, and everything that doesn't fit this three-part mold can only be foreign."

So you can see we have some way to go: we're doing our part; for goodness' sake, do yours.

CEQ
[Quebec Teacher's Union]

Members of the Centrale de l'enseignement du Québec (CEQ), the province-wide teachers' union, have been front-line participants in some of the major debates over immigration. The following is an abridged version of the brief that was presented to the Bélanger-Campeau Commission on Quebec's political and constitutional future and is reprinted with permission from Richard Fidler, ed., Canada, Adieu? Quebec Debates its Future *(Oolichan Books and The Institute for Research on Public Policy, 1991).*

Integration, not Assimilation

In the 19th century (and even the early 20th in some works, such as Lionel Groulx's in Quebec), the terms "race" and "ethnic group" were readily confused. For example, they spoke of the French and English races. Today the two terms have become specialized, and designate two different realities.

Race refers to a set of physical characteristics that are transmitted genetically. The concept is acknowledged to be of some use in animal breeding. Applied to the human species, it is of doubtful relevance. It can only be used to classify individuals, since there is no people that corresponds to a clearly determined race, no matter what characteristics one would use to define them (skin pigmentation, shape of skull, height, colour of eyes or hair, texture of hair, blood type, laterality, etc.).

Race therefore designates no actual community; it is purely a category for classifying individuals. From a strictly scientific point of view, it is impossible to define a people from racial criteria. Ethically, it is generally acknowledged that legislative or administrative attempts to promote the purity or improvement of the race would be incompatible with democratic ideals.

Nor has race anything to do with culture in the anthropological sense of the word. It refers only to what is transmitted genetically. And the fact that one has common family antecedents does not necessarily mean that there is a strong genetic resemblance.

However, an *ethnic group*, although it may be defined by dictionaries as "a group of families" and involve some common origin, has nothing to do in itself with physical characteristics or the genetic heritage of the individuals that compose it. Ethnic group refers to a cultural heritage and the affinities that are displayed between persons and families sharing that cultural heritage. Ethnic heredity is cultural, not genetic. One can find a great variety of physical types within the same ethnic group.

Whether or not a particular individual belongs to a given ethnic group is determined by his or her correspondence to a cultural profile. The community of culture on which the ethnic group is based is one of likenesses between the individuals and families within it (e.g., the same mother tongue, religion, family customs, eating habits, ways of dressing, memories of a common past, and the same hierarchy of values). The degree of likeness varies, of course, depending on the group observed and the way in which each ethnic group defines itself.

A *nation* is defined essentially as a society having its own culture as a society, not as a group of people having similar cultural traits as individuals. As the *Petit Robert* says, it is "a human group, generally quite large, which is characterized by a consciousness of its unity and a desire to live in common."

Ethnic culture is mainly transmitted by the family and the private institutions that gravitate around it. National culture is transmitted mainly by the national education system and through the operation of national institutions.

One's membership in a nation rests not on cultural characteristics inherited from the family milieu but on the implicit desire to live together, to constitute a true society, to share common institutions and adopt common standards of social life. In a normal situation this implicit desire is manifested by living in common in the same territory, defined in terms of the common culture erected on it. The nation is a work of reason and will, but a will renewed by successive generations – a synonym for historical continuity.

The Quebec nation

Insofar as the Quebec people defines itself as the entire population of Quebec, that is, all of the people who decide or agree to live permanently in Quebec and thus implicitly decide or agree to participate in its life and comply with its laws, it can be said to constitute a genuine nation. This people inhabits a territory that coincides with the sphere of influence of a distinctive national culture. It possesses a historical continuity going back to the 17th century. It has a national language that has accompanied it throughout its history and undoubtedly remains today the most easily recognizable aspect of its identity, to which it is very attached and with which it is spontaneously associated. It constitutes a distinct civil society, with its own codified civil law. It also has distinctive, original institutions – legal, political, educational, economic, cooperative, trade union, etc. And it is conscious that it constitutes an original society with a distinctive language, legal tradition and institutions.

The characteristics and attributes we have just referred to really belong to the entire Quebec society, to the Quebec people as a whole. Any Quebecer, even one who wishes it were otherwise, is affected and concerned by the fact that the society in which he lives has its own peculiar characteristics and a peculiar dynamic of social life. By agreeing to live in Quebec, no matter what one's origin, one accepts the laws of Quebec, short of helping to change them by becoming involved in the dynamics peculiar to Quebec's political and social context. To be a Quebecer it is not necessary to belong to the French-Canadian ethnic group, but to be a Quebecer regardless of one's ethnic affiliation is something quite different from being a Canadian or American. Quebec's national culture is the common property of everyone living in Quebec.

We said that the Quebec people indeed constitute a nation insofar as it is defined by the implicit will to live together and constitute an authentic civil, economic and political society. By this definition, we must acknowledge the special status of the aboriginal societies, which live collectively and to a large degree distinctly in the enclaves reserved for them in their own right. The Amerinds are ultimately subject to a law that applies only to them and imposes a particular political organization on them. Moreover, in many Amerind communities, and among the Inuit, there is a traditional political authority functioning parallel to the official political structure. Above all, in contrast to the situation of the other inhabitants of Quebec, their presence here cannot be interpreted *a priori* as a manifestation of an implicit will to share the institutions of the majority nation, since their societies already existed before the creation of ours. Their current societies are the extension of societies that never decided formally or implicity to merge with ours. That is why we say that the native communities will only be part of the Quebec people to the degree that they themselves so decide. We recognize their right of self-determination and will demand that this right be inscribed in the Constitution of Quebec.

The founders of New France did not simply open an area of immigration for Francophones from Europe; they created a distinct and original society. And not all of the immigrants who settled in New France were Francophones. Many, in all probability, spoke dialects or semi-dialects originating in the various provinces of France. Some were Italian, Spanish, German or Irish. The so-called "clash of dialects in New France" is comparable, in some respects, to the clash of ethnic languages in contemporary Quebec. The Quebec society of that day managed to integrate in French a linguistically diverse immigrant population speaking Norman, Poitevin, *gallo* (Breton), Picard and perhaps even Italian or Gaelic, and achieved its linguistic unity a century and a half before France. From the very beginning it sought to be a society with French as its common language, moving beyond the diversity of the languages of origin. Today's attempts to secure the integration in French, in the public schools and workplaces, of new Quebecers of every origin is consistent with the exemplary success achieved three centuries earlier.

The immigrants to New France came from provinces each of which had its own particular custom in the civil law. It soon became clear that the new society saw itself as a unified civil society with a correspondingly unified civil law. The *Coutume de Paris* was therefore recognized here as the ordinary law, laying the foundations of another major aspect of our national specificity. Contemporary Quebec's demands for exclusive jurisdiction over family and commercial law expresses the desire to protect and complete the overall coherence of our distinctive civil law, an integral part of our historical heritage.

And not only the civil law. It is no accident that Quebec is often the only province to demand exclusive power to legislate in many fields. Its aspiration is to build a fully coherent society by enacting laws that correspond to its national culture.

The desire to promote one's distinct legal coherence normally implies a desire for political autonomy. In this sense, in particular, the right of self-determination and the idea of national independence are grounded on the existence of a nation and of its distinctive national culture. Quebec, a nation in every sense, is now ready of its own accord to take its place in history.

Need for a cohesive society

The Quebec people are a multi-ethnic nation, in the sense that they have a distinctive national culture with which several ethnic cultures, including that of the majority group, co-exist.

Census information indicates that Quebec is now 83 percent Francophone and about 10 percent Anglophone. It appears that Francophones (defined by either mother tongue or language used in the home) will be in the majority for a long time to come. The percentage of Anglophones, on the other hand, has been declining for several decades. However, the percentage of persons whose mother tongue is English is declining more rapidly than the percentage of those for whom English is the main language used in the home.

In addition, many people and families in Quebec today have neither

French nor English as their first language, and there will be many more in the future. The low birth rate, and the high immigration rate we will continue to need as a result, indicate that Quebec will be increasingly multi-ethnic. And, on the international level, Quebec has a moral responsibility to do its part to provide a refuge for persons and families in distress who come from other countries. If we consider the ethnic diversity from the standpoint not of first languages but of ethnic origin, it can be anticipated that the descendants of the inhabitants of New France will long remain the largest group numerically, but in five or six decades will no longer constitute an absolute majority of the population.

There is no need, in our view, to regard this possibility, in itself, as a threat. We think the survival of the Quebec people and the protection of its common culture are not jeopardized by the presence in Quebec of persons of various origins, mother tongues or ethnic cultures. They could be jeopardized, however, by an ambiguity in the relationships between the ethnic groups and a larger society that is insufficiently defined. It is not a matter of indifference that immigrants feel they are joining a Canadian nation, rather than a Quebec nation.

What Quebec needs is not to be sheltered from immigration nor to be protected against the ethnic diversification of immigration. What it needs is full control over the tools it requires to build and assert its cohesiveness as a society over and above its ethnic, religious and ideological diversity.

There are ideological movements that base their defence and promotion of the Quebec identity on ethnic homogeneity. They demand that immigration be limited solely to European Francophones, for example. And they recommend that the people of disparate ethnic origin already settled in Quebec be systematically and rapidly assimilated. We disagree completely with this approach.

On the contrary, we think the diverse cultural contributions of the groups who join in the life of Quebec represent an opportunity for all Quebecers to enrich the national culture and open up to the world. We therefore advocate an open immigration policy that makes no distinctions on the basis of ethnic origin, without excluding, however, priority for those who, regardless of ethnic affiliation, already have a satisfactory knowledge of our national language. We also advocate a policy that values ethnic contributions, and promotes integration without assimilation. We support measures designed to promote the preservation of languages of origin. Finally, we support a policy of equal access for ethnic groups that suffer general discrimination in employment or are under-represented in specific jobs, for example in the public service.

A people's cultural dynamism is built not through levelling but through an emphasis on differences and building contacts between those differences and the common culture. Quebec's cultural dynamism needs all of the cultural resources of the peoples who make up its population. But it also needs to form a coherent society. Thus any policy of enhancing cultural differences must be accompanied by the promotion of a common culture and a common language. These two prongs of cultural policy are not contradictory, but complementary.

Hence Quebec's immigration policy must be accompanied by greater efforts than before to francize all manifestations and aspects of our collective life.

It is not enough that a prospective immigrant has heard of Quebec's French character in his or her contacts with the bureaucracy, or that he or she is offered French courses. The immigrant must see, hear and feel this French character everywhere – in everyday life, at work, in shops, in public services, in signs, in product labels, in corporate names, etc.

The goal must be not only to facilitate the use of French for Francophones in all of their activities, but to establish French as the common language, in fact and in law, for all of the inhabitants of Quebec. The alternative is the cultural dislocation of Quebec.

Translated by Richard Fidler

Boundaries of Identity

"Maudits Anglais?"

I'd like to say we've got no lesson on that score to take from the McConnells – from anyone that has been dominating Quebec like a bunch of Rhodesians – the white group! If we had colours here you'd feel it, and that is something we will not stand for any more, this paternalistic wasp – and it is that typically – the wasp arrogance of the ones who have been leading our government, and through the slush funds they contribute to, leading both of our hack parties by the nose for too long.

René Lévesque, politician
From *The Champions*, 1978 & 1986

F. R. Scott

A respected constitutional scholar, lawyer, poet, and translator, F. R. Scott (1899–1985) was a founder of the CCF and the NDP. Born and raised in Quebec, Scott became a Rhodes Scholar and graduated from Oxford University. He won his first Governor General's Award in 1977 for his Essays on the Constitution *and a second award for the* Collected Poems of F. R. Scott. *He received his law degree from McGill University in 1927 where he became a professor of Law and eventually the Dean of the Faculty of Law (1961 to 1964). The following poem is from* The Collected Poems of F. R. Scott *(1981). Used by permission of the Canadian Publishers, McClelland & Stewart, Toronto.*

The Social Register

(A Social Register for Canada was promoted in Montreal in 1947. On the Advisory Committee were names like Rt. Hon. Louis St. Laurent, Sir Ellsworth Flavelle, Air Marshal Bishop, Rear-Admiral Brodeur, Hon. J. Earl Lawson, Hartland Molson, and others. A Secret Committee was to screen all applicants. All quotations in this poem are taken verbatim from the invitation sent to prospective members.)

Reader, we have the honour to invite you to become a
"Member of the Social Register,"
For the paltry fee of $125 per annum.
This "work of art, done in good taste," and listing annually the
"Notables of the Dominion,"
Will contain nothing but "Ladies and Gentlemen pre-eminent in
the Higher Spheres,"
Who are "the very fabric of our country."
Thus shall we "build up in the Nation's First Families
A consciousness of their role in the life of a civilized
democracy."
Thus shall we bring "added dignity and profound significance
To our cultural way of life."
Through deplorable lack of vision, in times past,
Men who were "great Canadians, have everlastingly passed into
oblivion,"
Leaving no "footprints on the sands of time."
Somehow, despite their pre-eminence, they have disappeared.
Shall we, through "tragic short-sightedness," let the leaders of
this era
"Disappear into the realm of eternal silence?"

"Shall there be no names, no achievements, to hearten and strengthen on-coming generations in time of stress?"
If they have failed to make history, shall they fail to make The Canadian Social Register?
No – not if they can pay $125 annually,
And pass our Secret Committee.
For there is a "Secret Committee of seven members,"
Who will "determine the eligibility of those applying for membership."
Thus will the Social Register be "accepted in the most fastidious circles."
And to aid the Secret Committee you will send
The name of your father and the maiden name of your mother,
And the address of your "summer residence,"
(For of course you have a summer residence).
You may also submit, with a glossy print of yourself,
"Short quotations from laudatory comments received on diverse public occasions."
When printed, the Register will be sent,
Free, gratis, and not even asked for,
To (among many others) the "King of Sweden," the "President of Guatemala," and the "Turkish Public Library."

Reader, this will be "a perennial reminder"
Of the people (or such of them as pass the Secret Committee)
Who "fashioned this Canada of ours,"
For "One does not live only for toil and gain,"
Not, anyway, in First Families. It is comforting to believe
That while we "walk the earth," and pay $125,
And "after we have passed on," there will remain
"In the literature of the Universe," and particularly in the "Turkish Public Library,"
This "de luxe edition," "these unique and dignified annals,"
"These priceless and undying memories," with laudatory comments chosen by ourselves,
To which "succeeding First Families and historians alike will look,"
For "knowledge, guidance and inspiration."
Lives rich in eligibility will be "written large,"
(But within "a maximum of one thousand words")

"For all men to see and judge."
The "glorious dead," too,
These "selfless and noble defenders of Canada's honour,"
Will be incorporated in the Social Register
"Without any financial remuneration,"
Assuming of course, that they are all
"Sons and daughters of its Members."
Reader, as you may guess, the Register
Was not "a spur of the moment idea."
It was "long and carefully nurtured,"

And "counsel was sought in high and authoritative places,"
So that it may "lay a basis upon which prominent Canadians
 will henceforth be appraised
As they go striding down the years,"
Paying their $125,
And receiving a "world-wide, gratuitous distribution,"
Even unto "the Turkish Public Library."

"Si monumentum requiris, circumspice!" *
On this note, we both end.

* *From the* Gazette, *Montreal, February 25, 1967, reporting a finding of the Carter Royal Commission on Taxation*

David Fennario

The artistic director of Montreal's Centaur Theatre was so impressed by the strength of David Fennario's first play, Without a Parachute *– written as a class project at Dawson College in 1973 – that he decided to invite Fennario to become the Centaur's first playwright-in-residence. His first two plays at the Centaur,* On the Job *and* Nothing to Lose, *were hits with the public and toured the country. But it was Canada's first bilingual play,* Balconville *(1979), a portrait of working-class life in the Montreal neighbourhood of Pointe St. Charles, which established Fennario as one of the nation's leading playwrights. His most recent play,* The Death of René Lévesque *(1990) was reviewed harshly by French critics in Montreal. Fennario, who still lives in the Verdun-Pointe St. Charles district of Montreal, is an active member of the International Socialists and supports the right of native peoples and the Québécois to self-determination. The following article appeared in the* Montreal Gazette *(September 7, 1991).*

Black Rock Marks the Mass Grave of Irish Immigrants

A couple of years ago, I went down to St. Gabriel's Church on Centre St. in Point St. Charles and joined the members of various Irish societies in their annual march to the memorial stone marking the common grave of 6,000 immigrants who died here of typhoid fever back in 1847 when they fled the Great Famine in Ireland.

Wreaths were laid, speeches were made, but nobody cried when the pipers played. After all, the last survivors of the famine had died over 60 years ago, but still, the feeling was there – a need to remember a tragedy that has been largely forgotten or ignored by most historians and politicians.

I first saw the Irish Stone back in the 1950s on one of the bicycle trips I used to take with some friends of mine from the avenues in Verdun. Ten-year-olds pedalling our bikes along Bridge St. toward the Victoria Bridge in the heat and exhaust fumes of rush-hour traffic on a hot July day. We were heading down to the river to wash up before going home for supper, having gotten our jeans splotched with dirt from the old cattle pens near the Canada Packer's plant.

My friend Larry just wanted to go straight home because we were already late, but we knew we had to get the smell of manure off us, otherwise our mothers would know we had been down to the slaughterhouse, a forbidden place.

Danny, who loves animals, had been upset by what we had seen in the pens: cattle bellowing, pigs squealing, the stink and smell of shit and blood.

He wanted to go tell the police all about it because he was sure they would close the place down. But my other friend Bob didn't agree. "I think the cops already know about it, Danny," he said.

I was wondering how I was going to explain my missing shoe to my mother – already picturing in my mind the inevitable whack to the side of the head – when I saw Larry brake his bike to a halt on the sidewalk, about 100 feet away. He was yelling about something, but I couldn't hear him. Then I saw Danny pointing at what looked to be a huge black rock, stuck in the middle of a traffic islet that divides the left and right expressway lanes leading over the Victoria Bridge to the South Shore.

We stood there together, trying to read the inscription carved on the side of this strange-looking boulder. "To preserve from desecration, the remains of 6,000 immigrants who died of ship fever, AD, 1847. This stone is erected by the workmen of Peto, Brassey and Betts, employed in the construction of the Victoria Bridge, AD 1859."

Words like "desecration" and the AD's prefacing the dates had us a bit confused, but we did figure out that the great black rock was probably some kind of tombstone marking the grave of some 6,000 people. But who they were or where they came from or how they ever ended up being buried under an expressway was beyond our understanding.

Later, I went home with one shoe on, received the whack to the side of the head and had a nightmare in bed about that spooky black rock. Something about people getting slaughtered along with the cows and the pigs and nobody wanting to listen to me or Danny Casey when we tried to tell them what was happening down there on Bridge St.

Years later, I was to uncover the mystery of the black rock. I was in my teens, out of school, out of work and browsing around a lot of libraries because I like to read, especially history. Ever since I first asked my father where the sidewalks came from, I've always been curious about the past. Where did all this come from? But I didn't read much about Canadian history until I discovered the Salle Gagnon in the Cité de Montréal library, which specialized in Canadian history. Every day I'd sit there reading books about Montreal, instead of looking for a job, and I was surprised to see that my own community of Verdun-Point St. Charles got some mention in the records.

I discovered that the old legend I had heard about Griffintown being named after a guy who started a soap factory down there near the Lachine Canal was true. Then I came upon a book, *Loyola and Montreal*, by T.P. Slattery, published in 1962, which mentioned and even had a picture of the black rock.

Briefly, in a few pages, Slattery, whose family was from Griffintown, described the famine in Ireland brought on when the potatoes went bad two years in a row, with a million and a half peasants dying of disease and starvation between 1846 and 1851 and another million emigrating.

In 1847, 100,000 immigrants fled from Ireland to Canada on board ships usually carrying lumber. "Coffin ships," the Irish called them, because so many people died down in the holds from lack of proper food and ventilation. Others died in the thousands that year in quarantine at Grosse Île, located about 40 miles east of Quebec City, in the St. Lawrence. Those immigrants who could walk were shipped further west up the river to Montreal where the city fathers, worried about a possible epidemic, built some sheds to house the Irish out in Point St. Charles.

A letter of this period relates that "after a few weeks' service, these wooden structures contained colonies of bugs in every cranny; the wool, the cotton, the wood were black with them. Hundreds of the sick crowded upon straw; little children in the arms of their dead mothers . . . a chaos of suffering and evil odours."

Fifty to sixty died each day throughout the spring and summer of 1847 and were buried in a common pit lined with quicklime. A grave that probably would have remained unmarked if the workers who built the Victoria Bridge hadn't taken a boulder from one of the cribs in the river and erected it on the site. Not a memory in granite or marble, but a huge black rock that was pulled out of the water like a bad tooth.

Slattery, a successful lawyer and graduate of Montreal's Loyola College, places no blame on anyone for the tragedy he wrote about in his book. But other Irish writers and historians have pointed out that the famine was not just the consequence of the potatoes going bad; it was also a consequence of 700 years of British imperial rule over Ireland. They point out that while the Irish people were dying from starvation, food grown in Ireland continued to be exported out of the country by the British landlords, under the protection of British troops.

"During the winter of 1846-47," wrote Thomas Gallager in his book *Paddy's Lament*, published in 1982, "while over 400,000 persons were dying of famine or famine-related disease, the British government . . . allowed 17 million pounds sterling worth of grain, cattle, pigs, flour, eggs and poultry to be shipped to England – enough food to feed, at least during those crucial winter months, twice the almost 6 million men, women and children who composed the tenant-farmer and farmer-labourer population."

As I came across these facts during my reading at the Cité de Montréal library, I began to realize that the nightmare I had when I was 10 years old was not far from the truth. Horrible things have happened to people and are still happening today, but nobody seems to want to know about it. Too afraid or scared to admit what's going on around them, because they think or feel they can't do anything about it anyhow. Just like in a nightmare.

I wasn't sure then if I could do anything about changing the world when I was going through so many changes myself, but discovering what the Irish Stone was all about gave me a reason for becoming a writer. It made me want to tell the story of my community, a community that had somehow been largely left out of history.

I'm still trying.

GEORGE TOMBS

George Tombs is a Montreal journalist who works in English and French for newspapers, magazines, radio, and TV. His work also appears in the United Kingdom, France, and the United States. In 1987, he won a Bourse Nord-Sud (North-South travel grant to Argentina) from the Fédération professionnelle des journalistes du Québec. Other awards include the Michener Fellowship (1988) and the Michener Award (co-winner, 1990). The following is abridged from the author's original essay written in French for Cité libre *(vol. XIX, no.3, October 1991).*

THE ANGLOPHONE AND QUEBEC'S TWO NATIONALISMS

ARE ANGLOPHONES PART OF THE QUEBEC "NATION"? THEY USED TO BE CONSIDERED more British than Canadian. Now they seem more Canadian than Québécois. They live somewhere at the outer reaches of the nationalist universe. On an individual level, they are not viewed with any particular animosity. But their community is distinct enough to remain outside the nationalist model of "one land, one language, one culture." Besides, when people speak of the "society, collectivity and people" of Quebec, in the same breath as the "nation," they are hardly thinking of "les Anglais."

Do anglophones want to be Québécois? The answer depends on how we define the term. According to the broadest definition, a Québécois is someone who leads his life in Quebec. The individual has nothing to prove to anybody. He can be Québécois in his own way, and even Canadian, American or French at the same time. But according to the conditional definition, on the other hand, which is more widely accepted than we are led to believe, a Québécois is someone who has joined the nationalist and even the *souverainiste* movement. Such a huge condition excludes a good part of the population of Quebec.

In fact, there are at least two varieties of nationalism in Quebec. Although they are very different from each other, they occasionally work together for tactical reasons. The first variety accepts the fact Quebec is predominantly French. And yet it is based on the concept of a modern society built by freely associated citizens, regardless of their ethnic origin. This is the elective nation, a nation without boundaries. The anglophone goes wherever he wants with relative ease.

The second variety of nationalism is rooted in the organic nation, and holds that Quebec has a single, shared character, only one language, only one culture, common traditions and great ethnic homogeneity. This nation needs to separate and polarize people into clearly differentiated communities. The anglophone can't help stumbling over language, and has the choice either of being a member of a minority or being totally absent.

This ethno-nationalist Quebec has a hard time emerging from its ideology of exclusion. It can't see itself through the eyes of others. It needs to identify internal and external dangers in order to maintain group cohesion, so it makes them appear. It is an ingrown society and runs the risk of suffocation.

In order to grasp what life is like for Quebec anglophones though, it is important to leave aside all the surface arguments and explore the depths of Quebec's psychopolitics. The problem of "les Anglais" is at least two centuries old. Some might even say it goes back a thousand years.

Anyone who has hung around the anglophone community knows the WASP mindset has a number of cultural handicaps. The denial of internal and external problems, for starters. The silence of the anglophone community, in the face of nationalist demands, hasn't produced much in the way of results. The legendary refusal of anglophones to participate in the group, the way some of them seem to cultivate distance, is probably due to shyness, modesty, or quite simply to fear.

I have begun noting comments people make about Quebec anglophones. Here are a few of them. There's nothing scientific about my list.

Anglophones don't express their feelings enough, but when they do express them, they come on too strong. They are much too individualistic, which doesn't prevent them from having tribal instincts. They have no deep, emotional attachment to the English language, but boy, can they be exasperating when they insist on using it in public in Quebec. They make no effort to learn French. Their bilingualism is unacceptable. They are richer than francophones, but they have nothing but disdain for their own poor. They have nothing but spite for Quebec, but get too vehement when they claim to be part of Quebec. They have learned nothing and forgotten nothing. In fact, they have forgotten everything: their adaptation serves no useful function, since it has come too late. Taken on an individual level, they are an easy-going lot. But taken as a group they are the source of all the ills of a society which (admittedly) they helped build.

What a deep wound! In this list are subjective judgements, fears, assumptions, statements of fact, snippets of political speeches, the conviction that nationalism's new "règles du jeu" are threatened, as well as interpretations of history. And once we try to isolate some of these remarks, to check them out, we start to run into problems.

Question: *Wasn't the disdain of anglophones demonstrated beyond any doubt by the trampling of the Quebec flag in Brockville in September 1989?*
Answer: But that was a media event created by APEC discontents, actually a handful of retired Ontarians formerly of Quebec. And the event was manipulated by Radio-Canada starting in February 1990, in other words five months later, for clearly political reasons, in what was to have been the "final sprint" of the Meech Lake Accord. It was really a misunderstanding.

Q: *Isn't the wealth of anglophones amply demonstrated by the haughty existence of Westmount and the West Island, not to mention continual stories about anglo privileges in the media?*
A: All of a sudden, the 110,000 anglophones living below the poverty line disappear from sight. According to Richard Shillington, the best-known statistician of poverty in Canada, the rate of poverty is much the same among Quebec anglophones and francophones: 19%. French media generally ignore studies suggesting there is no longer any economic difference on an average basis between the two communities, once we take into account age and the number of years of schooling. Of course, the big anglo fortunes are still around. But the economist François Vaillancourt considers the increasing bilingualism of anglophones (60% are functionally bilingual) is starting to have an effect on their economic standing. This bilingualism offers an acquired advantage to replace the structural advantages formerly enjoyed by anglophones. ["Langue et disparités de statut économique au Québec, 1970 et 1980," Conseil de la langue française.]

Q: *"La politique québécoise de dévéloppement culturel," Camille Laurin's white paper, pointed out thirteen years ago the disproportionate number of English language radio and television stations in Quebec. Jacques Parizeau occasionally refers to this imbalance . . .*
A: The main commercial TV station, CFCF of Montreal, is controlled by Jean Pouliot, a francophone. CFCF is the main reason Pouliot has been able to keep his money-losing French-language network Télévision Quatre-Saisons afloat. The two largest cable networks in the province (Pouliot's CF Cable and André Chagnon's Vidéotron) have made CFCF and many other English stations more widely available than ever before. Two out of every three homes in Quebec receive cable.

I have been told so many times "you don't correspond at all to the Idea I had of anglophones." As if nature were supposed to imitate art. Until now, nobody has been able to tell me just who conforms to this "Idea people have of anglophones." The relationship always seems to be anonymous and generalized. Individuals who depart from the Idea are passed off as anomalies or eccentrics. At least the Idea itself is pretty straight-forward.

As we know, negative prejudices come in handy in politics. They condition public behaviour. Mythical thinking uses visceral images to describe the world. It appeals directly to the mind and directly to the heart.

Let's start with a first example. "Quebec is aging," said a morose Lise Payette, during the TV documentary *Disparaître*. "Some people even say we are going to disappear. Is it too late to stop our decline?" For anyone watching this Radio-Canada/National Film Board documentary, "Quebec" implicitly referred to "us," francophones of old stock. The film seemed almost apocalyptic in the way it presented the spread of parasites and foreign bodies on Quebec soil, while the good people of the land ran the risk of vanishing into nothingness.

A second example. Last year, the vice-president of the Parti Québécois, Bernard Landry, told me: "You English-speaking people control everything north of Rio Grande, except Quebec. So everything is in English elsewhere. In Quebec we have the image that Quebec is French." Quebec anglophones are a deeply-rooted community, whose language is known by 40% of the population. But in order to disqualify the linguistic claims of anglophones, Québécois nationalism reminds us of the world primacy of a foreign country, the United States.

People seem to forget the Anglo-Quebecer is neither a Californian nor a Texan. He lives in Montreal-West, Lennoxville or the Lower North Shore, not Manhattan. George Bush is not going to help maintain the community institutions of Anglo-Quebecers.

A third, last example. In her book *Le Québec, un pays, une culture*, Françoise Tétu de Labsade writes: "It shouldn't surprise anyone that francophones feel threatened. They get on the defensive and develop reactions which their frustration can even make violent. The 400,000 anglophones of British origin also face feelings of anxiety and frustration. They are the conquerors. For years they have tolerated these people who want to prevent them from living in English as they do elsewhere in Canada. . . ." [Boréal, 1990, p.102]

It would be hard to do a better job of discrediting anglophones! Such honors bestowed on the conqueror!

Reed Scowen, the new chairman of the board of Alliance-Quebec, told me this year "that it is perfectly futile to try to have our rights recognized in legislation or to encourage the francophone community to change its ideas about us."

Many anglophones wonder why francophones know so little about their quiet revolution over the last twenty years. Why do so many nationalists refuse to recognize anglo bilingualism? Anglo-Quebecers should be invited to the Francophone Summit. Is their French really worse than that of people represented at the summit table, like Equatorial Guineans, Egyptians, Laotians, or the inhabitants of Santa Lucia?

After all, wasn't the promotion of French supposed to be the whole point in Quebec? Wouldn't it be reasonable to openly recognize the adaptation of anglophones, and even to encourage them to participate in reinforcing and developing the French language?

In fact, those nationalists who still haven't acknowledged the bilingualism of a large number of anglophones probably feel it doesn't concern them. It's a little plus, but nothing major. It doesn't serve any of their goals, especially since, in one of the surprise consequences of Law 101, it seems to offer economic advantages to the "blokes." Besides, the fact that anglophones are bilingual can't hide the fact that they are opposed to a policy of French unilingualism.

Of course, elective nationalism would say "bravo." But ethnic nationalism is not defending French in the abstract. It is defending "our" French, the priceless heritage of a particular, organic and perishable society: Quebec.

"The struggle for French has not been won: it is a daily struggle," writes Françoise Tétu de Labsade, for whom abbé Lionel Groulx was a man of generosity and articulateness [p. 106]. "Francophone Quebec amounts to only 2.4 % of the anglophone North American continent; 6.5 % of Quebecers are still incapable, in 1988, of speaking the language of the majority."

So 6.5 % is a threat? Well that means being 93.5 % "francophone" isn't good enough. What do we need? 96 %? 99 %? The question can never be answered, because by its very nature ethnic nationalism cultivates feelings of insecurity.

Some *souverainiste* radio hosts in Quebec (for example Gilles Proulx of Montreal station CJMS) try to give their listeners an inferiority complex, by calling them cowards, rejects, jerks, cretins and zeroes. This crude language reminds me of abbé Groulx and his followers. These hosts project such insults, by a sort of ideological ventriloquy, into the mouths of anglophones. They do this in order to spread the sad, false belief that the "real" Québécois are abandoned, alone and detested, even at home. Strange how these radio hosts will approve of their listener on one condition: that he raise his lowered head and adhere heart and soul to the *souverainiste* movement. According to this view, anglophones are guilty until proven innocent. Taken individually, each one can be an exception to the rule. But taken together, without knowing it, and certainly without wanting it, anglos are the enemy.

Someone is going to point out to me that this strategy is not typical of the *souverainiste* movement as a whole. Which is true. But who will condemn a strategy that produces such splendid results?

The conditions imposed by nationalism don't stop here. We are beginning to see the emergence of a new attitude: "conditional tolerance," a sort of mirror-image of the conditional identity mentioned earlier. Many *souverainistes* hold that Anglo-Quebecers are the world's best-treated minority. Yet anglos will be better treated after sovereignty is declared someday. Which seems to contradict the idea of the world's best-treated minority.

In an article written for the *Montreal Gazette*, Daniel Latouche goes even further. He figures that a sovereign Quebec would be obliged by the international community to improve the status of its English-speaking minority. According to Latouche, who used to be one of René Lévesque's closest aides, a province can restrict language rights while an independent nation-state must demonstrate an attitude of generosity. After sovereignty, the sole rallying cry of nationalism – strengthening French at the expense of English – will have become an embarrassment.

But the risk with this attitude of conditional tolerance, and with all *souverainiste* thinking, is that it is "pie-in-the-sky," it is based on reassuring "maybes" off in some hypothetical future. What guarantees do we have that this sweet cooing of doves will one day become reality? We could just as well imagine that the economic sacrifices imposed by sovereignty, as well as the departure of many anglophone and francophone families and companies, would serve as a pretext for spreading the myth of English "spite."

When it comes to the imagery of nationalist myths, there's probably no point sorting out truth from falsehood. Ethnic nationalism will always feed on the image of the "maudit bloke" ("the damned Englishman"), whether the latter is in Quebec, in a towering, faceless English Canada, or in a unilingual, arrogant America. *Disparaître* added the image of the damned immigrant, a foreigner who is unable to become part of society. The goal of nationalism is not so much to prove the validity of ideas in the abstract, as to bond together and control a large community of people sharing the same blood.

We can always hope that the elective nation prevails! But it's a long shot. For Anglo-Quebecers, the idea of "belonging" is still adrift somewhere in the distant future.

HUBERT BAUCH

Hubert Bauch is a senior feature writer for the Montreal Gazette. *He has covered national politics for the* Gazette *and the* Globe and Mail *for the past twenty years, reporting from Montreal, Ottawa, and Quebec City. The following is abridged from the* Gazette, *April 13, 1991.*

THAT WHOLE HUMILIATION THING

ANYONE WHO HAS BEEN FOLLOWING THE CONSTITUTION DEBATE WILL HAVE NOTICED that there has been quite a run on humiliation in Quebec lately, most notably among nationalist politicians whose path to power lies in convincing Quebecers that the Meech Lake accord was confederation's last gasp.

"Never as a founding people of this country will we forget the many humiliations that were inflicted on us within this great country that we thought was ours," intoned Louis Plamondon, the member of Parliament for Richelieu, when he fled the Quebec Conservative caucus for the more flagrantly sovereignist Bloc Québécois after the Meech contraption came undone.

"The humiliation of the conquest; the humiliation of the Patriotes; the humiliation of the Act of Union; the humiliation of Louis Riel; the humiliation of conscription; the humiliation of the War Measures Act; the humiliation of the 1982 patriation of the British North America Act; the humiliation of the Meech Lake Accord."

And that's just the short list.

Plamondon doesn't even get into Lord Durham, the expulsion of the Acadians, the Manitoba schools question, the Rocket Richard suspension and the fat English salesladies at Eaton's.

Renewed federalism is a recipe for a new humiliation of Quebec, former Parti-Québécois minister Claude Morin told the Bélanger-Campeau commission. Its advocates, echoed Sylvain Simard of the Mouvement National des Québécois, "are leading us toward another collective humiliation."

"Your analysis is rife with elements that are humiliating for the great majority of Quebecers," declared Jacques Proulx, head of the Union des Producteurs Agricoles, after Julius Grey, a Montreal lawyer with a prominent civil-rights record on both sides of the linguistic divide, delivered a brief.

Grey had suggested that Quebecers, on the whole, have evolved an enviable lifestyle within confederation and that civil liberties stand a better chance in a federation than a unitary state.

"We must never forget that in 1982, Quebec was left alone, isolated and humiliated," said Brian Mulroney time after time as he tried to ram, squeeze and wheedle his constitutional deal through the ratification process. He went so far as to say that it was "the worst injustice ever inflicted on Quebec."

Now the prime minister has always had a bent for rhetorical overkill and his bluster might be laughable were it not for the fact that a great many people in Quebec are prepared, even anxious, to swallow this kind of hyperbole whole hog.

The main reason support for sovereignty has been riding as high as 60 per cent in Quebec polls recently is that hard-line nationalists, amply abetted by the prime minister, have put across the notion that the Meech failure was a rejection of Quebec by the rest of Canada, that it was the ultimate humiliation.

"It's come to the point," said frustrated Liberal leader Jean Chrétien, "that we're talking about humiliation on every street corner."

All this talk of humiliation must surely confuse English Canadians who look at Quebecers as people who share fully in the riches and freedoms of this country.

A great many are convinced that because of its special nature, Quebec is getting more than its share. They note that a Quebecer has been prime minister of this country for 31 years of the past half-century and that the leading alternative to the incumbent is another Quebecer. They see that the French language has never been stronger in Quebec or French culture more vigorous. They see Quebec anglos huddled anxiously in their shrinking enclaves, whimpering like whipped puppies. And that the last unilingual English saleslady at Eaton's is a long-retired grandmother.

And they wonder what's to be humiliated about.

Yet the fact remains that despite sweeping, fundamental changes during the past 30 years, despite the enormous power and respect Quebec has accrued, the culture of humiliation persists almost unabated.

Listening to the nationalist rhetoric, one would think nothing has changed in the land of Quebec.

"The basis of Meech Lake was that finally the recognition of Quebec as a distinct society would appear in a federal document," said political scientist Louis Balthazar of Université Laval. "But even that minimum was too much. Canada didn't want to recognize our cultural specificity, that we're not a province like the others. Instead, the rest of the country wants to impose a uniform federalism across the country. That's the heart of what we regard as a humiliation."

For Balthazar and most nationalists, francophone Quebecers are more susceptible to feelings of humiliation because of their minority status in the great anglo sea of North America. It is hard to find a francophone in this country who has not suffered some humiliation, great or small, for being French-speaking.

For Louis Balthazar, it was the scornful attitude of the fat-cat anglo clientele at the hotel in Mont Tremblant where he worked as a student. For Louis Plamondon, it was coming to town to shop with his parents and running into the wall of English at the big stores on Sainte Catherine Street.

Add to that the nationalist interpretation of Quebec history as the succession of humiliations cited by Plamondon, which also echoes throughout Quebec literature, and you have a powerful emotional reflex that is readily triggered.

"The way we've analyzed our history, the way it's taught to us, shows to what point francophones have always been humiliated in this country," Plamondon said. "What the rest of Canada wants is for us to take up as little room as possible."

To the beleaguered federalists in Quebec, this nationalist harping on humiliation is a dangerously cynical tactic, a shameful exploitation of Québécois fears that their language and community are fated to disappear, despite the screaming current evidence to the contrary.

"They refuse to recognize the progress that's taken place," said André Ouellet, the federal Liberal representative on the Bélanger-Campeau commission. "When I point out that 250,000 students are enrolled in French-immersion programs outside Quebec, that's not considered important. Instead, they blow the image of a few anglo rednecks walking on the Quebec flag out of all proportion because they know it'll get people's backs up. They're playing the humiliation card very deliberately."

"It is a difficult tactic to counter," said Senator Jacques Hébert, a Pierre Trudeau soulmate, because ultra-nationalists are rigidly *doctrinaire*. "It's like trying to argue economics with a Marxist-Leninist or religion with a Jehovah's Witness. You can't talk sense to them."

For nationalists, Hébert said, humiliation is a powerful lever. "They use it to make people believe that they are regarded as inferior, that they have lost face, which is a difficult thing for most people to accept. For some, it's about the worst thing that can happen. When they go on about humiliation, the separatist propagandists have touched a raw nerve."

But that doesn't fully explain the ready audience the humiliation argument has found in Quebec since June 1990, even though the death of Meech has caused no perceptible change in Quebecers' daily lives, save in the volume and tone of the political rhetoric. Yet there is undeniably a widespread perception that Quebecers were humiliated by the Meech exercise, even though few people can actually rattle off the accord's famous five points.

"The nationalists have convinced people that Meech was a slap in the face, period," André Ouellet said. "That's all they want to know."

At times it looks as though Quebecers almost revel in their humiliation. The fervor with which it is invoked by nationalist politicians; the way the videotape of the flag-trampling incident was lovingly shown over and over again on the French networks; the outrage that greeted languages commissioner D'Iberville Fortier's assertion that English Quebecers had been humiliated by Quebec's language laws, as though francophones should have a monopoly on humiliation.

"I don't take it back," Fortier said in an interview. "But maybe I could have used another word, like diminished or reduced, and it wouldn't have produced the same reaction. Quebecers can't imagine themselves humiliating anyone because they see themselves as the humiliated ones."

If humiliation has a distinct meaning in Quebec, it is because it has become, over generations, an integral part of the Québécois survival instinct. Humiliation may have been hurtful to the Quebec francophone psyche, but it has also served as a bonding agent for the community.

In a way, said Pierre Anctil, head of McGill University's French-Canadian Studies Centre, the perception of humiliation is vital to forging French Canada's will to survive. "It produces a sense of belonging," he said. "It echoes a very profound popular perception that can't be easily erased."

And it will persist, Anctil predicted, as long as there is a francophone community in North America.

"Despite what's happened during the past 20 or 30 years, Quebecers will always act like a threatened and insecure minority, no matter what happens."

Though Louis Hémon was essentially a French tourist writing for a French audience in France, his landmark 1916 novel, *Maria Chapdelaine,* artfully and powerfully encapsulates the spiritual dynamic of the francophone survival instinct that persists to this day. It comes near the end of the book, when the spirit of Quebec speaks to Maria as she wrestles with the choice of leaving her homeland behind or committing herself to stay: "We came here 300 years ago, and we have stayed. . . . We traced the map of a new continent. . . . But around us strangers came, whom it pleased us to call barbarians; they took almost all the power and acquired almost all the money; yet in the land of Quebec, nothing has changed. Nothing will change because we are a witness. . . . We have clearly understood our duty: to persist, to maintain ourselves. . . . In several centuries perhaps the world will turn to us and say: These are people of a race that knows not how to die."

Julius Grey

A member of McGill University's Faculty of Law, Julius Grey was president of the task force on Canadian federalism which presented its brief to the Bélanger-Campeau Commission on Quebec's political and constitutional future. He has been involved in many prominent civil rights cases in Quebec. The following is abridged from the Gazette *(October 9, 1991).*

Propitiating Nationalism

Ever since Quebec nationalism became a burning issue in the late 1960s, there has been a strain of thought among English-speaking Canadians which detractors would call "bleeding heart" and proponents "moderate" or "understanding."

The thesis espoused by believers in this philosophy was essentially composed of two propositions. The first was that Quebec nationalists had many good points, especially with respect to their claim of historical injustice and to the danger their culture faced. The second was that one had to grant most of their wishes, even ones which were unpleasant, in effect to foster the sense of security which would make them good Canadians.

We must say from the outset that it is to Canada's credit that such ideas became current. A tolerant, generous society naturally looks to peaceful and friendly ways to resolve acrimonious disputes. Further, it is of the essence of tolerance to view with some empathy the position of all sides, and not only one's own. In the early years of the Quebec disputes, the desire to conciliate certainly became the dominant sentiment among thinking Canadians. It manifested itself in the election of Pierre Trudeau and in the relative ease with which most Canadians accepted official bilingualism, even though it gave bilingual Quebecers of both languages an edge in the competition for public-sector jobs.

However, 25 years later one cannot help noticing the bankruptcy of the conciliatory position. Although everything that the nationalists initially demanded has been achieved, they are still unhappy and still in the habit of presenting constantly escalating demands. While it was possible to argue both ways about alleged historical injustice in 1965, today such a claim makes no sense at all.

It is also plain that there is no danger of French ceasing to be used, and that French has never been as healthy in Quebec as it is now. Quebec nationalists deserve no more sympathy, and in the last few years have been getting less and less. What remains is to draw the conclusions from this decline of sympathy. The obvious conclusion is that propitiating nationalism does not work. This can be demonstrated both by historical examples and by reasoning.

History cannot point to us a simple example of a nationalism which mellowed through satiation. The Austro-Hungarian empire attempted to cater to many nationalist movements, especially in Bohemia. It only succeeded in whetting the appetite for independence. Yugoslavia tried to woo Croatia by adding to Croatian territory. The result was an ethnic mix for which everyone is now paying the price. Innoculation with mild nationalism does not prevent the virulent variety but rather serves as a prelude for it.

Common sense tells us why this must be so. Nationalism, when divorced from its flowery propaganda, serves no useful purpose. It does not solve the problems people face. After the initial elation of success, there sets in an inevitable sense of disappointment. The nationalists thus face the choice of pressing new demands to stimulate flagging spirits or losing their support. They inevitably choose the first course. Moreover, consciously or not, moderate and extreme nationalists constantly replay the good cop/bad cop routine. What the moderate obtains, the extremist immediately brands as insufficient. A few months later the "moderate" goes back to the bargaining table for more concessions "to ward off the extremist."

Quebec has been very adroit at this, and therefore one must be especially careful in negotiating with it. If appeasing nationalism is not possible, there are countless examples of firmness leading to popular disenchantment with nationalist leadership and to real reconciliation of groups. It is obvious in the Canadian context that the rest of the country must refuse outright the massive decentralization demanded by Quebec and must demonstrate to Quebec the ultimate incompatibility of nationalism, its restrictive laws and petty preoccupations, with our ideals of individual freedom and social justice.

This does not mean undoing Canadian bilingualism as many mean-spirited Canadians would like. Granting equality to the French language and protecting French minorities was not a concession to Quebec. It was the right thing to do. It still remains the right thing and the process must continue and expand. Further, both the French language and Quebec are among Canada's most precious assets. To lose them would be the first step towards melting into the United States and losing our social programs.

It is a sign of respect that we do not mince words and hide our true opinion from someone for whom we care. We must, at last, show respect for Quebec by calling a spade a spade. That this is high-risk therapy is undeniable. But the alternative is immediate separation or a gradual, progressive dissolution of Canada.

Gregory Baum

A professor of Religious Studies at McGill University, Gregory Baum moved to Montreal in 1986 after teaching for many years at St. Michael's College at the University of Toronto. A widely respected theologian, he participated in the Vatican II and has written numerous books and articles on theology and sociology. He is now the editor of The Ecumenist. *The following is an excerpt from* The Church in Quebec, *published by Novalis (1991).*

Ethical Reflections on the Language Debate

The self-affirmation of French Quebecers in the Quiet Revolution (beginning in 1960) has created a new Quebec where the French-speaking majority plays the dominant role. This development led to several language bills, culminating in the Parti Québécois government's 1977 Law 101 which made French the public language and the working language of the province. English-speaking Quebecers retained their "historical rights" to English language institutions: schools, universities, hospitals and social service agencies can all operate in English. But public signs were to be in French only. Companies with more than fifty employees were obliged to carry on their work in French.

French Quebecers looked upon Law 101 as the charter of the French language that would give them a certain security against the assimilating power of the English language in North America. Law 101 was the public signal to immigrants and newcomers that their participation in Quebec society would be in French. Many Quebecers regarded Law 101 as a legal charter beyond political partisanship.

English-speaking Quebecers were unhappy with Law 101. Their main complaint was that public signs, including all commercial signs, were to be in French only. Some believed that this rule violated their human rights, in particular their freedom of expression. In the 1985 election campaign Robert Bourassa promised English-speaking Quebecers that his Liberal Party, once in power, would permit bilingual signs. Yet when he became premier, he hesitated. Realizing the enormous popularity of Law 101, he refused to touch the public sign rule.

Certain anglophone Montrealers took the matter to the courts. On December 5, 1988 the Supreme Court of Canada decided that it was indeed the task of the Quebec government to promote and protect the French language, but that the means employed in this endeavour had to conform to the charter of rights. The Court decided that the rule demanding commercial signs in French only violated people's freedom of expression.

The Bourassa government was in a bind. The great majority of Quebecers, including many Liberal members in the National Assembly, supported Law 101 as a charter that should not be touched, while the English-speaking population demanded that justice be done as defined by the Supreme Court. Mr. Bourassa sought a compromise solution. He introduced a new law, Bill 178, that endorsed most of the articles of Law 101 except the sign rule. Bill 178 allowed bilingual commercial signs inside the stores, but continued the requirement for unilingual signs outside. To make Bill 178 legal he invoked the notwithstanding clause of the Canadian Constitution (which Quebec has not yet signed) to limit the application of the Supreme Court's decision. Newspaper coverage gave the impression that the majority of francophones and the majority of anglophones were unhappy with Bill 178.

Human rights

What is sometimes overlooked is that the human rights tradition has its own complexity. There are personal rights that guarantee civil liberties: the freedoms of expression, of religion, of peaceful assembly and of organization. These rights were fought for, from the seventeenth century forward, against the *ancien régime*, the aristocratic rule that wanted to protect law and order by suppressing people's freedom to speak and act in public.

Secondly, there are collective rights that entitle peoples to cultural and political self-determination. These rights were claimed by peoples under imperial rule, for instance in the nineteenth century by the Irish under the British Crown and the Polish under the Tsarist Empire. In the twentieth century peoples struggling against political and economic colonial domination have demanded them. Peoples have the right to give themselves governments that protect and promote their values and their culture and the common good. These rights ratified by the United Nations have served as a basis for founding the state of Israel and many other states in Asia and Africa. These rights are not enshrined in a book of law, but they justify in universally-accepted ethical terms political struggles for self-determination and government actions to protect and promote the common good.

Thirdly, there are solidarity rights upholding the just claims of the weak against the power of the strong. These rights include, for instance, the right to eat, the right to shelter, the right to work and the right to form labour organizations.

Human rights, because of their complex structure, are often competing with one another. The Quebec language debate emerges from a conflict between collective rights and personal rights. French Quebecers regard Law 101 as an expression of their collective human right to define their own cultural and social identity, but many anglophones and other communtiies that speak English in public believe that Law 101 deprives them of certain personal human rights. Which human right has the priority here? Lawyers and courts tend to look upon this and similar questions from a purely legal perspective. They try to resolve such questions in terms of the existing legislation. But human rights are first of all an ethical reality; they are moral claims. Questions posed by competing human rights therefore call for ethical reflection.

Human rights are not absolutes. They are always historically situated. Human rights, moreover, remain ambiguous. Collective rights have been invoked by governments to suppress civil liberties. In the name of serving the public good or defending national security, governments have introduced repressive legislation. In Canada, for example, the War Measures Act allowed the government during World War II to intern and dispossess without trial Canadian citizens of Japanese origin. Another example is pre-Vatican II Catholic social teaching, which held that governments of Catholic countries had the moral right to protect the common good, including the established religion, by suppressing the religious freedom of Protestant minorities. In Quebec during the 1950s, this principle was invoked by the Maurice Duplessis government against the Jehovah's Witnesses.

It is also true that personal human rights or civil liberties are ambiguous. They can become part of a political strategy to undermine existing structures of solidarity and promote the individualistic free-enterprise mentality. Emphasis on civil liberties easily creates the illusion that the members of society are all equal and thus disguises the structures of economic inequality. On the basis of these civil rights, individual workers can take a labour union to court for giving financial support to the New Democratic Party without the approval of every member or even for violating the freedom of individual workers by imposing a closed-shop rule. Commercial companies can take the government to court for violating freedom of expression when it forbids advertising directed at children under thirteen or when it prohibits the advertising of cigarettes.

What follows from this is that from an ethical point of view the application of human rights, whether collective or personal, is never something unconditional: it always demands an ethical, rational justification. Similarly, conflicts between competing sets of rights must be resolved by ethical, rational arguments.

Is Quebec a nation?

In the case of the Quebec language debate we have to make certain historical judgements that have far-reaching ethical implications. The first question is: are Quebecers a people? Or are they simply French-speaking Canadians, an important minority in the country? We are often confronted with such historical questions. Are the Palestinians a people? Or are they simply groups of Arabs located in the area formerly called Palestine? The answers to such questions have ethical consequences. A people has the human right to self-determination; it is entitled to define its own cultural and political identity. According to the 1966 International Covenant on Civil and Political Rights of the United Nations, "All peoples have the right to self-determination: by virtue of this right they freely determine their political status and freely pursue their economic, social and cultural development."

Another way of posing the question about Quebec is to ask whether Canada is a nation state, a bi-national state, or a multi-national state? When we answer this question we must be careful not to forget the Native peoples who have lived here from time immemorial. It is not unfair to say that until recently, most English-speaking Canadians regarded Canada as a nation state – a state including a single nation – and considered French-Canadians an important and honoured ethnic minority, one of the founding groups of this country. Quebec was considered simply as one of the ten provinces.

It was only in the sixties, in response to the noise of the Quiet Revolution, that the federal political parties, especially the Progessive Conservatives and the NDP, began to recognize the peoplehood of French Canadians and to advocate a special status for Quebec within Confederation.

Are there norms that specify with some precision what peoplehood means? Usually peoplehood is defined with reference to a set of objective and subjective factors. The objective factors include a definable territory, common language, common culture, common history and the existence of political and economic institutions that bind people together and render them capable of acting in concert. The subjective factor is the collective will to constitute a people. This political will is usually generated by special historical experiences. Thus the Jews began to think of themselves as a nation in the political sense mainly as a response to the persecutions and later the genocide inflicted on them. The Palestinians developed a strong sense of peoplehood as a response to the powers that made them second-class citizens in their own land.

If this is a valid definition, it is difficult to deny that Quebecers constitute a people. Both the objective and subjective factors seem to be present. French Quebecers think of themselves as a people, even when they are convinced federalists and oppose the independence movement.

This conclusion has been challenged by an important argument. Pierre Elliot Trudeau has defended the view that French Canadians spread over the whole of Canada, not Quebecers, constitute a people. If this were true, then peoplehood would have a much weaker meaning. This sort of peoplehood would not ground the right to self-determination since French Canadians hold no common territory and have no political and economic institutions that enable them to act collectively.

An answer to this argument is that historical forces have so weakened the country-wide presence of French Canadians that there remains only one core territory, Quebec, where French Canadians constitute the majority and where the government protects the language and promotes the cultural institutions, such as colleges, universities, research institutes and publishing houses, that are indispensable for a modern, developed society.

A colonized people

The next historical question we need to examine is more controversial. The answer has important ethical implications. Is the self-empowerment of Quebecers in the Quiet Revolution part of a longer struggle against colonial subjugation starting with the British conquest? Were Quebecers an oppressed people? In other words, is the new Quebec with its dominant French presence in public life, industry, commerce and culture – including Bills 101 and 178 – the righting of a previous wrong? Is it, in part at least, redress of a colonial situation? Was the Quiet Revolution the outcome of a collective struggle against economic, cultural and linguistic hegemony exercised by the anglophone elite in the province?

Most French Quebecers believe that this is so. In particular, members of the older generation who remember inherited patterns of social inequality are keenly aware of the colonization inflicted upon their people in the past. They are able to muster strong, rational arguments drawn from Quebec history.

If this historical judgement is correct, then Bills 101 and 178 are a form of redress resembling other laws of affirmative action that seek to correct age-old structures of discrimination against women or blacks, for example. These regulations may inflict a certain injustice on individuals. The debates about affirmative action in Canada and the United States have made us aware that even justified and well intended rules for hiring staff or accepting members diminish the personal rights of some individuals, as do all quota systems. For the sake of overcoming massive historical injustice society is willing to impose certain minor injustices upon a limited number of people.

Redress of historical wrongs always inflicts some suffering on the innocent. The political and cultural shift produced by the overcoming of colonial conditions always causes some damage to ordinary people, workers and farmers, who through their ethnic or linguistic heritage were associated with the once-powerful elite.

There is another, quite different, interpretation of French-English relations in Canada. I call this the federalist argument. In this case it is claimed that the effects of the British conquest and the subjugation of French Canadians have been overcome through the social contract of the 1867 Confederation. Canada, the argument proceeds, has become a dominion of equals. Quebecers are seen as a free people because the British North America Act provided adequate protection for their language and culture. From this point of view, it no longer makes sense to speak of redress or righting previous wrongs.

The people espousing the federalist argument readily admit that, in Manitoba and other provinces, the French educational system has been dismantled despite the guarantees in the British North America Act. They regret at those historic moments the population of English Canada did not protest these political decisions. Yet the wrongs of the past, proponents argue, cannot be corrected through wrongs committed in the present by the injured party. They propose, moreover, that the exclusion of French from the economic elite in Quebec happened mostly because French Quebecers – influenced by their leaders, especially the clergy – defined their culture in spiritual, anti-modern terms. Thus the schools of Quebec offered classical education for the elite and only rudimentary instruction for all other people. Absence of worldly ambition and lack of scientific or technical training prevented French Quebecers from climbing the social ladder during the industrialization of their society. Since the modernization brought by the Quiet Revolution has overcome this educational handicap, Quebecers have become upwardly mobile and joined the economic elite.

Seen from this perspective, it appears misguided to interpret the Quiet Revolution as part of a long anti-colonial struggle. It also seems unacceptable to use redress as an appropriate category to understand the present situation.

There are important elements of truth in the federalist argument. Confederation did create legal guarantees for the survival of the French-Canadian people and their culture. Despite the limited nature of these guarantees and occasional violations, French Canadians in the province of Quebec enjoyed their own political and cultural institutions. They were not a disenfranchised people like the Mexican Americans, living in the territories annexed by the United States in 1848, who received no legal recognition and enjoyed no Spanish-language institutions of their own. It is also quite true that the Catholic church defined the collective identity of French Canadians in opposition to the Protestant and secular culture of North America and hence promoted spiritual ideals and cultural institutions that would prevent assimilation.

Still in my opinion the federalist argument does not stand up. It seems to me impossible to render an account of the patterns of exclusion imposed on French Canadians without recognizing the structures of colonization operative in their society.

Anglophone malaise

Redress of colonial subjugation is ethical, even if it causes some suffering to innocent people. People of modest means who are ethnically or linguistically associated with the colonial elite often suffer, though personally innocent, because they lose their sense of being at home where they live. They feel that the formerly colonized community, now liberated, accuses them of identification with the oppressor. They sometimes feel ill at ease.

The Anglo elite which exercised great power in Quebec was greatly puzzled by the Quiet Revolution. The families which set the tone in the past were pained by the new development challenging their hegemony. Yet it would be wrong to harshly judge the distinguished Westmount clique. These persons were heirs of a division of power in Quebec which they took for granted and did not question. The interrelation between unjust structures and personal responsibility is a complex ethical issue. Because the dominant culture tends to make the structures of domination invisible, it is very difficult to blame individuals who have inherited their elevated status.

Quite different is the situation of ordinary anglophone Quebecers, often working people, people without power, whose families had lived there for generations. They had felt part of Quebec society. Even though they lived at a great distance from the powerful elite and often suffered economic exploitation, the Quiet Revolution made them feel as never before that they were outsiders. They did not feel the excitement of the cultural, intellectual and artistic explosion in Quebec. The ordinary English Quebecers were often displeased by the new situation.

The shock made some English-speaking people self-critical. This happened in a variety of social contexts. Remarkable is the Black Rock Manifesto, issued by a group of radical workers, which acknowledges that they had occupied the more important positions in the work force because they were English-speaking. They had been the foremen, got the office jobs, stuck together and refused to extend their solidarity to French-Canadian workers.

In resounding prose the Manifesto analyses the previously unacknowledged complicity of the anglophone working class. At the same time the Manifesto also protests that now, after the Quiet Revolution, the class-conscious, francophone workers, organized in powerful unions, remain indifferent to the English-speaking members of their own class.

A scientific analysis of the Quebec labour force verifies the description presented in the Manifesto. Statistically, anglophone workers and employees had held the better jobs in the province of Quebec. Again, it would be quite unjust to accuse these workers of personal wrong doing. It is only at special historical moments when people are able to see through the system where they belong and recognize the structures of subordination from which they derive some benefits.

Irish Catholics were deeply hurt by the Quebec social system. As Catholics they had belonged at the margin of English Quebec and as anglophones they were treated as marginal in the Quebec Catholic church. Often they experienced the transformation of Quebec society as an added injustice.

The Jewish community felt threatened by the Quiet Revolution. The European nationalist movements against the domination of the Austro-Hungarian and the Tsarist Empires had always generated anti-semitism and feelings against outsiders. In Germany the liberation struggle against the conquest of Napoleon had produced a nationalist tradition, accompanied by anti-semitism, that would eventually come to flower under German imperialism. In Quebec itself certain priests had introduced anti-semitic motifs to strengthen the people's will to survive as a distinct cultural society. This is why the Jewish community, traditionally anglophone, felt uncomfortable with French-Canadian nationalism. By contrast the 20,000 French-speaking Jews who have arrived from France and North Africa since the Quiet Revolution have felt more at home in a Quebec committed to becoming a French-speaking society.

Immigrant families from Italy, Greece, Portugal, Poland and many other countries often felt frustrated. They were led to believe that Canada was basically an English-speaking country and that French was spoken only by a minority. This was the image at one time created at the overseas consulates. These men and women who had learned one language were now expected to learn another.

A variety of groups, a variety of malaise. What is the appropriate response to these disappointments? A period of mourning over the loss of one's cultural world seems quite acceptable, maybe even necessary. Yet if the ethical reasoning presented here is correct, it seems unacceptable to resent in principle the Quiet Revolution and the self-affirmation of the

French-Canadian majority. If there is room for anger, it must be directed not at French Canadians, but at the colonizing structures that humiliated them in the past and in which ordinary anglophone Quebecers were unknowingly and innocently caught.

Many English-speaking Quebecers have got used to the new situation. They feel at home in Quebec, they speak French, and they develop their English-speaking identity in their own cultural institutions.

Asymmetrical Canada

Quite apart from the answer to the question whether Quebecers were an oppressed people, there is no doubt whatsoever that the relation between French and English-speaking Canadians (whether of British or ethnic origin) is not a symmetrical one. French is threatened in North America and English is not. It is as simple as that. North America has defined itself as an English-speaking continent. This self-definition has produced a cultural and political trend that is still operative today. In the United States there is new "English only" legislation directed against Mexican Americans and other Hispanics. Quite apart from this, since the second world war English has become recognized as the world medium of communication. This is partly because of the enormous impact of American technological culture on all continents. That Asia recognizes English as the *lingua franca* is a heritage of the British empire. English has become the world language of science, technology, production and commerce. This is true to an increasing degree even in Europe. For the first time in world history a single language has acquired an almost universal status.

For this and other reasons, Canada is an asymmetrical political union. Thus the situation of the English-speaking minority in Quebec is quite different from the francophone minorities in other provinces. In Quebec, Anglo-Canadians were a thriving, wealthy community (although there was also a disadvantaged working class). The Anglo community built its own institutions, schools, universities, hospitals, social agencies, theatres, museums and publishing houses. A full cultural life was lived and is still being lived in English. Even the ardent nationalists of the Parti Québécois have always recognized the historical rights of the English-speaking community to its own institutions. Even as French became the language of work and of public signs, a full cultural life in English is a continuing reality in Montreal.

By contrast, the francophone minorities in the other provinces belonged to the more modest sectors of society. They could not build their own social and cultural institutions. For their survival they largely depended on the provincial governments. French Canadians were lucky if they got their own schools. But they lacked the set of institutions required for the expression of a full cultural life. If they became lawyers, doctors, scientists, engineers or successful business people in their own province, they did this, by and large, not in their own language, but in English.

This lack of symmetry is etched deeply into Canadian history. Ethical reflection on the language debate must take this into account. I will mention another example of this lack of symmetry. The immigrants who arrived and still arrive in this country tend to integrate with English-speaking Canada. This is a rational thing to do on this North American continent. In the past the newcomers who arrived in Quebec sent their children to the anglophone schools. In fact if the children were not Catholic, they were obliged to go to anglophone schools. When over the last two decades Quebecers realized that the influx of immigrants was starting to reduce their majority status in the province, they introduced legislation that all newcomers to Quebec must send their children to francophone schools. Since learning the dominant North American language gives the newcomers greater economic mobility and since they sometimes have relatives in other North American cities, they would often prefer to integrate with anglophone Canadian society. It is especially hard for them if they arrive from former British colonies and hence speak English fluently. There is the possibility of mutual resentment, the newcomers against those who force their children to learn French, and Quebecers against those who – quite innocently – become Lord Durham's agents of assimilation into English-speaking Canada.

The asymmetry of Canada is such that immigrants present no threat whatsoever to the English language, while they do offer a challenge to French Quebecers. Of course, French Quebec has its own lively multiculturalism among the communities that come from French-speaking countries or former French colonies and mandates, such as Haitians, Lebanese, North Africans, Syrians and Vietnamese. Moreover, an evergrowing number of immigrants belonging to other ethnic communities have come to identify themselves with French Quebec. Still, the lack of symmetry that is my subject creates a special challenge for Quebec society.

Competing claims

I now return to the competing claims of collective and personal rights. Quebecers regarded their collective right of cultural self-determination as the ethical foundation for their language charter, Law 101. Many English-speaking Quebecers, supported by the Supreme Court of Canada, judged Law 101 to be injurious to their personal rights, in particular to their freedom of expression. But I am examining the conflict from an ethical, not a legal point of view. Since Quebecers are a people they are indeed ethically entitled to collective self-determination.

What conditions make regulations protecting collective rights at the expense of personal liberties ethically acceptable? I will argue that such regulations are ethically justified 1) if there are good and urgent reasons for them and 2) when the imposed limitations are minimal, causing only inconveniences, or when they place more considerable burdens on a very limited number of people.

For instance, the War Measures Act made the government's action during the Second World War to intern and dispossess Japanese Canadians legal, but the action was unethical. Why? It was unethical because no good and urgent reason was convincingly presented and because the burden inflicted on these Canadian citizens was massive. On the other hand, I regard as ethical the decision of the Supreme Court in 1990 to defend the rule demanding forced retirement at the age of sixty-five, even though this violates personal rights protected by the Charter. According to the Supreme Court, the collective right of society to promote the public good, in this case the rejuvenation of institutions, has here precedence over the personal rights of a limited number of people even though for some the burden may be considerable. The seat belt legislation and the RIDE program in Ontario that limit personal freedom in the name of the public good are also ethical. There are good and urgent reasons for them, and here the personal burden is minimal. I would argue the same for the legislation in English Canada that radio and television programs must have a certain percentage of Canadian content. If someone took this legislation to the Supreme Court for violating freedom of expression, the Supreme Court might possibly decide that it was unconstitutional. Still, I regard it as ethically sound because of the good and urgent reasons in its favour and because of the minimal harm done to individuals. If, on the other hand, certain parents, for religious reasons, refuse to have their children inoculated, the Supreme Court of Canada might well decide that their right of refusal is guaranteed in the Constitution. I would argue on ethical grounds, following the principles set out here, that for the sake of the public good the government should invoke the "notwithstanding clause" and override the Court's decision.

Law 101

That there are good and urgent reasons for legal measures to protect French language and culture cannot be in doubt. Anglo-American technological culture is an omnipresent challenge. But what about public signs in French only? French Quebecers argue that unless the province's public face, especially in Montreal, is visibly and unmistakably French, the English-speaking communities and recent arrivals will think of Quebec as a bilingual society. It is true that many anglophones, especially the supporters of the Equality Party, oppose the idea of a French-speaking Quebec, even though the historic rights of their own institutions are recognized and protected. What these citizens want is a bilingual Quebec. In my own judgement, the above-mentioned asymmetry in Canadian society is such that bilingualism in Quebec would encourage immigrants to seek integration with the anglophone community and thus weaken the French majority: bilingualism in Quebec would open the door in other ways to the gradual take-over by the powerful, culturally dominant, omnipresent North American language.

More difficult from an ethical point of view is the second question whether the limitations imposed by Law 101 on anglophones and "allophones" are minimal. Do public signs in French cause only certain inconveniences? Or is the sign legislation insulting?

The Supreme Court looked upon the question simply from the legal point of view. Freedom of expression, a fundamental human right, is here understood as extending to commercial signs. The first purpose of freedom of expression was of course to make democracy possible, that is to allow public disagreement in the sphere of religion, ethics and politics. The extension of this freedom to commercial signs is recent. Thus a Canadian Court rejected the plea that advertising directed at children under thirteen be prohibited. I regretted this decision even though it was made in the name of freedom of expression. How will the courts rule when the producers of spiritous liquors plead before them that the law forbidding them to advertise is unconstitutional? Whatever the courts decide, it would seem, from an ethical point of view, that the freedom to communicate on commercial signs is not an essential part of the freedom of expression.

More serious is the argument given by some English-speaking Quebecers that the sign legislation of Law 101 and the present Bill 178 is insulting. This is an ethical argument. People have the right to be respected. Their human dignity demands recognition. Why do many anglophones regard the sign legislation as insulting? I do not suggest that the reason is a resentment-laden oversensitivity caused by the loss of their position of privilege. I presume good faith on all sides of the argument.

The British tradition and Anglo North American practice have always emphasized personal human rights while the continental European traditions and French Canadians had a much stronger sense of people's collective rights. Behind these traditions are different perceptions of the state: on the one hand, the liberal view that the role of the state is confined to protecting the rights of property and civil liberties, and, on the other, the more traditional view that the role of the state includes the promotion of culture and the common good. These different political philosophies have been generated by different historical experiences. It is perhaps the keen sense of civil liberties mediated by the British-North American tradition that makes some Anglo Quebecers feel that the present sign legislation is offensive.

At the same time, the preoccupation with personal rights can become obsessive. Some North Americans actually believe that medicare and interventionist economic policies violate the freedom of individuals. Occasionally angry citizens even argue that the seat belt legislation is fascist, at odds with the democratic freedoms.

There may be another reason why some English-speaking Quebecers find the language legislation insulting. An inconvenience is offensive when we detect behind it a lack of respect. We find a gesture insulting when we interpret it as part of an effort to diminish us. Some English-speaking Quebecers find the sign legislation insulting because they see it as an attempt by French Quebecers to teach them a lesson and to get even with them, innocent though they be, for humiliations inflicted in the past.

Anglophone Quebecers who admire the Quiet Revolution and sympathize with Quebec's historical project do not find the sign legislation insulting, even when it is occasionally inconvenient. These anglophones are confident that if they speak French and recognize French as the public language, they can live a creative cultural life in English in their own community.

The more serious issue that worries many progressive Quebecers, francophone and anglophone, is the growing indifference of society to the so-called solidarity rights: the rights of workers and the powerless to organize and demand that their just claims be recognized by the powerful. The debate about the conflict between personal and collective rights remains defective if it does not include concern for economic injustice.

What has happened in Quebec during the last ten years is the arrival of the world-wide phenomenon: the new, monetarist orientation of capitalism, characterized by the widening gap between rich and poor, the increase of unemployment and job insecurity, the decline of industrial employment, the shift to low-paying, low-skill jobs in the service sector, the feminization of poverty, the housing shortage, the roaming of the destitute in the streets and the hopelessness of ever-growing crowds of young people.

In Quebec as in other parts of the world, the left – the traditional defender of solidarity rights – has been decimated. The Parti Québécois has dropped its social democratic agenda. The radical parties and movements of the past have all disappeared. Many of the formerly left-wing intellectuals at the universities have turned to a post-modern interpretation of society, which looks upon social movements for structural change as useless and illusory. The Quebec newspapers have largely abandoned their role as social critics which they played so well in the past.

The surviving left in Quebec, though nationalist, is increasingly suspicious of the nationalism advocated by the two leading political parties and prominent members of the business community. What will happen to the workers, the unemployed and people on welfare in the new Quebec? The left is worried whenever nationalist goals are not joined to the socialist aim of economic justice.

Clifford Lincoln

The following excerpt is from Clifford Lincoln's resignation speech in the Quebec National Assembly on December 20, 1988. A popular Environment minister in the Liberal government, Lincoln's speech was in response to his own party's decision to re-enact the prohibition on English outdoor commercial signs and advertising following the Supreme Court judgement which ruled against such provisions in Law 101.

Rights Are Rights Are Rights

In my belief, rights are rights are rights. There is no such thing as inside rights and outside rights. No such thing as rights for the tall and rights for the short. No such thing as rights for the front and rights for the back, or rights for the East and rights for the West. Rights are rights and always will be rights. There are no partial rights. Rights are fundamental rights. Rights are links in a chain of fundamental values that bind all individuals in a society that wants to be equitable, and just, and fair. Rights are bridges that unite people in a society through a set of fundamental values, and the minute you deny those rights, you withdraw that bridge, and create a gap between members of that society by denying those fundamental rights that bind them together.

Rights are that delicate balance that equates the chances of people in a society, so that there is an equation between the rich and the poor, between the powerful and the weak, between the majorities and the minorities, between the State and the individual. Whoever tampers with a very delicate machinery of equality and justice in society, which is expressed through rights, sets in motion a chain of events which someone more audacious may tamper with even more. That chain of events could be disastrous for a society whose beliefs are based on a sense of equity and justice for all.

All of us are human beings first. We are not francophone, anglophone, rich, poor, weak and strong, first, we are human beings with rights.

Gretta Chambers

Chancellor of McGill University, Gretta Chambers is the first woman to hold the post. A well-known writer and broadcaster in Montreal, she was the chair of the 1991-92 Task Force on English Education set up by the Ministry of Education to study, among other things, the decline of the English school population in Quebec and its impact on English schooling. She is a member of the board of numerous organizations including the McCord Museum and the McGill Children's Hospital Research Institute. The following is excerpted from two articles which appeared in the Gazette *(December 18, 1991 & January 2, 1992).*

Collective Rights Would Benefit Quebec Anglos

In the constitutional reform of 1982, as in the building of Confederation, minority rights were at the heart of the negotiations. There was consensus that unfettered majority rule can always endanger the rights of minorities. That is why the idea of constitutional rights was developed.

Evidence of a majority's tyranny toward minorities is to be found today in the policies of the Reform Party, Confederation of Regions (CoR) and the Bloc Québécois, and in legislation like Quebec's Bill 178. The most notable historical minorities in Canada are native people, English-speaking Quebecers and French-speaking Canadians in the rest of the country. Which of these groups, based on their experience, would agree to a system of straight majority rule?

The issue of minority rights has lost ground in the years since the Charter of Rights took effect. Individual rights are now seen as providing protection against the tyranny of the majority. Today's national debate is more about the rights of competing majorities than about protecting minorities. Quebec and native leaders present themselves as representing their own majorities. Minority rights within these self-defined majorities have been dropped from the debate, their protection supposedly assured by the Charter.

Representatives of francophone communities outside Quebec went before the federal national-unity committee to plead for more collective representation, not only to ensure that their communities survive but to allow them to grow and flourish. Acadians and Franco-Ontarians both asked that francophones outside Quebec be given seats in the proposed new Senate, saying Quebec cannot represent them.

Interestingly, the commissioner who objected to this view was an English-speaking Quebecer. NDP MP Phil Edmonston was "somewhat offended" and did not understand why Quebecers could not represent Acadians. That is the old individual-rights syndrome. What Acadians want to protect and see flourish is their community in New Brunswick. For that they need collective rights, power as a group. If anyone should understand this, it is an English-speaking Quebecer.

French Quebec has not championed francophone minorities across Canada in the past. It is not likely to any time soon. As for English Quebec, it carries little weight in the country these days. Many English-speaking Quebecers have lost sight of the "collective" dimension of their aspirations for their community. It is often said in anglophone circles that there is no such thing as "collective" rights.

French Quebec talks a lot about collective rights superseding individual rights in matters perceived as vitally important to the majority community. To many anglophones, this sounds like rationalizing the tyranny of the majority. Only very late in the day are they beginning to grasp the idea that they, too, need to acquire collective community rights and to preserve those they already have.

Meanwhile, uncertainty continues to have a particularly schizophrenic effect on English-speaking Quebecers. When their political or linguistic interests are not being threatened, their sympathies tend to lie with the Quebec side of their dual personality. The more threatened they feel, the more Canadian they become. But the double discourse that has always been their trademark sounds like double-speak in today's climate of factionalism and political distrust. They are in danger of painting themselves right out of the picture.

To back up its claims of being an integral part of Quebec society, the English-speaking community is appealing to the resolve of "English" Canada. But the plight of English Quebec has never been a preoccupation of English Canada. The federal government and the other provinces will never refuse to make what they see as a good deal with Quebec just because anglophone Quebecers do not feel it gives their community sufficient protection.

The tendency of anglophones to fight all and any manifestations of Quebec nationalism puts them in a political class apart and reduces their ability to belong. Much of French Quebec sees the English-speaking community simply as an adjunct of English Canada rather than a part of its own reality. English Quebecers can repeat ad nauseam that they support the primacy of the French language in Quebec; that does not sound convincing when they say in the same breath that all measures taken by Quebec to preserve its language and culture are unnecessary.

The fact is that individual rights are not preventing Canada's linguistic minorities from being written out of these constitutional negotiations. It is the native peoples who have understood the power of the collective idea and used it to promote their status within Canada. They are now a principal player in the constitutional stakes. Their obstructionist tactics are only one aspect of their rising political profile. They have found leadership and a powerful spokesman in Ovide Mercredi, grand chief of the First Nations.

At what will undoubtedly go down as a "famous occasion," Mercredi and Pierre Trudeau crossed swords over "collective" versus "individual" rights at a dinner-discussion sponsored by the magazine *Cité libre*. Mercredi called for the entrenchment of collective rights in the constitution to protect native communities from the abusive power of the country's ruling elites. He claimed that "the assumption we are all equal as individuals" allowed for the domination of native peoples.

In answer, Trudeau reiterated his long-held view that pitting a large community against a smaller one would always result in total victory for the larger, and that individual rights are the only true protection against the tyranny of the majority. Natives, responded Mercredi, would never find justice by marching together as individuals. Aboriginals were driven by the same force as Quebec, the need to protect their collective difference.

If that is true, it also applies, for the same reasons, to English Quebec and the francophone communities across the country. The fathers of confederation knew this. Alexander Tilloch Galt, where are you when we need you?

Ron Burnett

Ron Burnett was the founder and editor-in-chief of Ciné-Tracts *from 1976 to 1983. He recently published* Explorations in Film Theory *with Indiana University Press, and his writing has appeared in numerous journals in Canada and internationally. He is currently the director of the graduate program in Communications at McGill University.*

"The Frontiers of Our Dreams are No Longer the Same"*

*(From *Refus Global* – quoted by Hubert Aquin in his essay entitled, *Literature and Alienation*)

It was an overcast day in 1977 when the great writer and Quebec nationalist, Hubert Aquin, committed suicide. I felt the pain of Aquin's death very deeply having followed his career and his writing for many years. While there was a profoundly personal side to Aquin's death, it was also a metaphoric and symbolic gesture, summarized by one of his most famous statements: "I am the broken symbol of revolution in Quebec, a reflection of its chaos and its suicidal tendencies."[1]

On the 19th of October, 1976, a few weeks before the Parti Québécois election victory, Andrée Yanacopoulo, Aquin's wife, wrote him a letter in which she implored him to change his mind about suicide.

> In Quebec we don't live a normal life like people do elsewhere. In more "stable" countries like France, England, or the United States each individual can, in an untroubled way, feel at home . . . but not here, not in Quebec. For many Québécois you represent the ideals of independence, the invincibility of a nationalist spirit. This only increases the meaning of your work as a writer. Your writing is, at one and the same time, authentically Québécois and universal.
>
> It is an act of escapism to commit suicide. It is an admission of failure. You have a responsibility to the Quebec community. If you commit suicide you will be killing a little bit of Quebec. You will be cutting off its future.[2]

She went on to say that his suicide would reinforce defeatist attitudes in Quebec which he himself had openly critiqued. She did not want to bring up their son in a country which wasn't capable of instilling national pride in its citizens. She equated his projected suicide (about which they had argued for many years) with the destruction of a collective identity still in formation.

There is a seductive romanticism to Yanacopoulo's equation of Aquin and Quebec. Aquin wanted total change. He wanted to rebuild Quebec society from the bottom up and this led him to analyze both the strengths and weaknesses of his own culture. He was alternately idealistic and pragmatic. His dilemma was that he understood the contradictions of his political position. In a Quebec which had become secularized, he was skeptical about any polemic influenced by religious thought, and this distanced him sometimes from the rhetoric which he used.

Paradoxically, with his suicide he offered himself to the Quebec people as the site of a symbolic *death*. But no one individual can ever be the nation, just as the nation can never be understood or experienced through one person. While it may be desirable to conceive of a national revolution through the eyes of one individual, it is a rather different thing to transform a community of six million people.

Aquin experienced the gap between his vision and the situation in Quebec in a very personal way. He grew frustrated with the slowness of change, with the time it takes for any community to alter its norms and values. His death was premature and a profound loss but its ambiguity may be at the heart of the dilemma which many people face in Quebec right now. The simple terms within which the national identity is presently being laid out means that any considerations about the future have to be deferred. It will suffice, the modern nationalist argument goes, to regain what has been lost, to live in our own country.

Reality begins to collapse into myth when the underlying argument in favour of a nation-state is seen as unproblematic or when the traditions which are supposed to unite an ethnic group are accepted as natural, inevitable. The notion of community in this instance pivots on assumptions of spontaneity and solidarity. Yet this is an historical period during which the very concept of the nation is undergoing complete change, when the ideals of the market economy have triumphed over all other ideologies, when Quebecers voted for a trans-national system of free trade. The result is that no border is secure and no identity will remain untouched.

Since 1759 Quebec has defended itself against its colonial heritage and that defense has centred on conservative notions of homeland and ethnic purity. Though Quebec long ago arose from the ashes of Duplessis and from the oppressive vision of Catholicism, the overriding premise of modern nationalist thought remains grounded in defense – in the barriers which have to be erected to protect a culture and a peoples under attack. The difficulty with this argument is that Quebec has thrived while under siege. The last thirty years have revealed a culture so rich and dynamic that only an extremely cloistered provincialism will undermine it. We are, to some degree, at the cusp of precisely such a retreat, a turning back to the ideology of the homeland, in which the distilled essence of Québécois identity will finally secure its borders.

But as the Uruguayan writer, Eduardo Galeano, has so brilliantly perceived: "What it all comes down to is that we are the sum of our efforts to change who we are. Identity is no museum piece sitting stock-still in a display case, but rather the endlessly astonishing synthesis of the contradictions of everyday life."[3] Is it possible that the lessons of the Quiet Revolution haven't been learned?

My voice is white, male, middle class, immigrant. I have spent most of my life in Quebec. I have married here, and my children go to school in this province. However, beyond the stridency and simplicity of labels like Anglophone or Francophone the question of my identity cannot be reduced to the *superficial boundaries* of the nationalist debate, and this applies as much to Quebec as to Canada. To say that I am either Québécois or Canadian is simply an inadequate description of my everyday life, a rather shallow and inept approach to the quandries of self and other. But I also recognize that the terms of the debate have been set, though the agenda remains uncertain. It is just not enough to respond to the national question in Quebec with an air of complacency, to retreat and then deal with all of the contradictions as if they have come from an *elsewhere* beyond intellectual reasoning or control.

To me the history of Quebec is full of extraordinary ambiguity, ranging from a long tradition of social justice to crass anti-semitism, from democratic practices to extreme forms of authoritarianism, from an exemplary openness to other cultures to narrowness and intolerance. This is not the place to examine all of these shifts, suffice to say that nationalists are rewriting this past in order to imagine a radically different future. Yet there is something troubling about the strategy of post-referendum (1980) nationalists, something which Aquin anticipated in the 1970's. There is a desire to downplay the *heterogeneity of identity*, to eliminate the contradictions of historical change, to freeze perceptions of Quebec's situation as if it has not evolved or undergone some fundamental shifts over the past thirty years.

"When we look at ideas about national identity, we need to ask, not whether they are true or false, but what their function is, whose creation they are, and whose interests they serve."[4] This point is at the heart of many of criticisms which have been made of nationalists in Quebec, but it leaves out the crucial need which the community of men and women in this province feel for some kind of place which they can truly call their own. Ownership of place is perhaps the biggest illusion, but it is also one of the most powerful. It is bound up with an imagined sense of community that exists beyond the more direct relationship of self to the immediate environment in which one lives.

We don't identify ourselves, in the sense of nationhood, with the street which we live on, or the highrise we occupy, or even the suburb we inhabit. It would be absurd to do so, and yet these are a few examples of more immediate attachments to community.

Concretely, we co-exist with small groups of people in relatively small social and economic configurations. Yet there is a longing to extend that into something greater, a sovereign realm beyond our immediate control. The only way in which that can be done is through an imagining, through a fantasy of place and then through a conferral of identity from self to another. Concretely this means giving over one's identity to politicans who are meant to incarnate what we ourselves lack, or cultural figures who are supposedly more in tune with what we share, than what differentiates us. But this conferral also produces a sense of loss, an almost inescapable feeling that *place* is not enough. The national imaginary is rarely satisfied with the geographic and psychological boundaries it finally creates, which may explain its link to expansionism and violence.

The "eternal" search for Quebec, for a sovereign nation somehow above and beyond the contradictions of class interest or gender or ethnic background, reflects a desire to create a homogeneity which the social, economic and cultural practices of Quebec have long ago left behind. But a crisis of identity, of self and community is characterized precisely by this kind of contradiction. This ambiguity is what drives nationalists to be caught in the past and to long for a utopian future; it is what allows projections into the past and future to effectively *deny* the present.

> Finally it [the nation] is imagined as community, because, regardless of the actual inequality and exploitation that may prevail in each, the nation is always conceived as a deep, horizontal comradeship. Ultimately it is this fraternity that makes it possible, over the past two centuries, for so many millions of people, not so much to kill, as willingly to die for such limited imaginings. These deaths bring us abruptly face to face with the central problem posed by nationalism: what makes the shrunken imaginings of recent history (scarcely more than two centuries) generate such colossal sacrifices?[5]

Hubert Aquin asked himself the same question in his very important essay entitled, "The Cultural Fatigue of French Canada,"[6] in which he responded to Pierre Elliott Trudeau's critiques of Quebec nationalism in the early 1960's.

> I agree with him that nationalism has often been a detestable, even unspeakable thing: the crimes committed in its name are perhaps even worse than the atrocities perpetuated in the name of liberty. In the nineteenth century, the resurgence of nationalistic feeling was marked by wars which gravely tarnished every possible form of nationalism and any system of thought stemming from it . . .[7]

At the same time, Aquin asserts that there is no necessary causal relationship between war and nationalism and that the concept of a national culture cannot be reduced, in a functional sense, to an anticipated future based on a sordid past. If nationalism is unpredictable, it is precisely because it unleashes forces of history which are already in place and which cannot be eradicated by an act of will or by legislation.

This is a crucial argument because it suggests that the errors of looking to the political arena for a solution to the national question are being replicated in the federal sphere as well. It makes little sense to argue against the nationalist use of the state in Quebec as a vehicle for independence, when the federal state is asserting its right to proceed in the same manner, albeit with a different concept of the national heritage.

Aquin is also very clear about the heterogeneity of Quebec culture and how immigration has changed the national character. The specificity of Quebec culture long ago dissolved into pastiche, into a hybrid of tendencies derived from many parts of the world. It took well into the 1960s before all of the historically embedded institutional practices of the state, the educational system, and the church recognized the characteristics of the shifts which had taken place. Quebec reinvented itself during the post-war period, and as it became more cosmopolitan, less xenophobic, more distinctively modern than any part of Canada, nationalists who were partially responsible for the changes grew fearful of the consequences.

In response nationalists turned to language as the unifying force upon which a new and more culturally homogeneous nation could be built. This assertion has been a consistent feature of the nationalist argument. I am by no means suggesting that language is not the focal point for a community's perceptions of itself and of others. But it is not the simple bulwark which nationalists have made it out to be. In fact language is a contradictory site of identity because there is no simple, transparent link between the rhetoric of the day and its interpretation by the community at large. More often than not language acts as a support for the community but at an abstract level. The lived relations which make up everyday life have a specificity of which language is a part, but not the whole. For example, the power relations in a factory will not change with language. Gender relations are not solely dependent on language. Language does not exist in a sovereign realm, and this is confirmed by the endless debates in the courts about the interpretation of laws or the circular arguments around the meaning of "distinct."

The power of language resides with its practitioners. Language is an expression of identity, and laws can be enacted to protect a language, but the law cannot reach into all the spheres which a community uses to define itself.

Continuity and discontinuity can co-exist. It is possible to be a nationalist and still long for the heterogeneity of many cultures. Simultaneously it is possible to deny the results of the mix, to deny difference, to be frightened by new images of self, negate the reinventions and transform the perception of change into a harbinger of danger.

Continuity and discontinuity. Part of what is so attractive about nationalism is the way in which it preserves the past, the way it transforms complex questions of identity into simple answers about community and self. Although, as Anderson has so cogently argued, adherence to a community larger than one's immediate circle is only possible at a mythic level, this doesn't prevent or inhibit large numbers of people from believing that the interests of the community at large are also their own.

Self and identity – these are fluid, ambiguous, often contradictory concepts yet they are bandied about by present-day nationalists as a currency of exchange, a political lexicon utilized to gain votes. But identity can no longer be talked about in the singular, for what is driving this nation-state-province forward at the moment are the many conflicting identities which are at its very heart. The desire to purify these conflicts, to rid the present of the differences which constitute it, to protect a culture which no longer carries the same messages it did even fifteen years ago, is rooted in a nostalgia for a past seen as simpler and more manageable.

The difficulty is that there is no turning back. As the environment deteriorates, as urban life becomes less and less amenable, as the complexity of modern life accelerates and solutions seem ever more distant, nationalist ideology seems to suggest the possibility, if not the probability, of *control.* No better evidence of this than the recent speech by Lorraine Pagé, head of the Quebec Teachers' Federation, in which she extolled the virtues of a Quebec somehow free of all the restrictions which now prevent it from realizing itself – a kind of pastoral myth of togetherness and harmony in a new Quebec produced by the magic of independence. Many of the submissions to the Bélanger-Campeau Commission echoed this concern, this need to create a new territory (both geographical and psychological) in which the sacred characteristics of the Québécois identity could be enshrined in a political form and in which a measure of the authority could be regained over social and economic processes which have become increasingly fragile.

The paradox is that there is a huge gap between the way individuals create their own identity and the way political institutions respond. The structural differences between community, family, the individual and the state are vast and usually fraught with contradiction and conflict.

What makes the nationalist movement think that these conflicts can be overcome? This, its seems to me is a crucial question which cannot be evaded, because it deals with power and the relationship between the state and the individual. Would a uniquely Québécois territory be different from the present? Are there political models being discussed which point the way to new social and economic configurations which would fundamentally transform existing power relations?

These questions mesh with another. What are the conditions upon which, through which the new self can be constructed? In other words, is the state, in its present form, a vehicle for genuine transformation? The tendency is to see this process as inevitable. Change will occur because the identification of the individual with the state will be so strong in an independent Quebec, it will overcome hitherto serious problems of an economic, cultural and linguistic nature. This leads to an even more complex irony. The state, now sovereign, will cease to be instrumental and manipulative and instead will work for the betterment of the social whole. Presumably these conditions are not in place at the moment, but this is a projection which can only be *tested* by the experience of independence.

As I have said, Aquin described a profound sense of fatigue among the Québécois, an ambivalence which simultaneously seeks both independence and dependence: ". . . they [Québécois] want simultaneously to give in to cultural fatigue and to overcome it, calling for renunciation and determination in the same breath. If anyone needs to be convinced of this, he need only read the articles our great nationalists have written – profoundly ambiguous speeches in which one can scarcely distinguish exhortations to revolt from appeals for constitutionality, revolutionary ardour from willed obedience. French-Canadian culture shows all of the symptoms of extreme fatigue, wanting both rest and strength at the same time, desiring both existential intensity and suicide, seeking both independence and dependency."[8]

At the centre of this malaise and ambivalence, lies a concern for linguistic sovereignty – language as the people – the identity of the people through their language. But any language is alive with paradoxes, not the least of which is that it cannot protect a culture against change, nor against a variety of evolutionary forces. The Québécois have always assumed that they live on a continent awash in English, but in fact there are hundreds of languages spoken in North America, and this is reflected not only at the level of dialect, but in the history of rural and urban settlement. English is dominant, but to what degree would independence change the defensive structures already in place in Quebec?

Crucially, language may be that which unites a diverse grouping of people into a sense of completeness, but it is also that which imprisons its practitioners. For language is never simply the site of a possession – language is not like private property. Language is not a "natural" characteristic of a community, it is the product of social practices which survive, of necessity, through consensus and conflict. There is no perfect moment of language as both the motor force and protector of a culture. And what must be understood here is that most languages develop through their relationship to other languages. This lack of isolation is creative and without it many languages would long ago have died out. The tension here is between that which is perceived to be foreign and that which is not, and the struggle to keep these elements separate and yet somehow contingently related, is at the heart of the fatigue which Aquin talks about.

There is a lack of stability to the relationship between identity and language, and this produces a profound sense of *dispossession.* It is as if there is a built-in limitation to what appears to be an almost natural linkage. Since identity is never stable and needs to be worked on in a continuous way, it becomes clear that the question of identity will never be solved. This may explain the repetitive and cyclical nature of the independence movement. But it does not explain it away. Nor should it.

> I myself am one of these 'typical' men, lost, unsettled, tired of my atavistic identity and yet condemned to it. How many times have I rejected the immediate reality of my own culture? I wanted total expatriation without suffering, I wanted to be a stranger to myself, I used to reject the very surroundings I have finally come to affirm. Today I tend to think that our cultural existence can be something other than a perpetual challenge, and that the fatigue can come to an end. This cultural fatigue is a fact, a disquieting, painful reality, but it also may be the path to immanence. One day we will

> emerge from the struggle, victorious or vanquished. One thing is certain: the inner struggle goes on, like a personal civil war, and it is impossible to be either indifferent or serene about it. The struggle, though not its outcome, is fatal.[9]

I am aware that I am treading through a minefield of complex issues here. I want to avoid the strategically chosen ahistoricism of many federalists. The pain which Aquin expressed has its roots in a set of memories which I do not share but with which I must co-exist. In this context it is just not enough to simply *acknowledge* that the British conquered Quebec in 1759. It is not enough to dismiss a crucial moment in the history of Quebec as if that dismissal will, in a simple sense, rid us of the memory.

In 1759 there was a war in Quebec, run by a military officer who had learned his tactics from the British Duke of Cumberland. General Wolfe served under Cumberland at Culloden in 1746 during which thousands of Scottish highlanders were brutally killed. It was a Catholic revolt led by Bonnie Prince Charlie, and it provoked the British not only to fight, but to practice a form of genocide, and this, on their own fair island. It is not surprising that Wolfe described the French settlers in Quebec as so much vermin, that he pillaged their farms and burnt them down. (One estimate suggests that nearly 1,500 farms were burned to the ground, an enormous number for such a small population.)

The memory of Culloden is etched into Scottish identity, inscribed in their sense of history and self. Why is it so inconceivable to the non-Québécois or to the anglophone living in Quebec, for the Conquest to be remembered in the same way?

Or what of the Patriote rebellion in 1837 and 1838? It is true that the convulsions of that period have been romanticized. It is also true that this was not exclusively or solely a French rebellion. Americans, Scots, Irish and Aboriginal peoples were involved. But this was a war of liberation, an attempt to take possession of Quebec, an attempt by a people to achieve, with violence, what they had not been able to achieve through peaceful means. Listen to Lord Durham in 1839 in response to the rebellion – the famous report:

> Is this French Canadian nationality one which, for the good merely of that people, we ought to strive to perpetuate, even if it were possible? I know of no national distinctions marking and continuing a more hopeless inferiority. . . . It is to elevate them from that inferiority that I desire to give to the Canadians our English character. . . .[10]

Durham clearly states that he wants to obliterate the *minority*. Why should these events be erased from the memories of the Québécois? This is a question which cannot be answered by those who do not share a similar sense of the past. The point here is that no one has the right to expect that the Québécois will simply eradicate that past to suit the present, in the same way that we would not want to eliminate the fact that in 1867 Canada was formed as a country. Certain historical moments take on a foundational character, and it is rather superficial to suggest that some should be eliminated while others are retained.

Aquin develops a stringent critique of the Patriote rebellion. He analyses the weakness of the leadership, the lack of battlefield strategy, the sense he has that the Patriotes were looking for defeat – a masochistic response to both the possibility and potential for victory.

> What pains me about this rebellion is precisely the passivity of the loser – the noble and desperate passivity of someone who will never be surprised to lose, but who will be all at sea should he happen to win. What pains me even more is that their carefully botched adventure perpetuates, from generation to generation, the image of a conquered hero. Some countries remember an unknown soldier, but we have no choice: the soldier we commemorate is famous in defeat, a soldier whose incredible sadness goes on working within us like a force of inertia.[11]

I have tried to experience this sadness. But I cannot share it with the same intensity as people whose experience of history has been forged from generation to generation in a cultural and social milieu very different from my own. I cannot expect myself, nor should others expect me, to internalize the history of Quebec as have the descendents of the original French settlers. Mine is an abstract reading born of a desire to know and understand. Similarly, there must be reciprocity, for if one national culture is to assert itself, with all of the contradictions which that entails, then it too must recognize other memories and other histories.

I am not one of those who believes that the national question can be obliterated. The struggle for identity can go in many different directions. At the root of this struggle, however, are the different strategies which we must all take to understanding, in a very personal sense, the role which we can play at the present time. Whether we are part of Québécois culture or not, we are still the recipients of the contradictions of memory, the idealizations and the errors of history and the ways in which history has been understood and acted upon.

Julia Kristeva talks about an *esprit général,* a collective state of mind, which she sees as operative within most societies. This state of mind cannot be legislated. It can't be created exclusively through political activity. It cannot be constructed through the idealizations of the nationalist perspective. All of these elements, taken together, constitute a fragment of what it means to build up and recognize one's own subjectivity. But the space for subjective growth must not be narrowed to suit the exigencies of the moment. It is precisely this lack of historical perspective which worries me and which characterizes the almost evangelical quality of present-day nationalists. The debate which we have entered into in Quebec seems to be codified along very constricted lines. It is increasingly monological and deferential (e.g. witness the August 1991 Young Liberal Convention in which anybody who was not a nationalist was shouted down). It is a debate in which the future is only being discussed in the most abstract of ways. This is as much a result of an impoverished Canadian understanding of the present and the past, as of an insensitive nationalist movement which does not want to look at the complexity of what it is proposing.

Notes:

1 Gordon Sheppard and Andrée Yanacopoulo, *Signé Hubert Aquin: Enquête sur le suicide d'un écrivain,* (Montréal: Boréal Express, 1985), p. 15.

2 Gordon Sheppard and Andrée Yanacopoulo, p. 41.

3 Eduardo Galeano, "Celebration of Contradictions" in *The Book of Embraces* (New York: Norton, 1991), p. 125.

4 Richard White, *Inventing Australia; Images and Identity 1688-1980* (Sydney: George Allen & Unwin, 1981), p. viii.

5 Benedict Anderson, *Imagined Communities: Reflections on the Origin and Spread of Nationalism* (London: Verso, 1983), p. 16.

6 Hubert Aquin, *Writing Quebec: Selected Essays by Hubert Aquin*, ed. by Anthony Purdy (Edmonton: University of Alberta Press, 1988), pp. 19-48.

7 Aquin, p. 21

8 Aquin, p. 42

9 Aquin, p. 42

10 Lord Durham's Report, quoted in *The Imaginary Canadian,* by Tony Wilden (Vancouver: Pulp Press, 1980), p. 71. This little known book deserves a larger audience. It was written by one of Canada's most brilliant social theorists, whose texts in Communications theory and Psychoanalysis have become classics and been recognized in most countries except Canada.

11 Aquin, The Art of Defeat, in *Writing Quebec,* p. 71.

Boundaries of Identity

Writing the Future

. . . the so-called unity of consciousness is an illusion. It is really a wish-dream. We like to think that we are one; but we are not, most decidedly not. We are not really masters in our house.

C. G. Jung, psychologist
From *Analytical Psychology: Its Theory and Practice,* 1935

LISE BISSONNETTE

Lise Bissonnette is the publisher of Le Devoir. *The following is abridged from her editorial on July 4, 1990.*

WHO SAID ANYTHING ABOUT REST?

WHEN THE SPARKS ARE FLYING, THE NATIONAL QUESTION MAKES JOURNALISTS, SOCIAL scientists, the political class in general, and activists in particular, very happy indeed. It would be an ideal situation, one would agree, if it did not make the majority so wretched.

Since the first waning of the Quiet Revolution, let's say towards the middle of the 1970s, Quebec has rushed breathlessly into all sorts of distractions to avoid a return to any broad-based thinking on its social organization. The march towards the 1980 referendum channelled intellectual energies, which subsequently fell into decrescendo mode while people contented themselves with a costume change, and a headlong plunge into the cult of the almighty dollar. With elites of all stripes enriching themselves, the Meech Lake Constitutional Accord came along at just the right time to save us from the existential void.

Now that the national question appears to have moved away from the soap-opera mode to a calmer conference mode, it would be good to refocus our energies on a few pressing issues, issues which are more than "dossiers," and which will have just as much influence on the future of Quebec as would a constitution.

The most urgent matter is that of the so-called "multi-ethnic and French" Quebec. Quebec has failed to build a nest somewhere between angelic interculturalism and racism. It is not enough to acknowledge that immigration is an alternative solution to the low reproduction rate of old-stock Quebecers. The model for integration remains vague and contradictory; it is not surprising that immigrants ignore it, or complain of a cold welcome.

Canadian-style multiculturalism, a high-minded endeavour, is presently being smashed and turned upside-down. When family traditions and folklore have been subsidized, one sees emerge, quite naturally, religious and ethnic claims of a more widespread, fundamental nature, which profoundly unsettle the welcoming society. Whatever is being said in Ottawa, in going from one concession to another, as in the curious "turban" affair, Canadian society continues to try to function as an American-style melting pot. Everywhere but in Toronto, a city that is metamorphosing before our very eyes, differences continue to destabilize society and resentment mounts.

What's more, the same thing is happening to the "first nations": nothing is more striking than the contrast between the compassionate elites who hid behind every available totem pole in objecting to the Meech Lake Accord, and the continuing discrimination displayed in even the smallest western cities towards the native populations attempting to live there.

Carried over into Quebec, this multiculturalism would be suicidal, since it tends to make francophones a minority like the others. But we are loath to adopt the model of the American melting pot. It is brutal: they are only now reluctantly resigning themselves to not brushing aside the language of the twenty million hispanics who call the United States home. So the Quebec dialogue unfolds along the blurred lines of cultural relativism, with each group claiming to "respect" the other, and no one actually doing so. Nonetheless there is no embarrassment in saying that Quebec wants to be French, that the francophone majority does not have to apologize for breathing its own air, and that different cultures can mingle with the French-speaking one.

Those who want to be Quebecers are Quebecers

At the same time, Quebecers of old stock, who are still too often the champions of racial prejudice, must stop seeing themselves as the nation's whole. Nowadays, nationhood is voluntary, as Charles de Gaulle proposed to modern France. Transposing his "those who want to be French are French" into "those who want to be Quebecers are Quebecers" could become a solid, viable plan. It supposes membership, rather than a simple, polite patchwork. All the while knowing, as the contemporary history of France reminds us, that this approach is not without pitfalls.

The racial tensions we now observe, mostly in Montreal, usually go hand in hand with poverty. The kind of poverty we can only talk about with statistics. According to federal surveys, it would appear that 600,000 people in the greater metropolitan region are living below the poverty line.

If that is true, how much longer can we wait before we start putting together a "new deal"? Without discrediting the "new guard" on all grounds, we can certainly reproach them for having marched forward pitilessly, and recognize that all Quebec embraced their credo without reflection.

A fascinating study by *Maclean's* magazine reveals that Quebecers are – by a wide margin in North America – the population most inclined to entrust its destiny *en masse* to businesspeople. This explains why the debate on free trade never took place here, except among like-minded types with their comforting mutual assurances. Nearly two years later, the shock seems to have been much harsher in Quebec than in Ontario, but the silence continues. And in that silence there is an imbalance of values, if not a hoax, that cannot last.

It is not to deny the dynamism of the new business class, or its basic role in Quebec's present awakening, simply to ask oneself to what degree the breakthrough of some was accomplished by leaving others behind. The image we get from the metropolitan region, to the extent that we want to see it as a whole, is that of a profoundly non-egalitarian and dangerously negligent society. More time and passion are spent discussing bike paths than health facilities or social service resources. All this, when we know that demand continues to put strain on the system, and that the erosion has reached our doorstep.

Sometimes our mistakes are distinct

And as for lost illusions, we might take a look at our finest plan of the 1960s, the reform of the education system. It is an unfinished revolution: our primary and secondary schools are among the most sound in North America, and are now returning to the basics, thanks to a remarkable consensus between the teaching body and the body politic at all levels. But post-secondary education, through which the intellectual and economic development of a nation flows, is still not equal to its claims.

Quebec made a mistake in creating the CEGEPs [community colleges], or at least in equipping them as a channel for general training intended as preparation for university, since they now function as an additional barrier to higher education. This is without taking into account the fact that these two years, often lacking precise objectives, disorient a number of students who have plenty of time to adopt the work and study habits that will carry over with them to university, or add them to the drop-out rates. Quebec universities, alone in North America, have also adopted a programming model that discourages full-time study and which, under the pretext of adapting to the adult clientele, takes away from young people an institution that should first and foremost be devoted to them. If, as we are told, the days of grand, overly expensive reforms are gone, the time has come at least to make urgent improvements, which will never cost as much, in the long term, as the status quo. There are certain "distinctions" that Quebecers can no longer afford.

And there are others that it could well afford. It is really quite curious that a society which considers itself full of vitality can find so little energy for doing some original thinking about its environment. It is one thing to know by heart your catechism of "sustainable development"; it is quite another to grapple with realities. Whether it's a question of reindustrializing east-end

Montreal, of pursuing the work on James Bay, of developing the aerospace industry, or of processing more aluminum, the projects that are bringing coalitions of people together to talk about the future have little to do with gentle technology. Between green nihilism, which fights guerilla battles on all these fronts, and the resistance of developers who consider ecological concern mere lacemaking, we are going nowhere. Few societies have so many big "ecological" decisions to make in such a near future, and are so ill-equipped to do so.

Artists bear the meaning

Culture, a sustainable development *par excellence*, hardly has any more importance than nature. Rarely has a nation produced so much creative work and found so little interest for it. Quebec is not absent from all these fields of activity, but it operates as a dilettante, almost as a sub-contractor. For the nation's political bigwigs, péquistes and liberals alike, culture is rarely more than a branch of our patrimony, a legacy from our ancestors that we put under glass for curious onlookers to admire. While shouting our approval for even the slightest exporter from the Beauce who finds some American customers, we think that cultural exports consist of the Cirque du Soleil, but today a multitude of home-grown artists, of all disciplines, populate the international avant-garde. Nothing does more abroad to dispel the clinging image of a shivering, closed, isolationist Quebec. Investing in culture here in Quebec would easily make it a unique centre of attraction in North America. But Quebec political culture is not cultural, except lately in Montreal where a sincere effort by the new administration is helping us to forgive the many mistakes of unimaginative bureaucrats.

Without some conviction as to the centrality of contemporary culture, all debates on the national question are merely fraudulent. Artists have always been the bearers of meaning of Quebec society. Whoever moves in their circles today can moreover benefit from a privileged view of the Quebec of tomorrow, of its language and its crosscurrents, all things that a constitution cannot foresee, but which it must not contradict, for fear of finding itself just as out of step as the Canadian constitution.

Translated by Christopher Korchin

ALAIN DUBUC

Alain Dubuc is the editor of La Presse, *Quebec's largest French daily newspaper. He is a widely respected commentator on Quebec politics. The following is abridged from* La Presse *(September 12 & 14, 1991).*

ONE MORE QUIET REVOLUTION BEFORE WE GO BUST

THE ECONOMY IS IN SUCH BAD SHAPE THAT WE MUST NOW ASK OURSELVES IF WE ARE willing to resign ourselves to poverty. Or whether we are prepared to do what we must in order to become once again a prosperous society, capable of creating stable, profitable jobs, and of protecting the least favoured. To check the flow it will be necessary to engage in what will be, for all intents and purposes, a second Quiet Revolution, with its own procession of groundswells and shockwaves.

Is this the alarmist stance? Quebecers have only to look around to see that something is not quite right. Workers have not made money since 1975. Or, when their purchasing power has risen slightly, the tax collector has been waiting at the other end. Most families can no longer make ends meet without a double income. The middle class no longer has access to what we used to consider a normal lifestyle. The army of the poor, the non-working and the unemployed is growing. Young people, no longer able to count on the stable, profitable jobs their elders were provided, are getting ready for a precarious future. And the State, unable to maintain the level of its services without asking even more of taxpayers who have already been picked clean, can do nothing about it.

So now we have to draw the necessary conclusions. The catastrophe is that we will never get back to where we were, just as the strong growth of the eighties was never able to bring us back to the levels of the preceding decade. On the contrary, the process of disintegration, which began imperceptibly fifteen years ago, is starting to pick up speed. The situation is hardly better in the rest of Canada.

How did we get to this point? Because natural resources, which once ensured effortless prosperity, no longer provide a strategic advantage. Because many of our businesses which, also with little effort, prospered in a protected world, are now dying in an era of global competition. Because too much of our energy has been devoted to squabbling over the sharing of wealth rather than the production of it. And finally because other countries, who have put in a great deal of hard work, do things better than we do.

Productivity is the measure of a country's talent. While other economies show rapid growth in productivity, ours is stagnant, so much so that Canada now ranks 22nd among the 24 countries of the OECD. The Canadian economy can no longer perform, and as a consequence it now boasts one of the worst rates of unemployment.

Nonetheless we are beginning to get a clear idea of the solutions that would enable us to reverse the trend. All of them are aimed at revitalizing our economy. . . . But a host of others affect our very values: rethinking the education system in order to put an end to the incredible dropout rate of 40 per cent; revising collective agreements; creating new relationships between employers and unions; forcing business to get involved in basic worker training; creating a climate of partnership; rethinking the role of the State so that it stops encouraging the dependence of a growing number of citizens who are paid to do nothing; and ensuring that social justice stops being synonymous with parasitism, on the individual as well as the corporate level.

Deeper still, these proposed changes are a question of reintroducing the work ethic, from high school to retirement. They all bear the same message: we can't hope to one day prosper without working at it. It is a message that has been understood by all countries, whether conservative or socialist, who are not, as we are, at the brink of the abyss.

In fact we are talking about a genuine Quiet Revolution, for it touches upon all facets of human activity. Even though the crisis is initially an economic one, the stakes are much higher than that. Can we seriously speak of culture in a world of illiterates and dropouts; battle poverty in an economy with no jobs; reform the health plan in a society with no funds?

The change in direction is necessary and urgent. Too many countries – in Europe, in Asia – are being profoundly overhauled. Their progress is such that if we wait too long the gap will widen and it will become virtually impossible to catch up to them.

But to get there we will have to overcome two obstacles. The first is fear of change. Many groups in society – businesses, unions, economists, political leaders – are increasingly aware of what is at stake. Yet we shuffle our feet: we know the answers, but we are still at the pious, vow-taking stage.

The second obstacle is the constitutional debate. How are we to view the debate on the future of Quebec and Canada when we know that the economies of Quebec and Canada are in a state of freefall? The problems threatening the Quebec economy are serious. So serious that, without a major shift in direction, we will be heading towards total collapse.

The constitutional talks, in their present form, are a luxury we can no longer afford. Not only because they are synonymous with instability and wasted energy. The new economic priorities we must set out for ourselves demand that we also rethink the way we look at our future.

Otherwise, all the constitutional debate will offer Quebecers and Canadians is the chance to choose the boat in which they want to sink. Against this perfectly gloomy backdrop . . . the plan for sovereignty ceases to be a beautiful dream. Rather, it risks becoming a nightmare. Friends and foes of sovereignty are in agreement when they allow that the principal economic cost of sovereignty will be incurred during the transitional period, a period of drift, several years long, during which we will have to digest financial instability, political tensions, the wait-and-see approach of investors, free-trade renegotiations, etc. . . . Some people put their money on the side of optimism; they expect a short adjustment period, during which we will naturally have to be willing to tighten our belts.

This makes sense only if you have some fat. In the context of an impending crisis marked by deindustrialization, closures, armies of unemployed, and impoverishment, "tightening your belt" really means losing your job. In a period of slippage, when the economy is fragile and vulnerable to upsets, a setback, even a temporary one, can only hasten the fall. Not just the fall of the economy, but also that of a State that is devoid of funds, a luxury Quebecers cannot afford.

The scenario is all the more troubling when one realizes that the time factor is not in Quebec's favour. Throughout the world, people are discovering that this decade will be crucial. During this time the balance of power between newly globalized economies will be decided – a race against the clock in which countries are expending gigantic amounts of energy to finish first. If Quebec were to separate, it would not be devoting these pivotal years to surging ahead, but to rowing ever harder merely to keep abreast and stay afloat. After that, it will be too late.

However, we have the resources to rethink our economic future. Thanks to its nationalism, among other things, Quebec is much better prepared than the rest of Canada to set about on a different course. The changes to be made are of an industrial nature, but they also must rely on new relationships between employers and unions, on dialogue between the State and its various partners, on cohesion and solidarity.

In this regard, Quebec has a solid head start. But now is the time to mobilize these resources. . . . There is no point in saying that the rest of Canada, in its present form, is not ready to face up to the economic impasse that is hitting it just as hard as it is us, as the collapse of invincible Ontario has shown. The crisis is pan-Canadian. It is Canada that is far behind in research, in training, in productivity. Unemployment is chronic.

In 1979, Canada was an economic model, in 1985, a symbol of failure. It is impossible to put an end to this headlong flight without rethinking the Canada that presided over this decline, the Canada of the Trudeau era. Two fundamental elements of the Liberal dream go a long way to explaining the failure whose effects we are now seeing. First, massive centralization, with its overlapping jurisdictions, its overmuscled and arrogant bureaucracy, which intensified the tactical errors. Second, a project for a just society that did not reach its objectives but which succeeded in creating from its scattered parts a culture of dependence: dependence of the regions, of the provinces, and of individuals. These two legacies are now the source of a profound rigidity, a fierce resistance to change, as we saw in the case of free trade.

This is why, in the rebuilding that awaits us all, and which must rely on flexibility and the ability to adapt, the first step – and it is essential – must be a large-scale decentralization of the Canadian decision-making process. As we know, the idea of a new division of powers is ill-received in English Canada. But if the efforts for constitutional renewal aim not to solve the difference of opinion between Canada and Quebec, but rather to save an economy that has been cut adrift, the outcome might be quite different.

If, in Canada and in Quebec, we understand the seriousness of the matter, the schedule defining our constitutional priorities will change rapidly. In such a framework, the interminable debates on the distinct society lose all meaning; the desire of the Quebec Minister of Communications to seize control of Radio-Canada becomes a monument of futility, as does the morbid fascination some current federalists have with the evils of the notwithstanding clause.

But on the other hand, the need to transfer to the provinces the responsibility for training skilled labour – which is at the very heart of an economic turnaround – would become clear. Not in the name of this or that ideology, but because it works.

To do this, you have to have the conviction that jobs for Quebecers who don't have them are more important than a few symbolic words in a constitutional text.

Translated by Chris Korchin

JACQUES RENAUD

Jacques Renaud caused a commotion in the Quebec literary world in 1964 with the publication of his first novel, Le Cassé, *which he wrote in* joual. *The book influenced dozens of Quebec writers, singers, and poets, including Michel Tremblay, Robert Charlebois, and Claude Jasmin. After writing for the Marxist, pro-independence publication* Parti Pris *in the sixties, his growing anti-nationalist opinions in recent years have made him less popular in Quebec. He has written ten books of poetry, as well as a collection of short stories,* L'Espace du Diable, *in 1989. Although he now lives in Ottawa with his family, he continues to publish his work in magazines and newspapers in Quebec. The following essay was published in* Cité libre *(vol. XIX, no.1, July/August 1991).*

GIANT-TOWNS

Thoughts on a Familiar Notion: The Nation

ONE CAN RECOGNIZE A NATION BY VIRTUE OF ITS HAVING A CERTAIN NUMBER OF CHARacteristics which, to one degree or another, are found in all nations. Broadly, these are: a common ethnic or racial descent; a shared language; a shared territory; a shared religion; shared customs and traditions; shared laws and institutions; shared historical memory; and shared political structures.

At first glance it all seems quite simple.

Quebec's "French-only" nationalists define the Quebec nation in an apparently unassailable manner: they define it, essentially, by language. One nation, one language; one language, one nation. This is the prevailing notion of Quebec nationalism.

Language

If we decided to extend this reasoning to its very extreme and fall in with Quebec's French-only nationalists, then the United States, English-speaking Canada, England and Australia would form a single nation.

If nationhood were based on language, there would not be a score of Spanish-speaking countries in Latin America, but just one – or at least there wouldn't be quite so many as there are.

In Canada, the Acadians of New Brunswick are francophones, yet everyone knows that they do not identify themselves as Quebecers but as Acadians. Franco-Ontarians, who identify themselves as such – or as Ontarians, or as Canadians, but not as French-Quebecers or as Quebecers – provide a comparable phenomenon.

Switzerland has four officially recognized languages. Italian-speaking, German-speaking, and French-speaking Swiss generally do not wish to become part of Italy, Germany, or France.

A considerable separatist movement exists in Northern Italy. It is grouped around a political party: the Lega Nord (the Northern League or Northern Coalition). The Lega Nord opposes Southern Italy and Rome-based centralization. If Northern Italy were to become a sovereign entity, either confederate or independent, it would obviously not be for linguistic reasons, and its foundation would certainly not rest on language: Northern Italians, like southern Italians, speak Italian.

Attempts to unify the "Arab Nation" (such as the United Arab Republic and the United Arab State, both founded in 1958) have been short-lived. "Arab unity" is a slogan that does not correspond to a common desire for national unity. Language counts for nothing, here, either "pro" or "con." Believing that a common language is automatically the basis for a nation falls under the category of myth. The problem is that demagogues exploit this myth and people continue to believe in it. It seems so simple, so natural. . . .

Ethnic or racial descent

Another characteristic that we sometimes attribute to nations is a common ethnic or racial descent. This is also a simplistic prejudice, one which obviously falls apart under scrutiny: today, a nation that is racially or ethnically homogeneous is a very rare, perhaps non-existent, phenomenon.

Territory

Defining a nation on the basis of its territorial identity means, roughly speaking, that "those who inhabit a territory with precise borders" form a nation. The pathetic case of refugees who, for centuries or more, had shared a territory with people intent on expelling them from that territory, categorically precludes any possibility of confusing territory with nation. Before being driven out, such refugees could be defined as "those who inhabit a territory with precise borders" just as easily as those who are bent on driving them out. The "persecuted" and the "persecuters" belong in equal degrees to the "national territory" that defines, in theory, the "nation." Is the nation composed of the expelled refugees, or of those who do the expelling?

Religion

The Muslim faith has never prevented Iran and Iraq from engaging in cruel battles with one another in the Middle East, nor did it prevent Iraq from attempting to conquer Kuwait and from massacring the Kurds, nor did it prevent Iran in 1987 from deliberately provoking a bloody riot (402 deaths, 649 casualties) at the very heart of Islam's most sacred sanctuary, Mecca, in Saudi Arabia, during the annual pilgrimage, and all of this under the inspiration of a charismatic Muslim leader, the Ayatollah Khomeini. Israel defines itself as a Jewish State, but hundreds of thousands of its citizens (the majority, in fact) do not practise the faith at all, and hundreds of thousands of others are Muslim, Druse or Christian Arabs who have the right to vote and the right to sit as elected members of the Knesset.

Any medium through which "collective identity" expresses itself is not identity itself

In fact, each of the "characteristics," or "bonds," we have briefly examined – language, religion, ethnicity, territory – rather than being inherent to the national phenomenon, seems instead to serve as a formal medium or a rallying symbol for a much more tangible, much more complex, much deeper and more distinct phenomenon: group identity.

What is group identity? Can it exist without a specific "bond" (such as language, religion, race, territory)? Can it exist without the mythical or even fanatical elevation of some shared characteristic?

Enormous questions.

To my way of thinking, while the potency of group identity may prevail, the media or "bonds" of identity are secondary, non-essential, "optional" – at the extreme, they are simply a pretext.

The "bonds" of group identity will evolve, change, sometimes even disappear, while the group identity itself may remain.

It's obvious that if the "bonds" of identity were an integral part of the "nation," then the "nation" in question would disappear with those bonds. Now, we know that a language may disappear, be "forgotten," or cease to be spoken, while the phenomenon of group identity still persists. Certain cases are well known: Gaelic (Ireland has been profoundly anglicized); Hebrew (a purely ritual language for over a thousand years during the diaspora, it has since been re-used and secularized in Israel); Amerindian languages (some of them have disappeared); Liberia (original tongues forgotten in America, replaced by English). None of which has prevented Ireland, or Israel, or native North Americans, or the Liberians from constituting national entities, or from identifying themselves as such.

The "bonds" of identity can disappear while group identity remains

Thus the "bonds" of national identity may be transformed and may even disappear over time. They do not constitute identity itself; they are not essential. The case of French Canadians is interesting in this respect.

For a long time, French Canadians from Quebec identified themselves primarily as "Canadians," then later as "French Canadians," and their identity was at once diasporic (in the North American and Canadian contexts) and territorial (Canada, province of Quebec).

Then, as the Canadian territorial identity gave way to the progress of Quebec's own territorial identity in the minds of French Canadians from Quebec, these people increasingly identified themselves as "Québécois." At the same time, a predominant feature of the collective French-Canadian identity, the Catholic religion, was disappearing, as was the notion of the "French-Canadian race." Another already-present bond of identity, language, gathered increasing importance at the beginning of the 1960s, taking the place of religion and the concept of race to the point of merging itself with the very idea of a Québécois territory. Language replaced race; language replaced religion. Group identity persisted and grew in intensity even though some of its "bonds" had disappeared.

Moreover, the superimposition of an exclusively French bond of linguistic identity upon the purely Québécois bond of territorial identity sowed the seeds for conflict: the inhabitants of the Quebec territory were not exclusively francophone. They still aren't. In renouncing the Canadian identity and in creating the "francophone" Quebec territorial identity, French-only Quebec nationalists eliminated several hundred thousand people from their "nationalist fantasy." The French-only Quebec nationalists "eliminated" the anglophones of Quebec just as they had gradually eliminated themselves ideologically from Canada by concentrating on Quebec. In doing so, they revived the old English-Canadian ideology of the linguistic primacy of English – an ideology which English-speaking Canada had been trying to rid itself of over the past twenty years, sometimes with success, as in Ontario and New Brunswick, but not without provoking some serious reactions. By adopting this ideology of linguistic primacy, Quebec nationalists awakened in the population of English Quebec the same separatist or partitionist thinking that the English-Canadian ideology had, over the years, awakened and strengthened in the minds of French Quebecers.

The nation is essentially a psychological phenomenon; nationalism is a matter of life and death

We could cite further examples which demonstrate that language, race, and religion, among others, cannot be viewed as fundamental, characteristic elements of nations: they are too fluid. They change, they evolve. They can disappear, while identity remains.

In this light, there is nothing more artificial, more void of meaning, than the notion of "nation." Nothing could appear more abstract. But from the psychological point of view, there is nothing more concrete. From this angle, the nation becomes a psychological phenomenon, an image, indeed a collective illusion. An immense subliminal comfort. A collective illusion that exerts a psychological pressure which, when the illusion is roused, can completely absorb the individual and estrange him from himself. It is essentially this final aspect that has struck me and preoccupied me most, especially since the end of the 1960s.

The nation is a symbol that reflects powerful subconscious contents associated with the idea of birth and also, implicity, with the idea of death. In the subconscious, opposites are absolutes. We are led directly to the level of myth, to the highly energizing universe of archetypes. The national delirium bears this out: the "nation" appears to conceive of itself in terms "of life and death." Everything becomes black or white. There are the faithful and the treacherous, the true Quebecers and the false Quebecers, the true Canadians and the false Canadians, the enemies of Quebec and the friends of Quebec, the traitors to the federation and the true federalists.

Nationalism is thus an archetypal phenomenon of possession that demands the resolution of a powerfully and dramatically polarized contradiction: life and death.

This polarization is too powerful. This contradiction "of life and death" cannot be resolved. In fact, only the individual conscience is capable of resolving such symbolic polarizations – so long as these opposites do not disturb one's consciousness or drive the individual completely mad.

This polarization is intolerable. The poles must separate from one another in the nation's mythical universe. One of them is projected onto a privileged, consecrated and magnified medium or "bond" of collective identity. This medium becomes the "totem," the magical bond, the very life of the "nation": language, for example. Language has become life, the vital pole; it is synonymous with life. Death is lacking. To accomplish the myth, the nation needs both poles. It therefore needs a mortal threat. The nation must not only "survive," it must also be "endangered" in order for the myth of birth or of nation to accomplish itself. Otherwise there is no national myth, there is no nation. The nation requires that the "vital bonds" on which its identity is magically projected – language, religion, etc. – be threatened.

In Quebec, language is the magical bond at the heart of which the question of life is mythically resolved. Language is invested with mythical importance. Language is the polarized element through which the "matter of life and death" is acted out.

The Salman Rushdie affair provides us with a non-linguistic example of such a magical bond. For the Muslims who have sentenced Salman Rushdie to death, it is religion, or the venerated image of the prophet Mohammed, which becomes the "matter of life and death"; if the holy image of the prophet Mohammed is suddenly no longer "venerable," the Muslim follower dies. The "survival" of the Muslim depends on the death of he who claims that the image of the prophet Mohammed is no longer "venerable": Salman Rushdie. In reality, it is the mythology of the "Muslim Nation" which needs a sacred Mohammed just as much as it needs an accursed Salman Rushdie in order to be complete. Victims – of one kind or another – are at the centre of this vortex.

The giant-towns of Clive Barker

A striking example of the double phenomenon of individual annihilation and mass bonding is given to us in Clive Barker's gripping short story, "In the Hills, The Cities." In the story, the inhabitants of entire villages skilfully bind themselves one to another through complex sets of straps and harnesses and thus transform themselves into monstrously tall and broad constructions which display all the attributes of a single gigantic human "being": arms, legs, head, etc. Each town-being then confronts the other in a "single combat." This activity is repeated in cycles, even though it brings unspeakable suffering. Let us note that the giant-towns are of no precise sex. We might say they are asexual. We might also say they are hermaphroditic, which is to say polarized. Nations.

The frenzied nation is an imaginary person, a chimera, an inflated construct filled with all the individuals who have been pushed back and then brought in line and harnessed. But alongside this frenzy, reality, for its part, remains implacable: a group is not a person. It never will be one, just as a forest will never be a tree. If the fantasy is pushed to the extreme, it will sooner or later crash headlong against this reality – like Clive Barker's giants who cannot prevent themselves from disintegrating, even though the cycle that drives the villagers to reconstruct themselves into giant-towns remains unbroken. Can the intelligence of the human being break this cycle? Or civilize it? "Nationalism must be regarded as a special case of the more general and permanent problem of group integration," says an excellent report on the question of nationalism prepared a long time ago by Members of the Royal Institute of International Affairs [*Nationalism*, Oxford University Press, 1939]. We might complete the last line as follows: ". . . of group integration and disintegration."

The willingness to live communally under a single system of fundamental laws

Of all the characteristics commonly attributed to nations, there is one that stands out, first and foremost, for me: the shared willingness to live together under a single system of fundamental laws.

Generally, whenever individuals refrain from losing themselves in the great national whole which swallows their freedom and makes them believe they are essentially a race, a language, a "culture," or a religion, it is this shared willingness to live together under a single system of fundamental laws that remains the surest way of defining, if one can, a "nation."

Why does this willingness exist? There may be several reasons.

One of these reasons – perhaps the most important and most decisive – seems to be the shared memory of an experience of battle against a common danger, a common obstacle, a common threat. There is nothing moral about this, nothing that necessarily guarantees or promises either democracy or dictatorship, freedom or repression, happiness or misfortune: Clive Barker's Yugoslavian villagers recall confrontations among giant-towns, yet they reagglomerate cyclically into giant "national entities" that bash one another up. Collective memory (I believe that we can validly hypothesize that something of the kind, in some form or another, exists – and this is precisely the problem) seems to hold a constraining, "atavistic" power. Whether latent, unconscious, or activated, this memory seems not to want to die. This phenomenon of a common, collective memory is peculiar to all groups who have been strongly bonded together by living through a shared ordeal (whether genuine, imagined, exaggerated or otherwise): it is not peculiar to "nations."

This memory may be exploited, transformed, coarsened, embellished: it is in large part imaginary. This mnemonic matter swirls, like schools of fish, in the structuring power of the collective imagination, and the dynamics of its metamorphoses are not without analogy to the dynamics that allow this same mnemonic matter to be transformed into great works of fiction.

By and large the nation is a creation of the mind. The golden rule that separates the rational individual from the madman is the ability, at once banal and decisive, to distinguish between the real and the fictitious, between what is human and what is mythical. The rational individual has a passion for verifying. The madman is possessed by a passion that the rational verification of facts would kill. Nationalisms are works of fiction, but ones which lie about what they really are in the sense that they claim not to be works of fiction. They are collective rituals subconsciously experienced, without knowledge of their profoundly mythological nature. Nationalism hands the human being, the human consciousness, over to alienating forces, to what used to be called the "gods." In that sense, nationalism transforms human beings into suggestible and delirious mobs – mobs easy to manipulate, mobs which easily yield to adoration, mobs which sometimes will go further, sometimes wielding knives, or tossing bombs, or acquiescing to deportations.

The shared willingness to live together under a system of laws based on the same fundamental principles should be the cement of a society and the basic definition of a "nation" (if we are to keep the term). Laws are important. They affect us personally; they have great practical and psychological influence. Laws have considerable consequences for the individual and for the quality of relations between individuals. Let's imagine for a moment a society in which theft, murder, or rape were not punishable crimes: every minute of our existence would be radically altered.

The importance of law is immense. But that is not all: the law must also be the same for everyone; equality of rights must be guaranteed. It is not enough to forbid theft, murder, or rape: they must be forbidden to all. Laws must also offer maximum liberty; a society's creativity, as well as material and spiritual prosperity, are derived from it. Whether or not the country I live in happens to be a "nation," I really don't care. I expect the laws of this country to guarantee to all citizens the rights and freedoms currently accepted as being fundamental: I won't allow someone sitting next to me to have fewer rights than I have. Otherwise, the shared willingness to live together – the consensus – dissolves: the inequality of rights means that we no longer live together. In human affairs, equality pure and simple is a myth; but the equality of rights is a psychological fact of great importance, and its practical consequences are considerable.

I do not want to live in a society that legalizes linguistic segregation (articles 72 and 73 of Law 101) and which makes informing a duty (article 78.1 of Law 101: "No person may permit or tolerate a child's receiving instruction in English if he is ineligible therefore."). I do not want to live in a society that claims to protect rights and liberties but which never stops praising the absolute right it holds to suspend them all at will, whether it is the freedom of expression and thought or the right to live and to be protected against cruel treatment (the notwithstanding clauses of the Canadian Charter of Rights and Freedoms, and of the Quebec Charter). Under the assault of such nonsense, through which the Canadian and Quebec political classes make their way like sleepwalking giant-towns, the shared willingness to live together is disintegrating. The demagogues will try to recreate it artificially by inventing collective dangers, exaggerated or imaginary, and always vampire-like: immense villages, stuck together and peopled with the good and the bad, the faithful and the treacherous. If that is a nation, I prefer a genuine jungle. Or a garden. Or an autonomous city-state buzzing with individuals, with liberty, intelligence, creativity, with daring, with humanity, a city without yoke and harness, the opposite of a giant-town.

The problems arise when laws intended to manage individual destinies begin encroaching on legitimate freedoms in matters of personal choice. State and religion should be separate, as should State and language. All constitutions should separate the State from these areas and should proclaim fundamental liberty and individual sovereignty in these domains. The problem, the discontent, arises in a liberal society, as ours is supposed to be, when laws are made on behalf of the "nation," or let us say for the benefit of an imaginary "immense person" at the expense of legitimate freedoms and the very concrete destinies of actual persons. I am perfectly indifferent to the idea that my children or great-grandchildren might one day speak a language other than the one I speak or they speak today, so long as the change is made on the basis of a free or rational choice, a choice that neither fanaticism nor legal inhibition has forced or perverted.

If laws go too far in suspending freedoms, if they categorically violate the laws of life or the "laws of the market," if they become too far removed from the natural milieu and from our legitimate desires simply to advance an abstraction, and if this abstraction violates the vital tissues, the flesh, the bones, the minds and the souls of a society of individuals, then these laws, somewhere, will hurt everyone – before they are brought down by a catastrophe and made to disappear.

As will one day be the case for the Indian Act in Canada after more than 115 years.

As attempts are being made to dismantle apartheid in South Africa after more than 40 years.

As will one day be the case for the recent (14-year-old) segregationist provisions of Bill 101 in Quebec.

As will one day be the case for the notwithstanding clause in Canada.

Because freedom is more powerful than Clive Barker's giant-towns. It is more powerful than nations. At least, I want to believe and hope so, for it is one of the foundations of what I am, first and foremost: an individual, a human being.

Translated by Chris Korchin

Referendum Speech 1980

"Mr. Lévesque said that Elliott is part of my name, and because Elliott is English that somehow explains why I'm on the No side, because I'm not a real Québécois.

"And this is the contempt the Parti Québécois shows, to say that some people are real Québécois and some aren't, but the Yes supporters have pure blood in their veins.

"Yes, my name is Elliott! Elliott is my mother's name. The Elliotts came here 200 years ago and settled in St. Gabriel de Brandon, and my name is Québécois!

"Here and now, I make a solemn commitment that the victory of the No vote will lead us immediately towards reform of the constitution, and we will not stop until this is accomplished."

Paul Sauvé Arena, May 15, 1980

* * *

Pierre Elliott Trudeau

Pierre Trudeau, the prime minister who brought home the Constitution in 1982, was a fierce opponent of the Meech Lake Accord which was eventually defeated in June 1990. The following essay in which he voices his objections was published by the Gazette *(Montreal, May 28, 1987).*

Canada in Weakling's Hands

"We have in our country the patriotism of Ontarians, the patriotism of Quebecers and the patriotism of westerners; but there is no Canadian patriotism, and there will not be a Canadian nation as long as we do not have a Canadian patriotism."

The late ***Henri Bourassa****, journalist and politician.*

The real question to be asked is whether we, French Canadians, living in Quebec, need a provincial government with more powers than the other provinces.

I believe it is insulting to us to claim that we do. The new generation of business executives, scientists, writers, film-makers and artists of every description has no use for the siege mentality in which the elites of bygone days used to nestle. The members of this new generation know that the true stakes of the future extend beyond the boundaries of Quebec, indeed beyond the boundaries of Canada itself. They don't suffer from any inferiority complex, and they say, consider as bygone the times when we didn't dare to measure ourselves against "others" without fear and trembling. In short, they need no crutches.

Quite the contrary, they know that Quebecers are capable of playing a leading role within Canada and that – if we wish it – the entire country can provide us with a powerful springboard. In this, today's leaders have finally caught up to the rest of the population, which never paid much heed to inward-looking nationalism – that sidestepping of reality in which only the privileged could afford to indulge.

Unfortunately, the politicians are the exception to the rule. And yet one would have thought that those who want to engage in politics in our province would have learned at least one lesson from the history of the last 100 years: Quebecers like strong governments, in Quebec and in Ottawa. And our most recent history seems to establish beyond question that if Quebecers feel well represented in Ottawa, they have only mistrust for special status, sovereignty-association and other forms of separatism. They know instinctively that they cannot hope to wield more power within their province, without agreeing to wield less in our nation as a whole.

Distinct society

How, then, could ten provincial premiers and a federal prime minister agree to designate Quebec as a "distinct society"?

It's because they all, each in his own way, saw in it some political advantage to themselves:

1: Those who have never wanted a bilingual Canada – Quebec separatists and western separatists – get their wish right in the first paragraphs of the accord, with recognition of "the existence of French-speaking Canada . . . and English-speaking Canada."

Those Canadians who fought for a single Canada, bilingual and multicultural, can say goodbye to their dream: We are henceforth to have two Canadas, each defined in terms of its language. And because the Meech Lake accord states in the same breath that "Quebec constitutes, within Canada, a distinct society" and that "the role of the legislature and government to preserve and promote (this) distinct identity . . . is affirmed," it is easy to predict what future awaits anglophones living in Quebec and what treatment will continue to be accorded to francophones living in provinces where they are fewer in number than Canadians of Ukrainian or German origin.

Indeed, the text of the accord spells it out: In the other provinces, where bilingualism still has an enormously long way to go, the only requirement is to "protect" the status quo, while Quebec is to "promote" the distinct character of Quebec society.

In other words, the government of Quebec must take measures and the legislature must pass laws aimed at promoting the uniqueness of Quebec. And the text of the accord specifies at least one aspect of this uniqueness: "French-speaking Canada" is "concentrated" in that province. Thus Quebec acquires a new constitutional jurisdiction that the rest of Canada does not have: promoting the concentration of French in Quebec.

It is easy to see the consequences for French and English minorities in the country, as well as for foreign policy, for education, for the economy, for social legislation, and so on.

2: Those who never wanted a Charter of Rights entrenched in the Constitution can also claim victory. Because "the Constitution of Canada shall be interpreted in a manner consistent with . . . (Quebec's) role to preserve and promote the distinct identity" of Quebec society, it follows that the courts will have to interpret the charter in a way that does not interfere with Quebec's "distinct society" as defined by Quebec's laws.

For those Canadians who dreamed of the charter as a new beginning for Canada, where everyone would be on an equal footing and where citizenship would finally be founded on a set of commonly shared values, there is nothing left to do but weep.

3: Those who want to prevent the Canadian nation from resting on such a community of values are not content merely to weaken the charter: They are getting a constitutionalized – that is, irreversible – agreement "which will commit Canada to withdrawing from all services . . . regarding the reception and the integration (including linguistic and cultural integration)" of immigrants. We can guess what ideas of Canada will be conveyed to immigrants in the various provinces, with Canada undertaking to foot the bill for its own balkanization, "such withdrawal to be accompanied by fair compensation."

Fair compensation

What's more, this principle of withdrawal accompanied by "fair compensation" is to be applied to all "new shared-cost programs." That will enable the provinces to complete the balkanization of languages and cultures with the balkanization of social services. After all, what provincial politician will not insist on distributing in his own way (what remains, really, of "national objectives"?) and to the advantage of his constituents, the money he'll be getting painlessly from the federal treasury?

4: For those who – despite all the Canadian government's largesse with power and with funds – might still have been hesitant to sign the Meech Lake accord, the prime minister had two more surprises up his sleeve. From now on, the Canadian government won't be able to appoint anyone to the

Supreme Court and the Senate except people designated by the provinces! And from now on, any province that doesn't like an important constitutional amendment will have the power to either block the passage of that amendment or to opt out of it, with "reasonable compensation" as a reward!

This second surprise gives each of the provinces a constitutional veto. And the first surprise gives them an absolute right of veto over Parliament, since the Senate will eventually be composed entirely of persons who owe their appointments to the provinces.

It also transfers supreme judicial power to the provinces, since Canada's highest court will eventually be composed entirely of persons put forward by the provinces.

What a magician this Mr. Mulroney is, and what a sly fox! Having forced Quebec Premier Robert Bourassa to take up his responsibilities on the world stage, having obliged him to sit alongside the prime minister of Canada at summit conferences where francophone heads of state and heads of government discuss international economics and politics, he also succeeds in obliging him to pass laws promoting the "distinct character" of Quebec.

Imposing heavy burden

Likewise having enjoined Newfoundland Premier Brian Peckford to preside over the management of Canadian seabeds, having compelled Alberta Premier Don Getty to accept the dismantling of Canadian energy policy, having convinced Ontario Premier David Peterson to take up his responsibilities in the negotiation of an international free trade treaty, having promised jurisdiction over fisheries to the East and reform of the Senate to the West, Mr. Mulroney also succeeds in imposing on all these little people the heavy burden of choosing senators and Supreme Court justices! And all this without even having to take on the slightest extra task for the Canadian government, be it national regulation of the securities markets, be it the power to strengthen the Canadian common market, be it even the repeal of the overriding ("notwithstanding") clause of the charter.

In a single master stroke, this clever negotiator has thus managed to approve the call for special status (Jean Lesage and Claude Ryan), the call for two nations (Robert Stanfield), the call for a Canadian board of directors made up of eleven first ministers (Allan Blakeney and Marcel Faribeault), and the call for a community of communities (Joe Clark).

He has not quite succeeded in achieving sovereignty-association, but he has put Canada on the fast track for getting there. It doesn't take a great thinker to predict that the political dynamic will draw the best minds to the provincial capitals, where the real power will reside, while the federal capital will become a backwater for political and bureaucratic rejects.

What a dark day for Canada was this April 30, 1987! In addition to surrendering to the provinces important parts of its jurisdiction (the spending power, immigration), in addition to weakening the Charter of Rights, the Canadian state made subordinate to the provinces its legislative power (Senate) and its judicial power (Supreme Court); and it did this without hope of ever getting any of it back (a constitutional veto granted to each province). It even committed itself to a constitutional "second round" at which the demands of the provinces will dominate the agenda.

All this was done under the pretext of "permitting Quebec to fully participate in Canada's constitutional evolution." As if Quebec had not, right from the beginning, fully participated in Canada's constitutional evolution!

More than a half dozen times since 1927, Quebec and the other provinces tried together with the Canadian government to "repatriate" our constitution and to agree to an amending formula.

"Constitutional evolution" presupposed precisely that Canada would have its Constitution and would be able to amend it. Almost invariably, it was the Quebec provincial government that blocked the process. Thus, in 1965, Mr. Lesage and his minister at the time, Mr. René Lévesque, withdrew their support from the Fulton-Favreau formula (a plan to amend the British North America Act) after they had accepted and defended it. And Mr. Bourassa, who in Victoria in 1971 had proposed a formula which gave Quebec a right of absolute veto over all constitutional amendments, withdrew his own endorsement 10 days after the conference. In both cases, the reason for backing off was the same: Quebec would "permit" Canada to Canadianize the colonial document we had instead of a Constitution, only if the rest of Canada granted Quebec a certain "special status."

"Wouldn't be nice"

The result was that ten years later, when the Canadian government tried to restart the process of constitutional evolution, it faced the roadblock of ten provinces which all wanted their own "special status"; inevitably, they had enrolled in the school of blackmail of which Quebec was the founder and top-ranking graduate.

The rest of the story is well known. The Canadian government declared that it would bypass the provinces and present its constitutional resolution in London. The Supreme Court acknowledged that this would be legal but that it wouldn't be nice. The Canadian government made an effort at niceness that won the support of nine provinces out of ten. Mr. Lévesque, knowing that a constitutional deal would interfere with the progress of separatism, played for broke, refused to negotiate and turned again to the Supreme Court to block "the process of constitutional evolution." He lost his gamble: The court declared only that Quebec had no right of veto (Mr. Bourassa had in any event rejected it in Victoria, and Mr. Lévesque had lost it somewhere in the west of the country), but also that Quebec was fully a party to "Canada's constitutional evolution."

A gamble lost, a gamble won – big deal! Quebec public opinion, with its usual maturity, applauded the players and then, yawning, turned to other matters.

But not the nationalists! Imagine: they had tried blackmail once again, but Canada had refused to pay. It was more than a lost gamble, it was "an attack in force" (law professor Leon Dion and many others), it was "an affront to Quebec" (Paul-André Comeau, assistant editor of *Le Devoir*). Because in addition to being perpetual losers, the nationalists are sore losers. For example, they didn't lose the 1980 referendum: the people made a mistake, or were fooled by the federal government. Likewise, after Robert Bourassa and René Lévesque had foolishly passed up a right of veto for Quebec, it was necessary to somehow blame it on the federal government: bid for power, affront!

The provincial politicians, whether they sit in Ottawa or in Quebec, are also perpetual losers: they don't have the stature or the vision to dominate the Canadian state, so they need a Quebec ghetto as their haunt. Think about it. If they didn't have the sacred rights of French-Canadians to defend against the rest of the world, if we could count on the charter and the courts for that, they would lose their reason for being. That is why they are once again making common cause with the nationalists to demand special status for Quebec.

That bunch of snivellers should simply have been sent packing and been told to stop having tantrums like spoiled adolescents. But our current political leaders lack courage. By rushing to the rescue of the unhappy losers, they hope to gain votes in Quebec; in reality, they are only flaunting their political stupidity and their ignorance of the demographic data regarding nationalism.

It would be difficult to imagine a more total bungle.

Mr. Bourassa, who had been elected to improve the economic and political climate in the province, chose to clash swords on the one battlefield where the Péquistes have the advantage: that of the nationalist bidding war. Instead of turning the page on Mr. Lévesque's misadventures, he wanted to make them his own. Instead of explaining to people that, thanks to the ineptitude of the Péquistes we were fully bound by the Constitution of 1982, Mr. Bourassa preferred to espouse the cause of the "moderate" nationalists.

Lot of good it does

A lot of good it does him now! The Péquistes will never stop demonstrating that the Meech Lake accord enshrines the betrayal of Quebec's interests. And a person as well-informed as newspaper columnist Lysiane Gagnon was able to scoff at Mr. Bourassa thus: "Quebec didn't achieve even a shadow of special status . . . the other provinces fought tooth and nail for the sacrosanct principle of equality. And they too will have everything Quebec asked for!" (*La Presse,* May 2, 1987). Does not the very nature of immaturity require that "the others" not get the same "trinkets" as we?

The possibility exists, moreover, that in the end Mr. Bourassa, true to form, will wind up repudiating the Meech Lake accord, because Quebec will still not have gotten enough. And that would inevitably clear the way for the real saviors: the separatists.

As for Mr. Mulroney, he had inherited a winning hand.

During the earlier attempts to Canadianize the Constitution, Prime Ministers MacKenzie King, St. Laurent, Diefenbaker, Pearson and Trudeau had acted as if it couldn't be done without the unaminous consent of the provinces. That gave the provinces a considerable advantage in the negotiations and accounted for the concessions that the Canadian prime ministers had to contemplate in each round of negotiations. It is likely, for instance, that if King had been prepared to accept unanimity (Mulroney-style) as the amending formula, the Constitution could have been repatriated as early as 1927.

But since 1982, Canada had its Constitution, including a charter which was binding on the provinces as well as the federal government. From then on, the advantage was on the Canadian government's side; it no longer had anything very urgent to seek from the provinces; it was they who had become supplicants. From then, "Canada's constitutional evolution" could have taken place without preconditions and without blackmail, on the basis of give and take among equals. Even a united front of the ten provinces could not have forced the federal government to give ground. With the assurance of a creative equilibrium between the provinces and the central government, the federation was set to last a thousand years!

Alas, only one eventuality hadn't been foreseen: that one day the government of Canada might fall into the hands of a weakling. It has now happened. And the Right Honorable Brian Mulroney, PC, MP, thanks to the complicity of ten provincial premiers, has already entered into history as the author of a constitutional document which – if it is accepted by the people and their legislators – will render the Canadian state totally impotent. That would destine it, given the dynamics of power, to be eventually governed by eunuchs.

Jean Paré

Jean Paré is an award-winning translator and the editor of L'actualité*, one of Quebec's most widely read news magazines. The following is abridged from his editorial in the December 1991 issue of* L'actualité.

A Distinct Society, Yes – And Then What?

When is a society so "distinct" that its political autonomy becomes necessary? Or inevitable? The Québécois were certainly just as distinct, if not more so, fifty years ago without there being political consequences. The more we delve into the expression – I don't dare say the concept – of "distinct society," the less we understand.

Specialists tell us that in every country, between regions, provinces or cities, even between neighbourhoods or social classes, there are differences due to language, religion, history, schooling, economic challenges, the environment, and most of all, to family structures.

The real reason for Quebec's gloominess is its deep sense of insecurity and lack of confidence in a Constitution that no one will agree to make into an insurance policy against assimilation, by such instruments (among others) as the right to veto or the double majority. Quebec fears the situation of minorities, the loss of political weight, assimilation – it's a fear supported by the example of the francophone minorities outside Quebec and the suspicion that the future is inadequately protected by a Constitution whose fundamental objectives do not include its survival. Quebec wants a constitution that will solve the complex equation which consists of giving the various groups comprising the Canadian nation both the ability to work together and the power for each one to control its cultural and economic future.

It's time to bury the idea of a "distinct society," a very recent one that's the straggly offshoot of the minimalist attempt at reform represented by the Meech Lake Accord. As recently as ten years ago, the Québécois still described themselves as a "people" or a "nation" – in the sociological if not the political sense of the word, as in the "associated states" of the Liberal party under Jean Lesage, or the "two nations" of the Laurendeau-Dunton Commission.

The current debate isn't settling the conflict, it's merely enlarging it, because the federal government, under the pretence of serving as a referee, is in fact both judge and judged, buttressing its own strength to the detriment of the elements that constitute the Canadian nation.

Translated by Sheila Fischman

George Stedman

A securities advisor in Montreal, George Stedman is a student of Canadian politics – to which he brings an economic perspective.

A Citizen's View of Sovereignty

"Ruling parties will always endeavour to maximize the power that is available to them. They cannot be expected to serve the interests of Canada as a federal society. They can only serve the interests of their respective governments. If Canada ever creates decision structures that are appropriate to constitutional decisions, referenda are apt to be among the repertoire of institutions to be considered. But referenda alone are unlikely to be satisfactory. Rather, referenda need to be viewed as elements in a more general structure of constitutional decision-making processes."

Vincent Ostrom. Letter to the *Globe and Mail*, May 9, 1980

Politicians today appear perplexed by the surge in demands from citizens for a decisive say in matters that concern them, issues local and national in scope. Canadians' post-Meech disgust with the sight of eleven first ministers making basic changes to the most fundamental law of the land was new. The dealing made clear the power of the eleven members of the exclusive club of constitution makers. It is a system of dominance created by the parliamentary structure of Canadian governments, an essential fact which, now that both federalism and political association are in question, is at last attracting attention.

There are a number of conventions of parliamentary government in Canada which work effectively to concentrate power in the first ministers in what the late Donald Smiley, one of Canada's most eminent political scientists, characterized as "executive federalism." In this system of executive dominance, cabinet ministers are collectively and individually responsible only to their legislatures; legislative decisions are made by majority rule. Ministerial responsibilities and the collective responsibilities of cabinets work to reinforce the hierarchal bureaucratic structure, secrecy, and the power of prime ministers. At the same time, patronage and party funds help to enforce party discipline and diminish the ability of cabinet ministers to represent regional points of view.

The most important of the parliamentary traditions that concentrate power in the eleven first ministers is the doctrine of parliamentary sovereignty. Henry David Thoreau observed long ago that in Canada people are subjects, not citizens. Parliamentary sovereignty gives Parliament the right to make or unmake any law, without being contradicted. The legal fiction that has been maintained in Canada is that each of the parliamentary governments is sovereign within its jurisdiction, with the Supreme Court's constitutional role being largely confined to settling jurisdictional disputes. People, according to traditional parliamentary theory, are the sovereign's subjects, and a government is elected not to follow, but to lead. The problem today is that as Canadians, we are seeing ourselves more and more as citizens, competent to decide our constitutional future.

If the colonists (with their loyalist and feudal roots) ever showed any inclination for democratic principles, the republican rebels, Mackenzie and Papineau, with their failed rebellions of 1837, made populist political ideas synonymous with treason. At the time of Confederation, British style cabinet government was a given, determined by the Imperial structure, although the contradiction of parliaments sharing sovereignty with other sovereign parliaments was apparent. The Fathers of Confederation, impressed as they were by the U.S. Civil War, gave primacy to the national parliament. But legal decisions of the British Privy Council soon made the provincial governments sovereign within their jurisdictions. This fundamental mix of federalism with sovereign parliaments has befuddled Canadian politics ever since.

There is a continuing reluctance of Canadian reformers to critically examine the evolution of parliamentary principles in Canada. Canadian proponents of federalism almost seem ashamed that federalism was invented in the U.S. It is as if advocating federal principles like the duplication of powers is akin to supporting unsavoury Americanisms like banning gun control. Instead, our parliamentary assumptions of sovereignty and hierarchy have been accepted as models of efficiency by critics whose imagination, when it comes to envisioning a "Canadian federalism," seems incapable of creative applications of the federal principle. For these critics, the elimination of duplication is the goal. Federal-provincial relations for sovereignists, as for advocates of a strong central government, are a question of centralization versus decentralization. By limiting our choices to only two repositories of political authority (provincial and federal), the independence of other democratic bodies like school boards, municipalities, and the First Nations, has been stifled.

The assumption that flows from prevailing notions of Canadian sovereignty is that the most efficient way for public services to be delivered is in a monopolistic way, by one government. This too is a fiction laid bare by the pace of technological change. Just as the complexity of change makes it virtually impossible to neatly assign or zone out exclusive jurisdictions for different levels of government, it also suggests that the appropriate economic scale of government services can change. An effective process for constitutional reform is essential if an initial constitutional agreement is not going to be outdated quickly by new circumstances, technologies and preferences.

The real benefit of federalism is that it gives citizens a choice between competing purveyors of public services. Choice implies flexibility. Federalism begins with the assumption that people are sovereign and competent to allocate responsibilities to their governments. In Canada, the First Nations are the first to make this claim. In demanding new techniques of local self-government, they have taken an important step towards transforming our colonial heritage of parliamentary sovereignty into popular sovereignty. Direct democracy via referendum is an obvious way for us as Canadians to demonstrate our authority to decide constitutional matters, and referendums can be an effective way to ratify constitutional reforms negotiated by others. However, for a fundamentally new constitutional foundation, a new form is called for, as Canadians will be suspicious of any major new deal put together by the First Ministers, regardless of how many commissions advise them.

A constituent assembly, elected only to strike a new constitutional bargain, composed of people who are not members of any of the eleven parliaments, would be free of parliamentary constraints. Members of a constituent assembly would not be caught between their interests in running the country and their interests in designing the government. The concerns of Quebecers and the hazards of majority rule could be addressed by ensuring that key decisions of the constituent assembly would require a majority of votes from Quebec delegates and a majority of votes in the rest of Canada. Quebec delegates might walk out, but the constituent assembly would still be worthwhile since a Canada without Quebec will still need to rethink its internal arrangements and terms of association. Either way, such a representative group has the best chance of producing a constitutional agreement that will be valued by future generations.

FILIPPO SABETTI

An associate professor of Political Science at McGill University, Filippo Sabetti is co-editor of Canadian Federalism: From Crisis to Constitution *(1984, 1988). A long-time associate of the Covenant Politics Workshop at the Center for the Study of Federalism, Temple University, Philadelphia, he teaches Canadian and comparative politics. This article draws in part on his essay "The Historical Context of Constitutional Change in Canada," published in* Law and Contemporary Problems *(1982).*

THE ABSENCE OF A COVENANTAL TRADITION

WHETHER THE CONSTITUTIONAL AND POLITICAL FUTURE OF QUEBEC AND THE REST of Canada will take on radically different sovereignist turns, or fall back on the status quo, it will not be for a lack of talks, public symposia and reports of one kind or another. Yet for all these talks and activities, there has been little or no public debate informed by covenant theory, and its relation to the Canadian admixture of federal principles with a parliamentary, majoritarian system. This is the missing element in the constitutional debate. From both a sovereignist and status quo position, serious consideration of covenant theory and its relation to Canadian federal arrangements is not necessary. Indeed, the maintenance of each position requires the avoidance of this issue. But any attempt at creating or recreating self-rule and shared rule among ourselves – in Quebec as in Canada – must be concerned with this question.

Generally, political scholars have defined a covenant as a morally-informed agreement or pact between people or parties who have an independent and sufficiently equal status. This agreement is based upon consent and established by mutual oaths or promises witnessed by a higher moral force, traditionally God. In its original Biblical form, covenant embraces the idea that relationships between God and humanity are based upon morally-sustained compacts involving mutual promises and obligations. In politics, covenant connotes the voluntary creation of a people and body-politic. The American Declaration of Independence is an example of the political application of covenantal ideas.

The emergence of covenant as a political language and factor is closely associated with periods when people find themselves faced with problems of reconstituting human relationships on the basis of mutual respect and reciprocal obligations. The spread of covenant ideas in the lands of the Reformation, first, and in American settlements, later is a novel reiteration of the Sinaitic tradition of the Hebrews. But people can develop on their own, without recourse to the revelations and prophetic teachings of Moses, covenantal ideas and concepts and apply them in the constitution of commonwealths.

The chief point is that the covenantal and the contractarian traditions in politics are not mutually exclusive nor antithetical to one another. Covenant, compact and contract are related terms. Both covenants and compacts differ from contracts in that they are constitutional or public in character and contracts are private. But a covenant differs from a compact in that the former's morally binding dimensions take precedence over the latter's legal dimensions. A federal constitutional order or compact (and I don't mean here Confederation) has been viewed as the most appropriate effectuation of a prior covenant. It may be worth recalling that the word "federal" is derived from the Latin *foedus*, which means covenant, and that the expression "federal theology" was originally used to refer to covenant precepts. The practical utility of such a "federal theology" and such a constitutional federal order lies in linking power and justice, politics and ethics, and self-rule and shared-rule, by pushing the logic of politics understood as power or domination off the stage of political discourse.

It is not entirely clear whether covenant ideas and concepts were critical factors in the creation of Canadian Confederation. The major institutional arrangements of the original colonies and territories were Crown- and executive-dominated, as they remained in post-federation Canada. The colonial masters were gone, but were replaced by a new indigenous set, consisting of provincial and Dominion elites. The persistence of this executive-centred system of government has led Mark Sproule-Jones to refer to Canada as "the Enduring Colony" (*Publius* 1984). He further suggests that much of the writing of Canadian political science reflects and rationalizes the operative assumptions of this executive-centered, colonial type of government system.

Covenant ideas and concepts emerge fully – but with unique twists – in political discourse only after Confederation, in response to basic problems resulting from the logic of executive dominance of the legislative process at the Dominion and provincial level. Two antithetical covenant languages emerged: "the compact of provinces" and "the compact of peoples."

The parliamentary nature of the Crown- and executive-dominated government system contributed in a significant way to the predominance of the "compact of provinces" as "the" political formula for settling or resolving questions of constitutional choice in Canada. As a result, much of the history of Canadian federalism is the history of successive efforts to adjust the structures of government in order to assert and strengthen the authority of provincial governments and executive dominance of legislative assemblies in general. While the compact-of-provinces formula emerged as an attempt to check and minimize the federal government's tutelage over provincial governments, the compact-of-peoples formula emerged as an attempt to check and minimize the consequence of the compact of provinces for the Francophone communitites outside Quebec.

The emergence of "the provincial rights theory" provided powerful incentives for a strict application of majoritarian legislative rule outside Quebec. The linguistic and educational rights of the various French communities were challenged by majoritarian rule. In an effort to prevent this tyranny of the majority, Francophone lay and religious leaders turned to another kind of covenant language – the compact of peoples.

Henri Bourassa, a Catholic thinker and founder of the Montreal newspaper *Le Devoir*, emerged as the most eloquent user and defender of covenant as the compact of peoples. He regarded – correctly – the compact of provinces as an erroneous formulation of the covenant idea, for it gave precedence to the legal dimensions rather than to the spirit of Confederation. He advanced the proposition that Confederation was, in the final analysis, based on a moral compact of peoples. The spirit of Confederation was for Bourassa best exemplified by what was taking place in Quebec:

> The vast majority of its [Quebec] people speak French, but they grant to the English-speaking minority the right to speak English freely, and they accord them in the local administrations, municipal or provincial, those facilities which we ask in federal affairs, not merely as a matter of right – I would never put the question on that narrow basis – but as matter of common sense, and true Canadian spirit, so as to spread out into every province of Canada the same spirit of Canadian citizenship which exists in Quebec, and should exist everywhere in the Dominion. (quoted in Cook, *Canada and the French Canadian Question*, 1966: 39)

Bourassa's appeal was not heeded, however, as it carried none of the powerful influences that were behind the acceptance of the theory of the compact of provinces. What became known as "the Anglo-Saxon Kulturkampf" or cultural struggle followed, to sweep away French-language rights outside Quebec. It has been suggested that, with the anti-French campaign outside Quebec, French Canadians now had the proof that the English Canadians did not accept French Canada as an equal partner. Yet, at least until World War II, most French-Canadian nationalists clung to the hope that some day they would receive more equitable treatment in the rest of Canada. Similarly, Quebec's failure to adopt the compact of peoples in any consistent fashion gave English Canadians "proof" that the Quebec governing class was like that of all other provinces.

The "triumph" of the compact of provinces as the formula for resolving constitutional problems has served to undermine not only the linguistic and educational rights of French communities outside Quebec, but also Confederation itself. Three different but interrelated manifestations of the crisis of Confederation can be observed today in Quebec's constitutional debate.

First, French Canadian nationalists have been led to identify their country with the province of Quebec alone – Quebec as the political expression of a nation as well as a distinct society. Second, the triumph of the compact of provinces combined with renewed concern about natural resources has strengthened the preemptive advantages given to the eleven Westminister-type parliamentary systems. In Quebec the distinctiveness of French culture has served to increase reliance on the Quebec government as the presumed universal problem solver in Quebec society and to create the potential for what Tocqueville called democratic despotism. A third, and perhaps most important, consequence is that contemporary political discourse in and beyond Quebec has little or no reference to a language of sharing, joint action and obligation. The language of sovereignty has, in effect, pushed the properly understood language of covenant off the stage of political discourse as well as discredited almost any version of the compact theory of Confederation.

In sum, covenant language itself is now viewed simply as a term of political controversy. Yet, covenant ideas and concepts properly understood are a vital set of tools for organizing political relationships in Canada and Quebec. A retrieval of this tradition of ideas is thus urgently needed in Quebec in order to link power and justice, politics and ethics, and self-rule and shared rule – in essence, to provide the moral and metaphysical base for whatever emerges out of the status quo. Of course, recourse to covenantal language is not by itself an assurance of covenantal arrangements. It would seem that covenant ideas and concepts, in order to form the basis of lasting political arrangements, need to assume "positive," and hence contractarian, characteristics. This is the sense in which covenantal and contractarian paradigms need not be mutually exclusive. The value of a written covenantal base is that it provides the foundation for making enforceable claims, and thus gives citizens a basis on which to resist the tyranny of the numerical majority or privileged minorities.

As a mode of political association, covenant contains a strong primordial element of kinship and communitarianism. The danger here is that this element of ethnicity or distinct society may rule out of the constitutional order people who do not share these kinds of covenants. For all the talk about the value of asymmetrical federalism, we are still left with the following question: what understanding and considerations apply to the covenantal base of asymetrical federalism *inside* a plural society like Quebec? An initial answer would be that a covenantal base does not have to apply to all considerations and all values of life, and there can be a limited covenantal base that allows diverse communities to share in more general communities of interest and a common political nationality. The American political experience, with all its shortcomings, suggests at least that. But a chief stumbling block to the emergence of such a limited covenantal base in Canada, as in Quebec, appears to be the executive-centered system of government based on majoritarian representation.

In sum, it is hard to avoid the conclusion that the present constitutional impasse is much more serious than is realized, for it involves some very basic ideas about federalism as they clash with the logic of executive dominance in government. The Canadian and Quebec political experience suggests that it is exceedingly difficult to fashion a limited covenantal base or community of agreement among communities of people who, driven by the logic of winner-takes-all inherent in parliamentary majority rule, have not maintained a continuing dialogue with one another. A language for understanding one another is a precondition for a language of covenant and, ultimately, for a common political nationality. And it is no accident that this perplexing problem is at the root of the Canadian and Quebec dilemma. A new language of constitutional choice is needed in Quebec, as in Canada. Yet this is nowhere to be found in the current political debate.

Charles Taylor

A professor of Philosophy at McGill University, Charles Taylor is considered a leading authority on Hegel. The Chichele Professor of Social and Political Theory at Oxford University for many years, he returned to Montreal to work on the federalist campaign in the 1980 referendum. He has been active in the NDP for many years and once ran against Pierre Trudeau as the federal NDP candidate in the riding of Town of Mount Royal. His recent books include Sources of the Self *and* The Malaise of Modernity, *the 1991 CBC Massey Lectures. A 12th-generation Quebecer, Taylor was recently appointed to the Conseil de la langue française. The following is abridged from his brief presented to the Commission on the Constitutional and Political Future of Quebec (known as the Bélanger-Campeau Commission).*

The Constitutional Problem

Quebec's constitutional problem can be summed up simply as the need to reconcile the imperatives that flow from certain fundamental facts. I see four such facts.

(a) Quebec is a distinct society, the political expression of a nation, and the majority of this nation lives within its borders.

(b) Quebec is the principal home of this nation, but branches of it have settled elsewhere in North America and mainly in Canada.

(c) Quebec must open itself economically, as must any society that seeks prosperity at the turn of this century.

(d) This economic openness must not be bought at the cost of political domination from outside. Such a danger exists by virtue of the fact that we share the continent with a superpower. Quebec therefore has an interest in political association with the other regions of what is currently Canada, so as to maintain a certain balance in North American political relations, and to enjoy a certain influence internationally.

In Quebec, some conflict has often been felt between these demands, and, in response to this conflict, some have preferred a radical option. This is the sovereignist position, as it has generally been defended over the last 25 years. To safeguard the full autonomy of Quebec as a political entity and to maintain the degree of economic openness already achieved, breaking all ties with francophones outside Quebec and abandoning all the benefits of a wider political collaboration with the rest of Canada is proposed.

But this would involve sacrificing some important benefits, so it would be essential to ensure that the radical option was really compelling.

Regarding francophones outside Quebec, it is not just a question of historical and cultural ties – these, of course, are important in their own right. It is also necessary to take into account that these communities represent the dissemination of French in North America. The stronger they are and the more recognition they gain for themselves in their respective provinces, the more they enlarge the French presence. And that is a great advantage for us in Quebec, who are at the heart of the francophone population in America. The pressure on us is reduced when we are surrounded by a demographic and political space that is not homogenous and monolithic.

Political collaboration with the other regions can also contribute to this dissemination of French. The process of bilingualism in Canada, the growing number of English Canadians who are learning French, the sometimes extraordinary expansion of immersion schools, all this is an undeniable advantage for Quebec francophones. Anything that enhances the prestige of French, that increases the number of people capable of communicating in French, diminishes the pressure that a minority language will always experience in North America.

These gains have been underestimated and insufficiently appreciated in Quebec thanks to the political context in which they were made. The Trudeau government is largely responsible for the growth of bilingualism. But this government linked the growth of bilingualism with a categorical refusal of any special status for Quebec. Bilingualism was defended in the name of a philosophy that relied on a rigorously symmetrical federalism. It was conceived as an individual right, of French and English speakers, and not as the recognition of a *community*, in this case Francophone, forced to protect itself and to ensure its growth.

The political dynamic of the Trudeau-Lévesque era has made us forget this program that is both logical and profoundly in tune with our historical aspirations. For the last quarter of a century it has been dismissed as utopian. We have felt compelled to choose between an anti-communitarian philosophy that recognizes only individual rights and that was dominant in Ottawa, and an independence strategy that gained ground in Quebec. It seemed that Quebec could only find the political status it needed at the expense of the dissemination of French outside its boundaries.

But this choice is not inevitable. It is no longer necessary to remain obsessed by the political configuration of the last 25 years. That era is finished. With the process manifested in the Bélanger-Campeau commission, we are starting a new phase. It is no longer a question of fixing our objectives against the background of a passing era. We want to define them for a future that is still undetermined. We don't have to constrain them from the start.

Now, apart from this question of the spread of French, there are some other advantages from collaboration with the other regions of contemporary Canada that must be taken into account. Without claiming to offer an exhaustive list, I would like to mention three.

First, Canada distinguishes itself from the United States by its social programs; for example, our old age pensions and our health insurance. Canadians and Quebecers hold these programs dear. But they are not guaranteed forever. In the context of North American free trade, there will always be a certain pressure on us to align our social spending and taxation levels with those of our powerful neighbours. The different provinces and regions of Canada have a common interest in resisting this pressure. There is a definite solidarity between them. To the extent that cooperation between the regions can support the maintenance of these programs, which was the argument made for equalization, cooperation is in the interests of everyone. Quebec should not become indifferent to the fate of the other regions in this regard.

Quebec is also different from the United States, and from the Anglo Saxon world in general, in its style of economic management. The state plays a much more active role. We need only mention the important role of the Caisse de Dépôt et Placement du Québec in our recent development. And, it must be noted that Canada has always offered a climate hospitable to this type of government intervention. For historical as much as geographical reasons, English Canada has always been more open to state initiatives than the United States.

Moreover, it is to be hoped that the other regions of Canada, and also a future federal government, will adopt some of the measures that have contributed to Quebec's economic success. One of them, the generation of capital from the citizens' savings, could enlarge the range of possibilities if practised on a wider scale. It could permit the financing of large scale projects or enterprises. For example, one resource that is currently under-developed in Quebec and in Canada is government-sponsored scientific research. Here, too, the results could be much more significant if we were to unify our efforts.

Finally, there is a very important reason for not withdrawing from the Canadian space to that behind our borders. The Canadian space contains vast resources, some still unknown. Rather than being forced to retreat, we must aim to participate in the development of the north. The advantages of such participation in terms of those factors and resources that we currently know about cannot be emphasized enough. The future wealth and opportunities of this vast space are in part unforeseeable. We cannot let ourselves be excluded from the game.

With the death of the Meech Lake Accord, something very profound happened in Quebec. Everybody feels it, but it is not easy to define. For me, the most significant element is that the traditional ambiguity of Quebec federalists has been resolved. I don't mean that they are no longer federalists. But the age-old uncertainty over whether it was necessary to make certain changes to the 1867 constitution or to remake our structures from head to foot, has gone. On June 23, 1990, the 1867 constitution died morally in Quebec. It is necessary to create anew.

Of course, it is quite possible that the old misunderstandings between Quebec and English Canada that destroyed the previous structures will survive them, that they will plague the new relationships that we want to establish. That's possible, but it's far from being inevitable. Some of these misunderstandings were tied up with the old constitution. The image of Canada as a "mosaic," the norm of equality of the provinces, the *idée fixe* that there was only a "Canadian" nation, all these elements were tied to the existing structures and to the way in which these structures were explained and experienced in the other regions. Canada created a certain expectation in the minds of a majority of English Canadians, an expectation regarding the provinces and other parts of the country, that Quebec couldn't violate. The advantage of creating anew is that new structures that break explicitly with the past can be proposed. It will no longer be a question of treason . . . but rather of building a new country.

Contrary to those who believe that English Canada, having refused Meech Lake, couldn't agree to bigger changes, there is a real possibility that deeper changes will be easier to accept, especially if they are proposed within the framework of a new constitution rather than as re-arrangements of the Canada of old.

It seems to me that the system that would best meet the four types of demands outlined at the outset would be a federal system that is more decentralized than the current one. The 1867 constitution is very supple in certain regards. The proof is that it was conceived as a very centralist system but has evolved over recent decades into a more and more decentralized one.

Quebec – and in the case of a symmetrical federation, the other members of the federation – would have to keep current provincial powers, plus a certain number of others, such as labour, taxation, communications, agriculture and fisheries (this is not a complete list). The federal power would control defence, external affairs and currency. There would be some areas of mixed jurisdiction as well, such as immigration, industrial policy (including scientific research) and environmental policy.

This distribution would put an end to certain useless duplications of effort that we currently have, but would not avoid all overlap. That would be impossible. The fact is that we don't live in isolation and even certain fully provincial powers can't be exercised without regard for what is being done outside. Take health insurance as an example. To maintain an open economy in Canada, we have to be concerned with mobility. Our health insurance system is our business, but we have an interest in extending it to others. The same applies to retirement pensions, labour policy and many other domains.

In some cases, coordination will occur through interprovincial agreements, but in others it would be better to imagine a shared or concurrent jurisdiction; shared power in the case of immigration, for example, because free movement of people within the federation requires legislation that is accepted by both levels; concurrent power in a domain like scientific research, because here our problem is not an excess of initiatives, but a lack of funds. As for ecology, some very obvious coordination problems exist. Regulation by inter-governmental agreements may be possible, as is currently the case between Canada and the U.S. for acid rain and purification of the Great Lakes. But the size and urgency of these problems, and the magnitude of the changes that must be made, favour a mixed jurisdiction. To some extent, even foreign affairs should be considered a mixed domain since Quebec has developed an international identity in some areas of jurisdiction, and any new federal structure would have to recognize diplomatic representations that are already being made under the current regime.

Another issue relating to the distribution of powers is the native question whose resolution will require the granting of some powers of self-rule to the aboriginal communities. A purely Québécois solution for the Indians and Inuit of Quebec, which would leave other regions free to legislate within their communities as they like, could be possible. But there are clearly some advantages to a common solution affecting all the native populations of the Canadian federation. One reason for this is that certain tribes cross provincial boundaries. But beyond such geographic considerations, two or more systems would always invite comparison, as well as demands and criticism that could render the new structures unstable and impair their functioning.

The new federal structures

A federation uniting whom? Who would be Quebec's partners? Unfortunately, it is impossible to specify at the moment. What's more, it is not for us to decide. English Canada itself, once it has understood and accepted that the country has to be remade from head to foot, will determine its identity and find its own articulations.

It is therefore necessary to examine several hypotheses, so as to measure their impact on the federal model just outlined. I rule out one possibility, a catastrophic scenario, according to which English Canada would disintegrate under the weight of its internal divisions as soon as it saw that the current structure will not hold. This is a possible, but not probable, scenario. But this is not the major reason for my ruling it out – it is rather that such an outcome would leave us without a negotiating partner.

I envisage three possibilities: (i) English Canada recovers its unity, either as a unitary state or a federation, and seeks to combine with Quebec in a federation of two; (ii) English Canada takes account of its own regional differences and restructures itself under three or four regional governments who would become Quebec's interlocutors; (iii) English Canada remains as it currently is, composed of nine provinces.

It is clear that the federal system wouldn't be the same under all three scenarios. Under (i), a perfectly symmetrical federalism can be envisaged, because it is obvious that a united English Canada would also push for a considerable decentralization of powers. Under (iii), by contrast, it is more than probable that the system would be asymmetrical. This means that only Quebec would exercise fully the powers that I attributed above to all the members of the federation, while the other provinces would opt for a centralization of several powers.

Hypothesis (ii) would probably represent a situation in-between. In this case the system would resemble a symmetrical federalism, but there would possibly be some minor differences in the powers that the different constituent members would want to exercise.

Quebec should decide the powers it wants to exercise, but not try to dictate those of the others. If the lists of powers differ, it would be necessary to build a system of asymmetrical federalism. English Canada could then evolve towards greater decentralization, or a centralization that is in accord with its own wishes and the needs of the time.

Is it as simple as this? Talk of asymmetrical federalism means a special status for Quebec. We all know how its very invocation provoked the resistance of English Canada, and how dangerous it still appears to some of our compatriots. The rejection of such a status was an important feature of the opposition to the Meech Lake Accord.

But we shouldn't automatically assume that asymmetry is impossible or unworkable. The fact is that Quebec enjoys a considerable special status *under the current regime*. We live every day with an asymmetrical federalism. Quebec is the only province that collects its own taxes, has its own pension plan, is active in immigration, and so on. This sums up what was at stake in the Meech clause recognizing Quebec as a distinct society. The resistance was not at the practical level. This was rather a principled resistance, a defence of the principle of equality of all provinces. It's as if we could tolerate considerable divergences from this principle in fact so long as provincial equality was safely protected in the texts. It's a resistance at the level of feeling. This is not insignificant, of course. But the obstacles it creates shouldn't be exaggerated. For one thing, the distinct society idea also has considerable support in English Canada. Furthermore, the resistance is linked, as mentioned before, to the expectations that the traditional idea of Canada has created in certain of our compatriots. It is a matter of convincing them that we are no longer playing the same game, that we are not proposing to repair the Canada of old. There is a new deal.

Beyond a certain threshold, a federalism that is too asymmetrical would create problems, so the best scenario for us would probably be an English Canada that formed itself into three or four large regions.

The status of minorities

While recognizing that French will dominate in Quebec and English elsewhere, Quebec and the rest of Canada should establish together a minority code that would prevent linguistic minorities from simply being crushed. This code would ensure that no matter which of the two traditional languages is in the minority, they will both enjoy special status and will not be treated as another immigrant language.

We have three major reasons for wanting to make such an agreement. First, by virtue of the imperatives mentioned earlier, our ties of solidarity and interest with francophones outside Quebec push us towards it. Secondly, a mean spirited and repressive policy towards minorities by one side or the other will poison relationships between the two societies, and good relations are important no matter what political regime prevails. Thirdly, Quebec itself, through several of its leaders including the Premier and the Leader of the Opposition, has recently declared that it considers the anglophone minority to be a traditional and integral part of Quebec society.

Consequences of new federation

With regard to our standard of living, I believe that a new federal arrangement of the type proposed here would be the most favourable. This is because it keeps the Canadian economic space intact and can better guarantee the integrity of this economic space over the years, and because a federation would be able to mobilize the resources of this vast country in the most efficient way.

As for the Québécois identity, there are two things that must be asked of a constitutional structure: first, that it recognizes fully and explicitly the specificity of Quebec; and second, that it gives Quebec the powers necessary to defend and promote this uniqueness. I believe that the proposed federal structure adequately meets these two demands.

Conclusion

There are some who want to convince English Canada of our seriousness, to induce them to negotiate, by taking extreme positions. It is said that the only way to make them negotiate seriously is to declare sovereignty first, and negotiate later.

It is necessary to find a way of alerting English Canada to the seriousness of the situation. However, we must avoid becoming embroiled in the maze of amendment procedures currently in place. The problem with these procedures is that they leave us with the status quo by default. They put the burden of proof on those who want change.

It may be necessary to propose to English Canada something like a rerun of the Charlottetown Conference of 1864 – negotiations whose defeat would not leave us with the status quo but would signify the end of the country. Of course, this ultimatum would have a shock-effect. But it is probably necessary, given the reluctance of English Canada to recognize the evolution of Quebec. On the other hand, a shock also risks damaging the interlocutor and leaving English Canada less inclined to talk.

It may be useful, therefore, to combine the ultimatum with an expression of openness, recognizing that Quebec is not alone in wanting to remake the country. Other regions have their own agendas, as we have ours, and we should declare ourselves ready to listen to their demands just as we expect them to listen to ours.

It is up to all of us in Quebec to decide what Quebec wants. But to achieve our goal, it is also necessary to take account of what the others want. Firmness doesn't mean closedness. At once determined and open, we can begin the political reconstruction of the north of this continent.

Translated by Ruth Abbey

DIANE LAMOUREUX

Diane Lamoureux is a professor in the Political Science department at Laval University. Her teaching interests encompass the Constitution and its bearing on individual liberty and women's rights. She has published two books, Fragments et collages: Essai sur le féminisme québécois des années 70 *and* Citoyennes? Femmes, droit de vote et démocratie, *in addition to many articles on feminist politics.*

A FORGOTTEN MAJORITY STILL

ONE DOES NOT HAVE TO OBSERVE THE POLITICAL SCENE IN QUEBEC AND CANADA FOR very long to realize that women are not included in the constitutional debate, a debate that is supposedly concerned with the fundamental organization of power in society, the recognition of differences, and the establishment of the terms of co-existence between different political communities. Could this be due to the fact that, as a social category, women do not need to speak up on what is at stake in the constitutional debate? Or could it be that women have been completely accommodated on the constitutional level?

Although these two types of arguments might seem far-fetched, this is what is implied by the constitutional silence surrounding women. When groups of women asked for representation on the Bélanger-Campeau Commission, they were bluntly turned down. This same Commission failed to address the matter of gender relations in its questions to the "experts." In addition, neither of the two parliamentary commissions formed after Bélanger-Campeau saw the question of women as an issue falling within the constitutional framework. The situation is scarcely more encouraging from a pan-Canadian perspective. The most recent federal proposals mention equality between the sexes on a few occasions, but contain no measures aimed at ending women's under-representation in political institutions.

This deafness cannot be attributed to silence on the part of women's groups. They have actively participated in the consultation process related to the Bélanger-Campeau Commission, despite the fact that their interventions were not always taken seriously. Women's groups everywhere across Quebec and Canada are demonstrating genuine interest in the constitutional debate, but the media remain silent on the subject.

It is difficult to inscribe the "woman question" within the constitutional debate because this debate is organized according to a logic which can easily make women invisible. Indeed, the debate is organized around the categories of ethnicity (anglophones, francophones, aboriginals), of territory (provinces, regions, central government), or level of government. Even if one accepts one or the other or all of these forms of logic, women can be passed over in silence because they are everywhere and scattered at the same time. And yet women, like Quebec and the aboriginal peoples, form a social group whose status must be guaranteed constitutionally. The current debate is attempting to deal with Quebec and aboriginal peoples, but for women there is still nothing to be gained from it.

It seems that for marginalized groups, the Charter, more so than the Constitution, is considered a means for collective advancement. This presents several problems: for example, it could sustain the marginalization of groups even while it diminishes the effects of marginalization; it could also mean that certain groups will be disenfranchised forever. The Charter's goal is the regulation of relations between citizens, female and male, and the body politic. It is therefore a protection mechanism whose paternalistic dimension cannot be overlooked. As for the Constitution, it regulates participation in power, and in this participation lies the possibility of ending marginalization.

In order to posit ourselves as a constitutionally-recognized group, we must think seriously about our relationship to institutions. Certainly we have created our own institutions, we have positioned ourselves in relation to the State, and we have even partially inscribed ourselves in the institutional game. But we are far from mastering our actions in this area and, in large measure, our actions uphold the State's paternalism towards us; we behave like "social beneficiaries" of the State – asking for its assistance – instead of behaving like citizens. And while thinking within this framework, we must take into account one of the main ruptures that feminism has introduced into modern political thinking, which is the necessity for the means to accommodate the ends.

What institutional reforms for women?

If we examine the federal government's most recent constitutional proposals, the offerings are very slim for women. Equality between the sexes is maintained in the Charter and the principle of equality would be included in the "Canada clause," but in the chapter on institutions, women disappear. The MP's free vote can have a positive outcome only if the number of female MPs increases considerably. Senate reform is being discussed solely on the basis of territory. As for the Supreme Court, given its role in the interpretation and implementation of the Charter of Rights and Freedoms, the majority of its members, if not all, should in my opinion be recruited from the "chartered" groups.

When we approach the question of women's constitutional recognition from the angle of Quebec's accession to sovereignty, we face even greater unknown factors. Generally speaking, neither the Bélanger-Campeau Commission report nor the Allaire report specify what a sovereign Quebec's institutions might be. And based on existing institutions, the future looks rather grim for women.

The only hope raised by this option is that a sovereign Quebec would want to think about its eventual political institutions and that perhaps, this time around, women will not end up being one constitutional metro stop behind. But on this matter, all we can do is hope.

From the institutional standpoint, it is quite clear that what is involved is a rethinking of the mode of representation. Because the present system is based exclusively on territoriality, groups that are geographically concentrated have their voices heard. However, this is not the case for women; there is no electoral riding where we can speak of a concentration of women.

In this context, the only way to ensure more adequate representation of women would be to include conditions for proportional representation. Such mechanisms remain to be determined and various approaches must be considered. But beyond the question of mechanisms, there is a need to rethink the meaning of citizenship. We presently live in a regime where citizenship is granted basically in terms of our needs, which has the effect of founding citizenship on a consumerist attitude toward the State. We must break out of this beneficiary mentality and the State paternalism it fosters, and seek to devise a form of citizenship based on participation and involvement in decision-making. No matter what constitutional choices arise, our political regime has not yet taken its democratic cure. It has to rethink its representational system in a democratic fashion.

Quebec women's groups and sovereignty

Several (but not all) of the women's groups in Quebec have come out in favour of sovereignty. This can be explained by the evolution of relations between women's groups and the Quebec State, by these groups' evaluation of their experience with shared jurisdictions and, finally, by their identification with the Quebec State rather than with the federal State.

Since the Quiet Revolution, the provincial "State" in Quebec has built itself up as a welfare State, a role previously played by the federal government. The major reforms undertaken in matters of health, education and social affairs can be seen in this light.

This was not a one-way process for women. On the one hand, many lost their positions of responsibility within these three important sectors. On the other, women's access to medical care, to education and to social services greatly improved. Moreover, women cannot, as main "consumers" of State services, remain indifferent to the government that provides these services.

If in previous times Quebec seemed to lag behind with regard to equality between the sexes or in matters of civil rights, this backwardness has largely been corrected over the last thirty years and, in certain aspects, has even been transformed into progressiveness. After several changes in legislation, there is no longer any discrimination in the area of married women's legal status, and Quebec is even willing to recognize the principle of no-fault divorce, something the federal government, which holds jurisdiction in this matter, still refuses to do. The equality of rights between men and women and even the illegality of discrimination based on sexual orientation have been included in the Bill of Human Rights since 1976. The right to abortion and to reimbursement by health insurance were acquired in 1981, well before the Supreme Court of Canada's ruling on the Morgentaler case.

As for shared programs and jurisdictions, the balance sheet drawn up by Quebec women is rather negative. Shared powers serve largely to keep the ball bouncing back into the other government's court and as a way of maintaining the status quo. So it is a sharing of irresponsibilities more than anything else. In addition, women often feel they are being taken hostage in these jurisdictional squabbles; they would rather know who to vent their anger at and not have to repeat the process twice. This might soon be seen as part of women's larger refusal to accept the double-shift. . . .

These are some of the probable factors explaining why certain women's groups identify with the Quebec State, while not turning their backs on the manna supplied by the federal State. For these groups, women's social experience is part of Quebec's distinct society. For this reason, they are preparing a feminist "projet de société" to be incorporated into the discussions concerning the future of Quebec society. They are certainly not so naïve as to think that sovereignty in itself will be sufficient to integrate women on the political level. However, they do believe that they will be able to take their place in the debate on the collective future of Quebec.

Translated by Susanne de Lotbinière-Harwood

ALAN CAIRNS

Alan Cairns is one of Canada's most respected political scientists. Among his works are The Politics of Gender, Ethnicity and Language in Canada *(1986)*, Constitution, Government and Society in Canada *(1988), and* The Charter versus Federalism *(1992). The following is abridged from* Disruptions: Constitutional Struggles *(1991). Used by permission of the Canadian Publishers, McClelland & Stewart, Toronto.*

DISRUPTIONS [A VIEW FROM OUTSIDE QUEBEC]

THE MULTIPLICATION OF SELF-CONSCIOUS MINORITIES IN AN INCREASINGLY HETEROGENEOUS society challenged the post-war constitutional world with its taken-for-granted's of federalism and parliamentary government, of a version of founding peoples' dualism in which the British were more equal than the French but both were more equal than others, of a quiescent and relatively invisible native population, and of a sexual division of labour and prestige in which the public sphere of politics and state affairs was *de facto* if not *de jure* reserved for men. Unlike Quebec nationalism and the aggressive provincialism of English Canada that challenged the constitutional order on, so to speak, its own traditional terms, these new or reinvigorated socio-political movements threatened many of the basic, often implicit, social assumptions on which the constitutional order had rested.

Perhaps appropriately, the massive decline in the deference accorded to men by women, to Anglophones by Francophones, to the rest of Canadians by aboriginal peoples, and to the French and the English by those who came later coincided with the attenuation and then virtual disappearance of the political and emotional significance of the formerly potent British connection. The traditional elitism of the constitution was no longer legitimated by its now fading British imperial roots. After the domestication of the amending formula in the 1982 Constitution Act, Canadians could no longer avoid the self-examination and the self-responsibility for their constitutional identity and evolution that had been possible as long as major constitutional amendments required the passage of legislation by the British Parliament. Belatedly, more than a century after Confederation, Canadians were on their own, freed from the external (if only symbolic) authority that had previously acted as a mild restraint on centrifugal pressures. For example, after the passage of the 1982 Constitution Act, status Indians, who could no longer look to the British Crown as the protector of their treaty and other rights, became much more politically aggressive.

As the British past became more memory than living reality, the explicit language of rights displaced the implicit trust in authorities and the related hierarchical community assumptions formerly fostered by a monarchical tradition. Concurrently, as Canadians moved toward final control of their constitutional future, their domestic heterogeneity was both more pronounced and its component parts more politicized than previously. Consequently, the voyage of constitutional self-discovery on which Canadians embarked went far beyond the federal-provincial dimensions of their existence to the exploration of the political consequences and constitutional significance of sex, race, ethnicity, language, and other cleavages of contemporary Canadian society.

Since the Charter's arrival, it is no longer possible to think of the constitution almost exclusively in terms of federalism and parliamentary government, the institutional arrangements in which executive dominance flourishes – in the former by the practices of executive federalism that bring governments together to manage their inescapable interdependence, and in the latter by the theory of responsible government and the instrument of the disciplined majority party on which it is normally based. The Charter selectively challenges executive dominance in both these arenas – in the former by affixing a taint of illegitimacy to the practice of first ministers deciding on the substance of constitutional amendments in secret, which they then announce as a *fait accompli* to citizens viewed as spectators, and in the latter by giving individuals and litigation lobby groups the capacity to challenge government legislation in the courts.

By the time of the Meech Lake Accord, the traditional dominance of governments in formal constitutional change no longer appeared legitimate to the representatives of the numerous groups that challenged its substance and process. The leading actors in the governments that structured the Meech Lake process drastically underestimated the Charter's impact on the constitutional culture of Canadians, especially in English Canada. Clearly, the constitution was no longer a concern only of governments. On the contrary, women, visible minorities, the disabled, and others felt that they, too, now had stakes in the constitution, and they inevitably assumed that changes in the constitution that might weaken their rights were by definition not matters to be decided by governments alone. Thus, one of the most dramatic developments of the seventies and eighties was the enlarging of the cast of would-be constitutional actors.

Our understanding of the new reality produced by the emergence of these new players is hampered by the too-easy availability of the traditional inherited language of federalism and the natural tendency of governments to justify their constitutional objectives as being no more than readjustments of federalism that properly concerned them alone. This explains the early tendency of governments to discuss, explain and justify the Meech Lake Accord in the federalist terms of bringing Quebec back into the constitutional family, as if that task could be pursued without any repercussions for the aboriginal peoples and the various interests that cluster around the Charter. Feminist groups, aboriginal elites, a vast array of ethnic organizations, Charter activists, and others bluntly denied that such a segregation of their concerns from those of governments was possible. They were convinced that their constitutional rights and agenda were or might be threatened by the Meech Lake Accord. By both words and actions they denied the hegemony of federalism issues, and the implicit claims by governments that the constitutional management of federalism could be neatly compartmentalized from the concerns of these emergent constitutional clienteles.

The Charter also challenged the belief that the representation of territorially-bounded populations by leaders of the governments of Canadian federalism was an adequate response to the representational requirements of constitutional bargaining. With the Charter in place, it was now a criticism, not simply an observation, to note that, unlike first ministers, not all Canadians are "white, male, able-bodied, middle-aged, and Christian." Further, those who accusingly proffered these observations had few doubts that their constitutional concerns would be overlooked if one of their own were not at the table.

The unwillingness of various groups that formerly could be excluded or ignored to accept any longer their sideline status is a remarkable constitutional development. It reflects the convergence of several inter-related factors. The new aggressiveness of women, aboriginals, and others and the rhetoric of rights that they wielded were in broad terms supported by changes in the international environment. The idea of rights was vigorously championed by the United Nations in its Charter, in the 1948 Universal Declaration of Human Rights, and in an ever-growing list of rights covenants that were frequently followed by consciousness-raising ventures, such as International Women's Year in 1975 and the Decade of Disabled Persons (1983-1992), to stimulate positive state action. The ending of European imperialisms and the delegitimation of the racial hierarchies on which they had been based made an independent contribution to the attack on ethnically or racially based inequalities within Western states. This cultural shift was of special significance in Canada because of the profound ethnic and racial transformation of Canadian society from the mid-sixties to the present.

In the Canadian case, the opening up of the constitution stimulated a specific constitutional self-consciousness in the innumerable groups that paraded before the hearings of task forces and federal and provincial constitutional committees that were a pervasive feature of the seventies and eighties. Inevitably, the participants came to see the constitution not as a permanent, unchanging part of the institutional landscape but rather both as a potential policy instrument for their particular goals and as making the most fundamental statement that a society can about who counts, and how much.

The federal government viewed the Charter positively as a nation-building instrument. Many of the provincial governments viewed it apprehensively and with hostility as province-weakening. For many of the citizen groups, however, it was profoundly status-enhancing. For the first time they had a major place in the constitutional order. The constitution spoke to them generally in the language of rights, and often specifically to particular groups by individual clauses that pertained especially to them. The sense of entitlement and recognition held by such groups was enhanced by their almost universal belief that their particular clauses had been only reluctantly granted in 1980–82 by at least some of the governments, rather than graciously awarded. Thus women, the disabled, and aboriginals, for example, came to feel that particular constitutional clauses or phrases belonged to them, that they had hard-earned niches in the constitution and possessed constitutional stakes, indeed had constitutional identities. Accordingly, it was only to be expected that they would come to think of themselves as constitutional actors, especially if formal constitutional change looked as if it might weaken what they had already won or, in the case of aboriginals, was necessary to add constitutional specificity to the abstract recognitions they had received.

The magnitude and significance of this transformation in constitutional culture was not appreciated by the political managers of Meech Lake. We know with some confidence what is behind us, and we can make plausible, if contestable, statements about what caused the Meech Lake failure. The future is more of a question mark, although it is reasonably certain that the Quebec/rest of Canada relationship will be much looser than was true of the first century and a quarter of our common existence. Each increment of prediction beyond that generalization is a hostage to fortune. . . .

The disagreement between Quebec and the rest of Canada over the desirability of the Meech Lake Accord will be repeated in divergent answers to many of the retrospective questions that can be addressed to that searing experience. Meech Lake will join the Durham Report, Confederation, the hanging of Riel, and conscription in two world wars as key historical events whose competing interpretations underline the perennial French-English dualism of Canadian life.

If the country breaks up, what will initially be seen by many Quebecers as an escape into freedom will be experienced very differently as a defeat in English Canada. The latter's identity and *raison d'être* have always been much more bound up with Canada as a coast-to-coast nation, and with a strong central government, than has been true of Francophone Quebecers. It is possible, of course, that English Canada, digesting its lengthy education in a failed attempt to patch up the existing constitutional order, may come to see an independent Quebec more as a blessing than a defeat.

Uncertainty about the future of English Canada, that ambiguous entity that Quebec with its solid Francophone majority defines as the other national partner, is compounded by its lack of cohesion. English Canada is geographically fractured by the massive presence of Quebec sprawling astride the St. Lawrence and separating Atlantic Canada from the five provinces to the west of Quebec. Further, English Canada is no longer British, and its future will be even more multiracial and multicultural than is already the case. The remarkable contemporary experiment in the mixing of peoples that is occurring in many Western states is far advanced in English Canada. While a similar future awaits Quebec, its impact so far is less pronounced in that province. Thus, English Canada is called upon to redefine itself vis-à-vis Quebec while its own ethnic demography is unstable.

An effective response is further hindered by English Canada's political fragmentation into nine provinces and two territories, with an additional substantial minority within Quebec. A provincial premier can speak only for the provincial dimension of the local citizenry. The multiple provincial and territorial voices portray English Canada as a discordant babble. The federal government cannot speak for English Canada as such. Its inescapable mandate as long as Canada survives is to represent all of Canada, which necessarily includes both Quebec and Francophones outside of Quebec.

Thus, the structure of the federal system deprives English Canada of any single official actor or centre of power to articulate its concerns. By contrast, the Quebec Francophone population is singularly privileged by its decisive majority status within Quebec and its numerical weakness elsewhere in the country. Premier Lévesque used to complain about how federalism divided Quebecers by pitting their federal against their provincial selves. English Canada is subject to far more profound and disabling divisions, mute testimony to which is offered by the absence of an English-Canadian counterpart to the Quebec Premier to address the problem in English Canada. The divisions in English Canada are not a problem to any government, and that is the problem. Hence, the requirement for English Canada to inform Quebec "what English Canada wants" is a far more difficult task than its reciprocal.

Further, English Canada in some ways has fewer intellectual or psychological resources on which to build a more independent future than does Quebec. Quebec, ever sensitive to its minority condition, is not thinking of independence, sovereignty-association, or a distinct status for Quebec in federalism for the first time. For Quebec, the politics of disentanglement posit an exciting goal, one that builds on an historic and continuing strand in Quebec political thought. Canada-outside-of-Quebec has no such intellectual heritage or minority ambitions on which it can build. As a complacent majority, English Canada has historically been committed to the whole and has not seen the country's break-up as probable or desirable. Should the Quebec response to the perceived Meech Lake rebuff lead to demands for an extensive constitutional separateness of or sovereignty for Quebec, English Canada is unprepared by disposition, by its past pan-Canadian identity, and by the virtual absence of a helpful intellectual heritage for the unsought goal of virtual *de jure* independence for itself.

To some extent, the Charter strengthens the civic identity of English Canada. It has generated a much greater sense of connection to the constitution for English Canadians than formerly prevailed, a recognition that the constitution is not a distant, detached arrangement of supreme indifference to daily life, but on the contrary is the expression of the normative order by which Canadians are supposed to live and by which they define themselves. On the other hand, that consciousness of a constitutional connection is often highly particularistic, stronger at the level of women, ethnic groups, and aboriginals (although their linkage is not primarily with the Charter) than at the level of English Canada as such. In any event, as long as Canada survives, the Charter applies to all of Canada, not just English Canada.

The constitution is no longer a prosaic document that instrumentally only packages government jurisdictions in separate federal and provincial boxes. It now makes the most authoritative statements available to free societies about the relative status of the various major categories into which the citizens can be divided. Consequently, it taps deep emotions of identity and concerns for status and recognition. Thus, those who are satisfied or dissatisfied with their constitutional treatment employ the language of honour, shame, and betrayal. Mulroney's consistently reiterated goal was to get Quebec to return to the constitutional family with "honour and enthusiasm." Elijah Harper, the aboriginal MLA who thwarted legislative discussion of the Accord in Manitoba, did so in order "to symbolize that aboriginal people are not being recognized as the first people of this country and not being recognized as founders of this country." The then vice-chief of the Assembly of First Nations, Ovide Mercredi, asserted that Prime Minister Mulroney had "insulted and hurt aboriginal people by [prematurely] praising Meech Lake as a victory for all Canadians."

This emotional language of identity, hurt, self-esteem, and indignity powerfully indicates how the constitution and our psyches have become intertwined. It underlines the difficulty of constitutional change. One can split the differences in dollars and powers, but pride and dignity are less easily divided.

My response to the dramatic events through which Canadians have lived is intimately linked to my attitude to Canada, the state and its people that have been the patients of so many recent constitutional doctors. Trudeau was fond of quoting Thucydides, who attributed greatness to Themistocles, a man who could dispassionately accept that Athens was not immortal. To an all-seeing god, who has observed so many Ninevehs and Tyres reduced from greatness to dust, the future of the little Canadian experiment may scarcely deserve an entry in the divine logbook that spans millenia. Even three Canadian historians taking the long view recently averred that if Canada "were to disintegrate Canadians would probably continue to live in much the same way as they do now. And it is the lives of persons, not nations, that really matter."

For most of the professoriate, however, who are neither gods, historians, nor Themistocles, such divine disinterestedness or *insouciance* is neither what we feel nor seek to attain when our own country is our subject. The Canada that is being left behind was not, in spite of many scars and blemishes, a place and a time for which Canadians need be ashamed.

Oren Lyons

Oren Lyons is Six Nations Iroquois Confederacy spokesperson and faithkeeper for the Onondaga Nation. The Mohawk nation is one of the six that make up the Iroquois Confederacy, the traditional government of the "Longhouse" people, whose central fire is at Onondaga. The following talk was part of a conference, "Lessons From Oka," organized by the Aboriginal Law Association of McGill University on February 13, 1991.

Sovereignty and the Natural World Economy

SOVEREIGNTY IS A TERM THAT WE HEAR APPLIED ALL THE TIME TO INDIANS. IT'S A term that should be applied to Indians. But I have noticed in the past ten years or so a certain change in terminology. Nationally and internationally, the term sovereignty is often being replaced by the term autonomy.

But what is the difference between the two terms? What is sovereignty? Well we have always taken a rather sophistic view. We said that sovereignty is the act thereof. You are as sovereign as you are able. Generally, sovereignty is applied to nations and today, to nation-states. Indians have always perceived themselves to be nations, sovereign and independent. Indian people, of all people, really understand the concept of freedom and being born free, of having been born with rights.

Columbus landed here 500 years ago. Across America and the world there was a tremendous preparation for 1992. I know that the president of the United States set aside some $82 million for this "celebration" as he called it, and Spain has spent even more than that – all of the world has really become involved: the Catholic Church, for obvious reasons; Italy and the United States, Central and South America, everybody . . . and why? Well, we can look at 1992 as the year of assessment, where we stand back and look at 500 years of activity here in the Western hemisphere and assess what condition we are in. It can be a year of atonement for what happened to the indigenous people who caught the brunt of this invasion, or it can be a year of commitment to see that the next 500 years are going to be better than the last 500.

This process of reflection will have to involve Indian nations. We have to make our own assessment of our condition. We have to present a position to challenge this idea of a celebration, to challenge this idea of a discovery. A very arrogant perception – that we were discovered, sort of like the flora and fauna of North America. In truth, there were free nations here with a real understanding of government and community, of the process and great principles of life. In fact, on the landfall of Christopher Columbus, freedom was rampant in North, Central and South America. Everybody was free and living in a natural world economy where they had economic security in perpetuity. They had adjusted themselves to working with the land, understanding every year that the land renewed itself.

Now coming across the water was somebody with a different perception about economy. As a matter of fact, up to the present day, the governments of Canada and the United States have spent their time trying to get our people involved in this economy. They have spent a lot of time trying to tell us about the importance of private as opposed to community property. We hear terms like development, progressive development, sustainable development, but if from our perception they don't operate around the real laws of the universe then you are challenging fundamental cycles that you depend on for life.

So there was obviously a conflict between Christopher Columbus's perception, and the people that he met. All of the writing says, here were people who were healthy, happy and well-fed, and not overly inclined to warfare. Those were the first people he met, and yet the process began immediately. He said, well these would make good slaves. That was his first message back to the Queen. We can make slaves of these people since they are easily subjugated, and they don't know much about warfare. Any ten of my men can take over this island with the technology and weapons we've brought over.

The basic conflict relates to economy because Indian nations operated under the basis of a natural world economy. They had ceremony; they had Thanksgiving ceremonies that went around the clock and around the calendar year. Something is always coming up so there is always Thanksgiving in this economy. It was part of the structure of a community. It was an instruction to respect what was growing. This was true across the Americas. Everyone had it, everyone believed it. But our white brother was telling us there is a better way. "Get rich," he kept telling us. Our people had a hard time with that. They said, "No, our land is held in common, everyone owns the land. Water is free, air is free, everything you need for life sustenance is free." And he said, "I would like to buy your land." They said, "What do you mean by buying?"

As we sit back at 500 years distance and assess that, let's look at what has happened to our people. How have the Indian nations fared? How have our children? How are our institutions? Are they holding up? How are our principles? Are they holding up? We have to look at ourselves because as tough as these last 500 years have been the next 500 are going to be tougher, and maybe even the next 100 years and the next 60 years.

There is a real fundamental discussion here that we have to look at because human beings are displacing life around the world. Huge populations are displacing life whether it is trees, the elephants in Africa, the tigers in India or the buffalo in this country. They are not here anymore. But there are more and more people. There is a displacement going on here of things a fundamental economy needs. The Indians understood one thing, they understood that the law of flesh and blood and bones is common to all living beings. We are under one common law here. We are animals, but we are animals with intellect. Intellect is what makes us dangerous because we have the foreknowledge of death. Animals know when death is coming, and they prepare for it. We know from a very young age that we are going to die. This is a tremendous knowledge, but how do you use that knowledge? How do you work with it?

When one speaks of generations the way the Indians speak of them, we must see that the next generations, those faces coming from the earth, have the same good that we have and can enjoy the same law that we do. Well, in assessing 500 years in this country, we see that the next seven generations are not going to enjoy that. Every day at least six species of life become extinct. But when you talk about the philosophy of sovereignty, you are talking about longevity and the future. This is the common sense that comes from the long experience of Indian nations being in one place – if you don't work with the laws that surround you, you will not survive. That's quite simple. We know that there is no mercy in the natural law whatsoever. It will exact retribution in direct ratios of violations. You can't discuss this – there are no lawyers, there is nothing, only the retribution. The problem here is that we visit this retribution on our children and on our grandchildren. We leave them the problem of our excesses.

I never believed the white man when he said his way was better. I never believed it. I always believed that our way was better, maybe just because I knew more about it. The truth is, if we are going to sit back and really look at it, there is some hard news here for all of us no matter who we are. As human beings, there is some very hard news to look at. I think that when we speak of sovereignty, we have to have a large conceptualization of what it is we are talking about. With Indian nations, it's not really a political term, it's a spiritual term as well. It may even be more spiritual than political. One of our people once said that spirituality is the highest form of politics. So let's keep the parameters of what we are talking about clear.

The parameters are beyond the oceans that surround us, and they're beyond our time here on earth. These parameters we are discussing reverberate into the future. If your economy doesn't function within those parameters then you are shortchanging those future generations we talked about. Maybe it's only the Indians that talk about the seventh generation. I don't know. Since we have talked about it a lot, I've heard it again and again. I hear it from strangers, I hear it from strange places. But why not? It seems to us common law and common sense. And so, shall we say that sovereignty is common sense in its most basic fundamental form; common sense and respect, respect for one and all and for life.

Boundaries of Identity

Between Ourselves:

An Inconclusion

Ruth Edwards Abbey

A doctoral candidate in Political Science at McGill University, Ruth Abbey has been living in Montreal for five years.

Between Ourselves: An Inconclusion

The "other" is never outside or beyond us; it emerges forcefully, within cultural discourse, when we think we speak most intimately and indigenously "between ourselves."

Homi K. Bhabha (From *Nation and Narration, 1991)*

This anthology is animated by a strong dissatisfaction with the public debate about Quebec's political and cultural aspirations. It is as if an either/or mentality has been constructing the questions being asked about the future of Quebec. In these polarized terms, people are perceived to be either for or against Quebec nationalism, and being for nationalism is usually assumed to be the same as being in favour of independence.

But this either/or framework is both simplistic and divisive. It occludes a whole range of positions integral to Quebec's culture and politics. For example, it should be possible to support the preservation and promotion of Quebec's culture, or cultures, without believing that some form of independence or "sovereignty-association" is the only way to do this. Likewise, it should be possible to support Quebec's cultural aspirations while harbouring reservations about the way they might infringe upon individual rights. As this anthology demonstrates, such diverse positions do exist in Quebec society, and this book is by no means an exhaustive collection.

At first glance, the way in which different perspectives have been presented in the anthology might appear to reproduce the very homogeneity supposedly being challenged, for the presentation seems to imply that there is a native voice or a women's or immigrants' perspective. However, each of the book's divisions offers a variety of conflicting positions. Each section presents a series of perspectives that reinforce and challenge and confront one another, either by addressing similar questions or rousing different ones. Thus, although none of these pieces were written with the others in mind, each can be read as being in dialogue with those around it.

At the most general level, all of the book's contributors are addressing, whether implicitly or explicitly, one of the fundamental issues of politics: identity. And, in the particular context of Quebec and its future, a related question that tacitly unites these contributions is what form of society can best host all the different identities that currently constitute the population of Quebec.

Of course complexity and multiplicity also exist at the level of individual identity. To be identified as a woman or a native or an immigrant in Quebec society tells us something about who that person is, but it is still only a partial representation. As David Fennario's play *Balconville* clearly reveals, any individual's identity is a composite of forces like gender, age, class, religion, ethnicity, and so forth. These different aspects both divide and unite us in ways that shift as issues and situations change.

The "spirit" of the "meeting" that this book represents cannot be summarized in a few closing sentences. Nor is the purpose here to try and answer this question of what form of political organization is most conducive to letting different groups feel at home in Quebec. However, much will have been achieved by merely putting this question on the agenda. Expanding the debate about Quebec's future by including more perspectives and increasing the number of issues to be discussed obviously does not simplify matters, but it does give us a more faithful picture of a pluralist society in the 1990s that is undergoing an important process of self-definition.

Yet there is an important sense in which the very acknowledgement of identity as multiple and protean, both at the level of the individual and the collective, does tell us something about how a truly free Quebec would be. In such a society, as many people as possible would feel at home; they would feel welcome and accepted in terms of who they are, who they were in the past, and who they might become. The "Québec libre" would acknowledge that it is not only Francophones for whom the phrase "Je me souviens" is central to identity. As this anthology reveals, there are many histories to be remembered by Quebec's citizens.

Paradoxically, a nationalism that embraced Quebec's population in its diversity could thereby ensure a healthy future for itself. If newcomers to Quebec, from the rest of Canada or the world, feel accepted here, they are more likely to feel a loyalty to Quebec and a desire to preserve and promote its distinctiveness in a far more powerful and enduring way than measuring centimetres on public signs could ever do.

In the late twentieth century, not many people are born Quebecers in the sense of being descendants of the founding families of New France. But there is another history of Quebec that immigrants could come to identify with: the affirmative history of a culture that has struggled against great odds to retain and to go on creating its identity and to have its distinctiveness recognized by others. This ongoing history of Quebec is one that many newcomers could be proud of and participate in.

Printed in Canada